RUNNING
CONVENTIONS,
CONFERENCES,
AND
MEETINGS

RUNNING CONVENTIONS, CONFERENCES, AND MEETINGS

Robert W. Lord

A Division of American Management Associations

Library of Congress Cataloging in Publication Data

Lord, Robert W
  Running conventions, conferences, and meetings.

  Includes index.
  1. Congresses and conventions. 2. Meetings.
I. Title.
AS6.L63   060'.68   80-69704
ISBN 0-8144-5643-X

First Printing

to Barbara

Preface

More than 30,000 conventions are held in the United States each year. Their cost is well over $8 billion, with more than twice as much spent in related services. Hundreds of thousands—probably millions—of people attend. In addition, there are innumerable smaller meetings, ranging in attendance from several hundred people down to the small committee.

Over many years of attending and running meetings, I have observed a frequent lack of expertise on the part of meeting planners and managers. With so much money at stake, and with so many people spending time at conferences and conventions, there is a need for knowledge about handling the many details that make a successful meeting. Providing such knowledge is the purpose of this book.

The book is written with business executives in mind. They have to run meetings in house, for customers of their firms, for professional organizations to which they belong, and for civic and other organizations in their private life. Anyone who has to run a meeting—business executive, professional organization director, or other program or conference chairman—can profit from this book, whether he or she is a neophyte or experienced at managing meetings.

There are many types of conventions and meetings—business, nonbusiness, professional, trade. They may last an hour or several days, and the refreshments provided can range from a glass of water to a full-scale banquet.

This book deals with all these types of meetings. It treats as many aspects as possible, but omits those subjects that can become outdated, such as recommendations for specific hotels or convention bureaus.

What is good today may have different management or personnel next year. I trust, however, that the meeting manager will find all the information needed to help run a better meeting.

Some principles apply to all meetings. Certain actions must be taken by the meeting manager or planner in any case, whatever the size and type of meeting.

The plan of the majority of the book applies these principles and "must-do" actions to the larger meeting, leading the meeting manager through the earliest decisions that must be made, planning and promotion, the meeting itself, and the post-meeting wrap-up.

Small and special types of meetings receive attention in one separate chapter, and another is designed to help the person who attends a meeting get the most out of it.

The final chapter contains tips to assist the traveler, whether he or she is attending a meeting or not. I hope the meeting manager will pass some of these tips on to the people who will be attending the meetings, and that the travel tips will make the manager's journeys easier and more pleasant.

This book is based on a newsletter I produced twice monthly for several years.

I wish to acknowledge the assistance of Thomas J Lewis, editor and publisher of *International Insurance Monitor,* and my wife, Barbara. Both read the manuscript and made many helpful comments.

Robert W. Lord

Contents

RUNNING CONVENTIONS, CONFERENCES, AND MEETINGS

1
Advance Decisions

Why have a meeting? Meetings are held to gather, impart, or exchange information, to sell services or products, to make money, to transact business of a company or organization, for sociability, and for other reasons. A meeting is successful if the reasons for holding it substantially outweigh the objections and difficulties, if it is planned in effective and timely fashion, and if it is run efficiently.

Some meetings must be held because of custom, an organization's constitution, or sheer necessity. This is true of all sizes of meetings, from the country's Democratic and Republican political conventions held every four years down to the small committee in a company department that must meet immediately to deal with an *ad hoc* problem.

Many other meetings should not be held at all. Where an organization, company, or committee has a choice it must weigh the factors, including cost, pro and con. Does it have someone who can run the meeting? (By the time you have finished this book *you* will be in a much better position to do so.) For an "optional" meeting I know no better criterion than this: *Will there be substantial benefit for the people who attend?*

For example, a consulting firm in a highly technical field considered running a seminar on compliance with government regulations affecting its industry. The firm was frank in its hope to make some money from the meeting. But a number of other organizations in the field were sponsoring seminars that touched on this subject. The consulting firm finally decided to go ahead with its projected seminar. It felt that the fact that competing meetings were being held was a positive factor—it indicated keen interest in the regulations. The program was designed with the benefit of the audience, not financial gain, as the primary object. Good speakers dealt in depth with their subjects. Audience orientation made the meeting successful, and it made money as well.

Once you decide to have a meeting, there are many decisions to make: the theme, the length of the meeting, its date, the site (geographic area, city or resort), pricing, and the make-up and function of the meeting committee.

Theme

Most conferences and conventions are helped by having a theme. The meeting manager who sets a theme and then selects topics and speakers within the limits of that theme, and with the purpose of supporting and reinforcing the theme, is at one time disciplining himself and sharpening the effect of the meeting.

The theme must encompass the purpose of the conference. It must be acceptable to all who might be expected to attend. It must move people to action—that is, get them to attend the meeting because they believe it will improve them, help improve the work they do, or enable them to do a better job by helping people for whom they are responsible.

The theme must be carefully thought out. It should arise from a serious consideration of the purposes of the conference. From the objectives of the meeting you should try to synthesize a thought that will dramatize the overall aim of the conference. This is the theme. Often the theme evolves in a committee meeting concerned with the coming conference.

Is this theme necessary? Not every meeting needs a theme. For some people this statement is the rankest heresy. But themes should not be foolish, trite, or too limiting. Some meeting managers sweat hours trying to get a catchy combination of concatenated concepts that can be heralded in hot headlines. They would be better off telling their prospective conventioners that they will have a good program, with this and that topic and such and such capable speakers, that the location is great, for the following reasons, and that anyone who passes up this year's meeting will be sorry.

If the theme comes hard to the meeting manager or the convention committee, the remedy may not be more thought. The subjects which have to be covered at the meeting may simply be too diverse to be contained in a theme. It may be possible to encompass all the topics in a description pulled over them like a blanket, but this description cannot be reduced to the précis-like status of a theme. Better not to use a theme in this case than to fall on your face with a poor one.

What it's not. Before going further with selecting a theme, we should know what a theme is not. As I have said, the theme arises from the purpose of the conference. But the purpose is not the theme. Nor is a theme necessarily a slogan. A theme may be a slogan, but it usually is not. Would anyone call *It Floats* or *They Satisfy* a theme?

A theme is not a symbol. A symbol can illustrate, dramatize, or personalize a theme, but symbol and theme are not identical or even interchangeable. A symbol is visual, a theme verbal. Appropriate symbols have power, however, and should be used where possible.

The location of a meeting is not connected to the theme. Usually, subject matter and setting are largely independent of each other. The exception is where plants, activity of government, or some other aspect of the site have been chosen as major subjects of study at the meeting. Even such local interest may not involve the whole conference program. If it does not, the theme should not be tied to geography. *Higher aspirations in Asbury* makes little sense if the aspirations could be easily raised in Omaha. But an attractive site symbol can nevertheless aid your promotion, unifying all the literature you distribute about the meeting.

Elements of a good theme. A theme should carry the idea of movement, action—the feeling that *We're moving forward together*. It can be a lure to action—*New horizons for achievement in. . . . Spring training for increased sales*, with the whole program following a baseball format, might be an effective theme.

Since a theme appeals to our better instincts, it must be honest. Hypocrisy or glibness shows through. This is as true for a sales meeting as for any other conference. Maybe company president Sinister is flattered by the theme, *Salute for Sinister*, but the theme will not go over well if Mr. S. is hated by everyone in the firm.

A theme must be comprehensive of the subject matter of the meeting. It helps if the theme is catchy. These two characteristics make a theme memorable.

Don't choose a theme that overstates your meeting. If there is no crisis in your occupation or profession, don't let the theme say there is; it invites ridicule. Also, overstated themes year after year tire people and turn them off. Do not let the theme promise more than the meeting will deliver.

Here are some themes that do the job, though they are not flashy. Note that they are fairly specific.

Better Personal Administration Through EDP
Practical Approaches to Energy Saving
Managing the Investment Process in the Eighties.

Others, of a general rather than specific nature, convey a more abstract idea:

Independence Through Interdependence
Education Is the Key
Milestone Year in 1982

Some themes, especially where they are specific, can double as the title for the conference.

If you do not have a theme for your entire meeting, it is still appropriate to have one for your entertainment evening. The entertainment theme may or may not be related to the location of the meeting. If you are in Philadelphia and can get the Mummers to furnish music, you can have a Mummers' Evening. If you are at a place that does not have famous local entertainment, your party theme may be something appropriate like *Venetian Nights* or *South of the Border*. People like escape. They also like to recognize, in an entertainment theme, the conception they have of what a romantic evening in Venice or Mexico is like. This conception can work for you when you promote an event that has an exotic theme.

Sometimes a theme will have influence long after the meeting is over. At the 1932 Democratic National Convention the musical theme, *Happy Days Are Here Again*, helped create a mood that led to irresistible victory in the campaign which followed. The song generated a spirit of optimism in the public. Many years earlier, however, a national party held a convention at which a current popular song was played over and over again. The song was called "Don't You Kick My Dog Around." The song is reported to have roused delegates to a high emotional pitch, but its influence, and relevance if any, ended with the convention.

Themes that are relevant, comprehensive, and catchy will be remembered and will continue to benefit your organization or company long after your meeting is over.

How Long a Meeting?

Some years ago the five-day meeting was not very unusual. The long meeting, however, is costly—in time as well as money. A meeting of three full days or more is a long one now. A conference that draws out-of-town people is likely to run two or two-and-a-half days. Consider the extent of your subject matter and schedule the length of time accordingly, but try to have the meeting run no longer than necessary.

If you are holding a two- or three-day meeting, and you wish to attract out-of-town people, have the meeting begin on a Monday or end on a Friday. Presumably you will choose a location that has attractions. By having your meeting follow or precede a weekend, you will give those attending the opportunity to enjoy the attractions. These may be golf, beach, sightseeing, big-city entertainment, or something else.

This kind of scheduling also suits the meeting-goer who has come alone and wants to be home on the weekend.

The only drawback is that Sundays and Fridays can be tough days to get seats on planes in a hurry. This points up the importance of advance planning. Conventioners should reserve their seats far ahead of when they will need them.

The middle of the week is often good for one-day meetings, where most of the audience would normally be in town for business anyway.

Because midweek is slow for hotels, they will sometimes offer special rates for a meeting beginning on Tuesday and ending on Thursday. This scheduling, however, is likely to hurt attendance at the meeting.

Date

The time of year you hold your convention or meeting depends on the needs of your organization, company, and industry. Site may also be involved, to the extent that special off-season rates are available at resorts. For example, you may wish to stay out of hot places in the summer.

Conflicts. What is more important is that you avoid conflicts with holidays and possible competing meetings. No one would hold a meeting on Christmas or the Fourth of July, but too often nobody checks out the Jewish holidays and as a result a date is scheduled that conflicts with them. If your group includes a lot of men, avoid conflicting with the World Series, or speakers will be talking to empty rooms.

It is also necessary to avoid competing with other organizations. All large associations—and many smaller ones—must make sure that they will not have competition for the city and hotels they wish to use at the time the meeting will be held there, or competition with other organizations anywhere that might hold conferences that could draw part of the audience away. The competition for site can be easily checked out with hotels and convention bureaus. The competition for audience is an entirely different matter.

In clearing a date the meeting manager will do well to proceed as follows:

1. Decide on the best date for the organization's convention. Have at least two alternate dates in reserve.

2. Check with hotels in the desired city to see if these dates are open.

3. Make a list of every organization that could possibly compete for this audience. A good deal of work should go into this list. At first thought it may seem that there are very few organizations to worry about. Often overlooked, however, are those associations that hold meetings in different fields. For example, if you are planning a convention of hospital administrators, you should include on your list organizations of such medical professionals as doctors and public health experts. Go on to think of consumer organizations that may run meetings on hospital costs, and conferences of government officials that may deal with the same subject. (Hospital costs are being borne more and more by government.) The list of possible competing organizations should be as inclusive as you can make it, as long as there is any possibility—however small—that the group could hold a meeting that might interest some of

your audience. While you're making the list, include addresses and phone numbers. Avoiding a direct conflict in date is not enough. You don't want your meeting too close to the date of a strong competitor's, either.

4. Check out the meeting dates, by phone, with the meeting manager (often the executive director) of every possible competitor. Don't use the mail. It takes too long and is too frustrating. If you have a competitor for your dates you want to know quickly. Keep good notes of your telephone conversations. It will be useful to know later when other meetings are going to be held. Such information can help you to schedule your own promotion so that it will receive the best attention from your prospective audience.

In checking out the dates you will find that the further ahead you are working, the less likely you are to find real competition, except from those organizations that "always" meet at that time.

5. Immediately upon determining that your date is clear of competition, inform everyone on your list of potential competitors of the date. Do this in writing, and do it fast. A photocopied letter is an acceptable way to do the job.

6. Send a news release to the professional or trade press informing them of your date and the place of the meeting. If the date announced is some years hence, include, too, the dates and places of the meetings that are closer. Since the publications may not carry the item, or may not print it for some months, and the item may not be read by everyone, do not rely too much on news releases to get the word around. I recently saw a meeting go down the drain because of direct competition. I asked one of the men arranging the canceled meeting if he had checked with competitors. He said he had sent out a news release, and thought that was enough. The best one can say about this is that it was incompetent.

Tell your membership the date and the site. Remind them frequently. If they are all aware of the approximate date—"We're meeting in San Diego in September '84"—they can act as so many watchdogs, speaking up when they hear of possible competition for the date. Use your own publications and those of the profession or industry to spread the word. But more of that later, under the heading of "Promotion."

Site

It is often not possible to separate consideration of a meeting city or resort from the hotel or hotels where the conference or convention will be held. It is convenient, however, to consider first the kind of site—general area, type of climate desired, urban or resort—to be chosen and then the criteria important in selecting a specific hotel. The latter is discussed in the next chapter.

Consider Climate. Some people say that climate makes no difference. This is simply not true. I have seen meetings turn into disasters because climate was not taken into account. Take two cases:

Case number one. A publishing firm that had held some conferences decided to hold a new meeting, in a field in which it had not previously held conferences. The company depended on subscribers to its magazine to form the core of its registrants for the meeting. The firm got a good deal with a hotel in Miami Beach—in July. Virtually no one signed up. An established meeting might have made it, but not a new one.

Case number two. A large international organization (United States and Canada) held a January meeting in Quebec City. People came, but the Floridians and southern Californians froze. They simply did not have the clothes for those frigid temperatures.

Both meetings were in great places. But in each case the time of year was wrong.

Facilities. When you choose a site for a meeting you should be concerned first about adequacy of meeting facilities, guest rooms, and other essential needs for the business sessions. It is frequently necessary to take into consideration the amount of traveling that members or delegates will have to undertake to reach the conference site—a consideration quite important in our energy-conscious times.

Cities and Resorts. But it is evident that besides these considerations some organizations and companies hold their meetings in obviously workaday cities, say Chicago and St. Louis, and others head for places associated with pleasure—for example, Las Vegas and Miami Beach. Chicago, St. Louis, and similar cities have many places of interest and often have more nightlife than resorts, but there is nevertheless a difference in kind. Perhaps as important, the executive who says he is going to Chicago for a meeting does not arouse the envy and possible criticism of his associates to the same extent as the one who says he is going to Miami Beach.

Organizations tend to meet in predictable types of places. Insurance and mutual fund organization meetings go to large, metropolitan cities—New York, Chicago, Montreal, Dallas, St. Louis, Atlanta, and maybe San Francisco, Miami Beach, San Diego, and Honolulu.

Company sales meetings go to sedate resort areas like Williamsburg and Monterey, if the company is in the financial field. Product manufacturing companies that entertain their salesmen—and their potential customers—hold meetings in livelier places.

Large organizations tend to meet in a few cities—usually five or six—that tend to become a closed ring. The association moves from one to another each year until it is back at the first, to begin the swing again. While this makes an extremely burdensome job easier for the convention manager of the organization, it tends to encourage sameness not only in the choice of location but also in the way the convention is conducted and in the program as well. It would be good for every large organization to try, at least once every five years, to hold its annual meeting in a new city, or if this is impossible in one that has not been its convention site in many years. This would shake things up, force a new look at old ways of doing things, reawaken the interest of the members, and perhaps increase attendance.

But back to the question of city versus resort.

Although rarely discussed in the open, there are two schools of thought in contention.

One school might put its position this way: Our organization is strictly business. Let's keep it that way and go only to cities that people do not think of as resorts. Caesar's wife must not only behave, she must be above suspicion. Sure, we could hold our meeting together at a resort, but why try to do it? We avoid criticism by staying away from resorts.

The pro-resort side might state its case this way: By going to a place with good golf or beach facilities we make the location itself an attraction to draw attendance. There are no more distractions there—in fact fewer—than in a big city. We get more spouses this way, which keeps the convention on a higher plane. We meet just before or after a weekend, giving our members a chance to spend some time on their own—and at their own expense—on the golf course or the beach. We don't give them time off during the meeting.

There is logic in both positions. If your organization's purposes and desires are better served by holding your meetings in nonresort locations, by all means do so. I do not feel, however, that possible adverse criticism should count as too large a factor if logic otherwise indicates going to a resort.

For example, a bankers' association hesitated about meeting in Las Vegas, for fear people might think it unwise for those who handle depositors' money to go to a gambling resort. I would not have chosen this city for that group, but it went there without apparent ill effects.

Another association convinced regulatory authorities that it could meet more inexpensively in the Bahamas than on the mainland and held a successful convention there.

A small group, particularly, can benefit by using resorts. First, it is easier to hold the members together than when they are dumped in an overwhelmingly large city. Second, if a very large city is chosen, there are relatively few cities the membership will want to go to. This means that the meeting manager has to keep repeating at well-known cities—not the best way to build attendance. The small association can meet in a different resort each year for several years without having to repeat.

This brings us to the question of whether meeting at resorts builds attendance. I cannot give a definitive answer. No doubt it depends a great deal on the nature of the organization and the character and ability of its governing executives. Consider the following, however, which relates to two large organizations:

One association is over 80 years old, the other 25. Both are strong, active organizations, of great service to their membership. The older association grows nearly every year, until now its membership is 130,000. The younger group has a membership in the 20,000 to 22,000 range, also exhibiting excellent membership growth.

Now comes the difference. The group with 130,000 members meets annually, in Boston, Philadelphia, Chicago, Cincinnati, Los Angeles, with a rare year in Miami Beach. Twenty-five years ago it had an attendance at its annual convention of 3,000; for some years now it has been 2,000. The smaller group meets in San Diego, Honolulu, Miami Beach, San Francisco, and occasionally New York, and has an attendance of 6,000 at its annual meeting. There is no proof that the difference in location has caused a difference in attendance, but we must consider the possibility. The larger association must, too, have taken a look at its sites, because this year, for the first time, it is going to Honolulu.

Sites are not limited to big city or resort. You can take your meeting to sea. For many years some meetings have gone down to the sea in ships. A shipboard convention fosters a sense of community and you have no reason to worry that your membership will wander off—they're all there. It may be a cliché to say that a ship is a floating hotel, but that is just what it is. It has meeting rooms, guest rooms, meal service, entertainment, and sports. In addition, because it travels, conventioners can sightsee and shop in ports of call.

A variation on the cruise meeting is to rent a ship for a day or two while it is tied up in port during its turn-around period. Small charter boats also make excellent settings for programmed entertainment some evening.

Besides the factors I have already discussed that can influence your choice of a site, the following thoughts arose from some meetings I attended or was involved with.

Why don't large, serious organizations get out of the rut of the few big metropolitan cities where they place their meetings? First, of course, any place they go must have enough beds, but perhaps the organizations cannot change. Maybe the membership does not want to. Or the wives or husbands of members don't want them to.

The small organization has a large advantage over the big one. Because of its size it has a choice of many more sites and hotels.

Inevitably, the convenience of the location is important for the membership or company representatives.

Kind of meeting. Another consideration is the nature of the meeting. If it is all work and no play, if you expect no one to leave the hotel from the time he arrives till he departs—and there are such meetings—there is no use going to a resort that has beach, golf courses, tennis courts, and swimming pools.

As touched on before, there may be regulatory restrictions, too. Insurance organizations involving companies subject to regulation by strict insurance departments will want to make sure that a conference can be run more cheaply in a resort than in some city in the middle of the American continent.

Membership wishes. Another consideration really extraneous to the main purpose of a meeting, but which you must pay attention to, is where your membership wants to meet. We know a small meeting that could go anywhere, but goes to New York City every year. The men in this all-male organization are used to going there, their wives look forward to shopping in the city, and neither members nor wives want to change. After 20 years New York has been institutionalized as a site. Objectively, it looks as if a meeting manager who might wish to switch this group to another place would have his work cut out for him.

The officers and directors of the organization may have strong feelings on site.

Is the nature of the site city changing? Will it be a desirable place for a meeting five years from now—when the convention is scheduled? The Old Super Majestic Hotel has been the organization's headquarters for its annual meeting for 25 years. The owners admit that the hotel is getting a little tacky. How serious are they about the promised renovation? Will the new Hilton be built in time? This organization can meet only in unionized hotels. That one needs a city with a good teaching hospital—for field trips by members. Another association received a lot of flak from the ranks about the indifferent service in the hotels the last time the association met in a particular city.

There are so many variables and uncertainties that the meeting manager or meeting committee will do well to get opinions and advice from the membership and from officers of the organization or company. The members, however, cannot be allowed to make the decision on a site and should not be allowed to vote. The decision must be made by the meeting manager, the committee, and—very likely in the ultimate stage—by a top executive or board.

Pricing

In these inflationary days, any absolute dollar figures suggested as the price to charge people attending a meeting would rapidly become outdated. I can, however, suggest some principles.

Anyone "costing" a meeting wants to be fair, but what is fair? If the conference is being run for profit, what price will draw the largest number of people, or make the most profit? If your organization is nonprofit, do you want to subsidize the meeting from dues in order to encourage attendance?

Let us look at the smaller meeting, then the larger one.

The smaller meeting. A small meeting, especially the luncheon or one-day meeting, should pay its way. In fact, the one-day conference should normally turn a profit, even if the sponsor is a nonprofit organization. To load meeting deficits onto dues would be to charge everyone, including those who could not attend the meeting, for a benefit received only by those who were there. Also, if you start the business or organization year by charging a little more than necessary, you can absorb moderate increases later as costs for your meetings rise. This keeps the customers happier than they would be if they were exposed to frequent price increases for their luncheons and other meetings.

If your meeting is nonprofit, determine all your costs, add a little, and, hopefully, that is your price.

If the intention is to make a real profit, the rock-bottom price you can set is the one that, in the aggregate, will return out-of-pocket expenses. From there you go up, with a respectful regard for the law of the effect of rising price on demand.

Larger meetings. The two-day meeting should not cost twice as much as the one-day conference (excluding guest-room hotel cost, or course). There will be lunches and coffee both days, but if there is one cocktail party it will be on the first day. If the meeting runs two-and-a-half days and if there are two cocktail parties, one of them will probably be a cash bar.

Another consideration in pricing is who is going to benefit from the conference. If those who attend will receive the main benefit, shouldn't they pay for it? If you are going to sell them something, shouldn't *you* pay? If the cost is too much for you, consider omitting lunch, or alternatively, keep the luncheon price moderate and split the cost with the audience.

Inevitably, price has an effect on the meeting—where it goes, how long it lasts, whether you can afford to pay speakers, and whether you provide entertainment. With that interrelationship in mind, you can focus on these major factors in pricing: the cost of putting on the affair, whether making money is a consideration, and who will benefit from the meeting.

One other matter—price your meeting in even amounts—that is $200, not $195; $350 and not $349.50. Charging odd amounts detracts from the image you should wish to create for your meeting. Nothing is really gained by doing it. With merchandising of tangible goods the practice is well established, but I doubt that it is useful with intangibles and services such as meetings. I suspect that no one is fooled by such a price and some people would react negatively to the idea.

Working with a Meeting Committee

Happy is the meeting manager or association executive who has a completely free hand with meetings. Such a person has complete responsibility and total authority, drawing on the help he needs and deciding where, when, and what for all major aspects of conferences. If the meeting manager is knowledgeable and competent, this autonomy results in good conferences, probably the best.

Such an ideal situation, however, rarely exists. Often the meeting manager has to deal with executives of his company or organization, or with a formal committee. How can a meeting manager best work with these people who are also charged with decisions, in order to evolve the most desirable meeting for the company or the organization?

Two Kinds. There are really two types of meeting or program committees:

1(a). The type that is chaired by an executive who is not a meeting professional. This person is usually a vice-president of the company or of the organization whose area of responsibility is considered to include conventions and meetings.

These people are usually effective executives, but it is the duty of the knowledgeable meeting manager to see that the committee chairman is sufficiently briefed on what he needs to know to have a successful conference, and that other members of the committee feel free to speak up and make their contributions during committee sessions.

The meeting manager's role in the committee is to propose valid options of time, place, hotel, program content, and scheduling. He should be prepared to make recommendations and back them up with reasoned arguments. He is likely to find that the executive/chairman seems predominantly interested in costs, and the meeting manager should be particularly well prepared, not only to present basic figures, but also to answer follow-up questions on the more detailed costs that the meeting is likely to incur. The meeting manager must also be prepared for the real possibility that the chairman will brush off some matters of importance because he cannot see them as falling into areas that require discussion by the committee. If the meeting manager is to handle such matters himself, he should see that the chairman tells him in open meeting to do so, and that the person taking notes on the meeting records this action.

A meeting chaired by a nonprofessional in the field of discussion tends to get off the track. The meeting manager should unobtrusively prod things back into line when this happens.

If you have done your homework well for this kind of committee meeting, you will have prepared an agenda two to three weeks in advance of the meeting and circulated it through your chairman. Try to see that everything you considered of prime importance on the agenda gets acted on. Naturally, these should come up early in the meeting.

It sometimes happens that the meeting manager is designated chairman of the conference committee, only to find that an executive to whom he has to report is taking action on his own. This man or woman has a brainstorm for a speaker and calls him directly, without consulting the meeting manager as to whether the speaker will fit into the program. Or the executive decides to change the menu for lunch the second day, makes a quick phone call, and that's that. This is very frustrating for the meeting manager. Whether he thinks he is chairman of the conference committee or not, in reality he is not. In my opinion, his best course of action is to recognize that he is part of an informal committee with the executive as chairman and try to get the executive to call formal meetings, with the executive in the chair and the meeting manager as a member of the committee, where things can be accomplished in an organized fashion.

1(b). There is another type of executive-chaired committee meeting dealing with conferences. The executive committee of an association may meet to handle the subject. The meeting is naturally chaired by the president, and important decisions may be put to vote of the executive committee. The meeting manager and perhaps others are present.

A meeting of this type may be very productive. Three people or so in authority, instead of one, are propounding ideas. And somehow the knowledgeable manager of meetings gets a better hearing at an executive committee meeting than he does in one dominated by a sales manager or company treasurer. Because the members of an executive committee represent different constituencies, and have collectively attended many conferences (unless the organization is new), they will have a good idea of what has been successful at past meetings and will have worthwhile suggestions for new conferences.

A major advantage of having a company executive or an executive committee in the driver's seat in planning your conference is that once he or they are sold, your worries with regard to any particular problem are over, except for the follow-through. Budgetary obstacles, too, are fewer and lower.

2. The other major type of conference planning meeting is the type in which you, the meeting manager, are the chairman.

Meeting Manager as Chairman. Here your function is to gather information, using your committee members as advisers and as a sounding board for ideas. Ultimately, they will carry out your instructions as you delegate areas of work and specific jobs. In all important matters you will make decisions yourself, not asking for votes within the committee.

Even if you have to report to a superior and get his approval on actions you take, if your consultation and deliberation are conducted in a committee that you truly chair, you are the person responsible for the recommendations and for all but the ultimate decisions. Your approach and methods are the same, whether you have the final say or have to get your decisions initialed upstairs.

Run your committee meetings well. An agenda is just as necessary as with any other committee meeting. Start on time, discuss every question you intended to. Defer all new items to the next meeting (and another agenda). Allow no interruptions. Keep a record, and close on time.

Draw out every member of your committee to secure his or her ideas and to determine the strengths each has. Give each a job to do. Try to stimulate your committee to collect ideas from others that can be of value. Even though you will have final decision-making power, attempt to get a consensus from your committee. They will support you more enthusiastically if they are convinced of the rightness of the decisions and actions adopted.

If your committee deals with meetings held on a regular basis, such as annual conventions or sales meetings, you should make a practice of securing reaction sheets, critiques, or whatever you wish to call them, from the people attending. In preparation for one of the early conference committee meetings, have a member of your committee tabulate and summarize these questionnaire answers. This is true no matter how the committee is organized. Any good conference should take into account what people ought to hear or learn; it is certain to fail if it does not give them what they want, and pay some attention to their wishes as to where they wish to hear it. It pays to listen to your audience when it speaks back.

Often meeting managers fail to take advantage of knowledgeable people in their memberships who are not members of the conference committee. How about asking spouses of some of the members who live in the city that will host the convention for suggestions about a spouses' program and entertainment? This is especially important if most of the membership is male. You can get their ideas in writing and possibly in person, if one or more of them has to visit your city for another reason.

If there is a printer among your membership, his advice can be of value when you are discussing how best to keep costs down on your promotional material.

If the conference will have the help of a public relations professional, it goes without saying that he should be in on the planning sessions at the earliest possible time. Encourage him to be more than a reporter taking notes to write news releases and advertising. His ideas can be of real value in a number of areas important for a conference.

There is a tendency among some professionals—and there may be meeting managers who are guilty of this—to take ideas from people and present them in committee, but to exclude the originator of the ideas from access to the committee meeting. This betokens insecurity on the part of the professional, while the committee loses the benefit that it could derive from being able to discuss ideas with the person who thought them up.

In any session of the conference committee, save a few minutes toward the end for summing up, for laying out the work to be done by committee members before the next meeting, and for a rough outline of what is to be accomplished the next time you get together.

As soon as possible after the meeting, each committee member should receive a full report or copy of the minutes. Don't forget to get the OKs and initials or signatures of company executives, the president of the organization, or whoever is responsible for approvals for all important steps you take—especially where money is involved.

If a meeting is to be successful, one principle must never be compromised. Whether ultimate approval is in the hands of a company executive, an organization president, or an executive committee, one person and only one can be responsible for organizing and running the meeting. This will be you, the meeting manager, whether your everyday title is executive director or program chairman, or some other. To divide authority is to work at cross purpose, cause confusion, and lead to a conference that fails to accomplish its objectives.

2
Planning,
Part I

Once you have made the initial, advance decisions, you must decide the subjects to be discussed on the meeting's program, secure speakers, decide whether you will use the services of a convention bureau, and you must select a hotel or motel as a site and make preliminary arrangements with its management. These matters will be the subject of this chapter.

In Chapter 3 I will take up such housekeeping matters as advance registration, badges and signs, kits for those attending the meeting, spouse programs, later arrangements with the hotel, and relations with the press.

Subjects and Program

A program is built around subjects. You determine what your audience should hear and what you think it wants to hear and then decide who is going to tell them these things. (Exceptions to this rule are the celebrity who may talk on a subject with little or no relation to your field and the company official who may be expected to speak at a meeting of his firm.)

Let's look at the larger meeting. Much of what we say will apply to the smaller meeting and the sales conference. There are in addition some good ideas usable by the small meeting that the large one cannot use, that will receive particular attention in Chapter 8.

As you plan your meeting bear in mind that the amount of ground you wish to cover can affect the length of the meeting, but you have already pretty well determined how many days the conference will run. You can allow 20 to 30 minutes, usually, for each speaker, plus five or ten minutes of questions. Headliners will probably speak at lunch, but you do not have to have any luncheon speakers, and you must allow for breaks, to rest people.

Let's suppose that the meeting manager is responsible for a program of two or three days' duration and that he wishes to choose speakers and subjects that will in the main appeal to all those who attend. In addition, he wants to allot some time to narrow, in-depth discussion of specialties that will interest limited groups. What procedure to follow?

Brainstorm a list. First, compile a list of every possible subject that might appear on the program. Some of these will definitely be borderline, but will be written down because they may ultimately suggest better topics. The list is an accumulation of notes made during the preceding months or year. It incorporates every idea you have or have been able to garner from others. You have looked at past programs of your own organization and competing associations or companies. And the list is compiled without any eye to organization or possible speakers for the subjects. The list should include at least three times the number of topics that can be treated adequately in the time available for your conference.

The next step is to organize the topics in a logical, outline-type form, retaining every topic on the list. The organizing is not difficult. If the hardware business is suffering a recession, and yours is a conference of hardware people, a talk about the present state of the business would precede discussion of what to do about it. If a subject will not fit at all into the organization outline, put a question mark beside it. Perhaps it does not fit the meeting, either.

Now, mark the topics for "old" and "new." Old subjects are those that are always with your industry or profession. They are matters of continuing interest or are problems that just will not go away. There must be something new to say about them if they are to be on the program and not put the audience to sleep. New topics are ones that have not been discussed at previous meetings and that are more likely to reflect recent developments of a more topical interest.

A desirable program has something old, something new. New subjects are great for catching the eye and promoting a program. People will not attend in large numbers, however, if the subjects and problems that are a continuing concern are not treated. On the other hand, if only old topics appear on the program many potential conference-goers will see no reason to attend this meeting if they went to the last one. People need to leave a conference feeling that they have received benefit in fundamental and temporary aspects of their field of interest.

General vs. specific. The next step is marking each item on the list to indicate whether it is of general concern to the people who will attend or of interest to only a limited number. The general subjects are candidates for the auditorium sessions that will be attended by everyone. The limited, special-interest topics will be considered for small, perhaps simultaneous, sessions.

At this point you still have a long list of topics, far too many to cover in the period of time available. This list, however, is now organized, with indication for each subject as to whether it is continuing, basic to your business or profession, or important but of mainly current interest, and the list is also marked so that you can tell whether a particular topic is of general interest or should be dealt with in a small session.

Condense and eliminate. Now, cut the list down to size. What topics must necessarily fall by the wayside? What related subjects can be combined, to be treated by one speaker in the same time slot? What related subjects should be discussed by two or three speakers? Should they follow one another, giving independent talks, or should you put them together on a panel?

It is now that you pull out the specialized subjects that are to be handled in smaller, separate sessions. Try to find enough of these so that each person attending will be involved in at least one of them. Do your best to see that any simultaneous sessions you arrange are noncompetitive. That is, a convention-goer should not feel frustrated by wishing that he could be in two sessions at the same time. Also, bear in mind that simultaneous sessions require more speakers than general sessions do.

Next, enter into an intensive study of the tentative subjects you have chosen for the conference. How much time does each topic require for adequate treatment? Where a subject is controversial, do you need pro and con views? Are any of the subjects being treated in competing conferences? If so, do you need to cover the same topics for the sake of completeness, or are you wasting time rehashing material the audience will have heard enough about? This aspect of planning is so important that it should be spread over several days. It is helpful to consult with other knowledgeable people. Examine the prospective program in depth. This is when you decide on program topics—catchy titles welcomed—and they are assigned time slots.

Before I go on to discuss speakers, I should say a little more about simultaneous sessions. (Meeting managers and hotel people also call these breakouts.)

There should be a positive reason for splitting your meeting into pieces. As noted above, varying interests and differing capabilities or expertise of people in the audience may call for this. If a large number of subjects simply must be covered, simultaneous sessions will be inevitable. Or, if you have so large a group that any general session is impossible, you must divide into smaller groups.

Simultaneous sessions place a greater burden on you, the meeting manager, than do general sessions alone. You need more speakers and equipment (audiovisual and other). You have less control over the meeting. Special hotel accommodations are necessary, but more about them later.

As mentioned above, a problem is the possibility of competing simultaneous sessions. You're lucky if your audience is truly diverse. I mean that those interested in the California condor couldn't care less about the brown pelican; the ear, nose, and throat men would have no interest in beri-beri; and the men charged with investments in bonds will not feel deprived if they cannot hear the expert on real estate investment trusts.

Another problem is estimating the size of the audiences in simultaneous sessions, but I will discuss that under hotel arrangements.

Simultaneous sessions are not hard, but they are more work than a general session occupying the same time slot. If you have simultaneous sessions, plan, stay on top of them while they are running, and find opportunities to get your entire group together during breaks.

Speakers

It is finally time to put speakers' names alongside the topics. Of course these are tentative, and you should put down as many names as possible for each topic.

Where do you find speakers? If you have been storing up names over the months before you formulated your program you have a good start. Consult past programs and competitors' programs, just as you did for topics. Consult your public or business or professional (e.g. law) library, searching out periodicals in your field to get ideas for speakers. Authors of books often make good speakers.

Maintain a file. Besides managing meetings, I have for many years attended meetings sponsored by associations and firms. I maintained a card file for every speaker I heard, listing name, affiliation, address if readily available, the name of the conference at which he spoke, the date, the topic, and a few confidential words about his ability as a speaker. I supplemented this card file with information that came to me about other speakers and authors who were potential speakers. I marked the subject of the talk or article in the upper righthand corner of the cards and filed them alphabetically by subject. The file reached several hundred cards, and I was never at a loss for a speaker, as each subject could be covered by any of several capable people. This kind of depth gives you confidence, and a file of this kind is invaluable to a meeting manager. I might add that with such a file I rarely had to use a speaker I had never personally listened to.

Speaker bureaus will help you if you pay an honorarium.

Your own members. One good source of speakers that organizations often overlook is their own membership.

Are meeting managers prejudiced against using members of their own organizations as speakers at conferences? Is the only true expert the one who comes from at least 500 miles away? I think not. I believe most meeting managers recognize that there is value in using their own people on the podium. The problem is really ferreting out good speakers within the company or organization. They certainly are there, but how can you find them?

There is no substitute for a wide personal acquaintance with members. If you know their personalities, their specialties, and a good deal about their daily activities, you may frequently see opportunities to enrich your programs. In conversation with them you can often determine, too, whether they can really talk.

A second source of tips for speakers within your own organization is data sheets on the members or employees. Some associations require that an applicant for membership meet rather strict qualifications. Information about the experience and qualifications of the applicant should be retained in the file once he becomes a member. These membership applications are a gold mine for the speaker hunter. Likewise, job résumés and personnel information forms are a useful source of speaker possibilities for the meeting manager who is constructing a program for a commercial company.

Occasionally, a survey of members, conducted to determine opinion, activity, or financial status, will turn up speakers for the alert meeting manager. This is more likely to happen if the meeting manager has a part in framing the questions to be asked than if he is not given that opportunity. If the organization is not very large, the meeting manager may create a questionnaire to get a "profile" of the membership. If he does this, he should make the tabulated results available to others. (Remember that the results of any survey of the membership are themselves the basis for a good meeting topic.)

If the organization or company has its own publication, the editor and the files of the magazine, newspaper, or newsletter are all good sources of tips for speakers.

Criteria for speakers. What criteria do you apply in selecting speakers?

■ Does your potential speaker know his subject thoroughly?

■ Is he a good speaker? Does he have something of value to say? Can he be heard in the back of the room? (This is more important than you might think.)

■ Is his name well known to the potential audience? This criterion is not essential as a factor in your choice, but popularity helps. At the same time, avoid the speaker who has had a great deal of recent exposure.

■ In choosing Speaker A over Speaker B, have you thought about diversity in your program? That is, diversity from the standpoint of geography, industry, company, and point of view.

Inviting the speaker. Only one person should decide on the list of final speakers. This means you, or someone you designate. Divided responsibility results in speakers' duplicating one another's efforts, holes in the program, or other forms of disorganization. Suggestions are fine. Volunteers to do legwork are fine. High-placed intermediaries *may* be fine. But keep your selection committee down to one. That person alone should make final decisions.

Only one person should approach potential speakers to invite them to talk at the meeting.

Start with the speaker you want most, though you may have to settle for less.

If you know your potential speaker personally, there is no question but that you should pick up the phone and call him or her. Give the details—the sponsoring organization, the purpose and nature of the meeting, nature and size of the audience, the place and dates for the conference, the date and time that the speaker is scheduled, the topic, the length of time allowed, whether to expect questions, the honorarium, if any, and certainly expenses. It may be useful to mention other speakers you have already secured.

Barring a conflict in your potential speaker's appointment book, you are almost assured of an affirmative answer, if not immediately, in a few days. It is almost impossible to say no to a friend. Of course, if he says yes, follow up with a confirming letter.

If you do not know the man or woman you are inviting to speak, write a letter. The reason is that in this situation you have a triple selling job—you have to sell yourself, your organization or company, and your meeting. This is too much to accomplish over the phone. In your letter, supply the same information about the conference that you would have supplied if you had phoned. If you are in a hurry for a reply, you can indicate that you will phone when your potential speaker has had a chance to receive your letter.

Timing is important. A two- to three-day meeting frequently requires initial planning a year in advance, especially with regard to reserving a hotel. Program decisions can well be made at that time, in no case later than six months before the start of the meeting. The timing for securing speakers is also 12 to six months before meeting. Work on the earlier side. A few potential speakers get irritated if asked a year in advance, but you will get no flak if you invite them eight months ahead of time. Wait any longer and you will find that some other meeting has sewed them up.

Contact. Now begins what could irreverently be called the care and feeding of speakers.

The relationship of the meeting manager and his speakers is close, though temporary. Continual contact is important. This begins with the confirming letter. I have made a practice of sending our speakers copies of the programs of the preceding two or three meetings of the kind in which they will participate. (Allow for this in the print run for your programs.) If your company or association is not well known to a speaker you should send a fact sheet or other background material. (Sometimes it is useful to send this in the letter in which you invite him or her to speak.) In return, get the speaker's biography and picture.

Certainly the speaker who has promised to address your audience should receive all publicity material you send out, as well as any copies of your publication that mention the meeting. If other publications mention your conference, send all the speakers copies of the clippings of the news stories.

Keep your speakers apprised of the development of the program for the meeting. Usually this can be accomplished by seeing that they receive *advance* copies of mailing pieces.

One of the first concerns a speaker has after he has agreed to talk is how he is going to get to the meeting. One of your early letters should tell what airline, train, or whatever he or she should use, or the routing if the speaker is going to drive. Ask if he wants you to make plane reservations. You will, of course, see to hotel reservations. Some speakers will want to bring wife or husband. Make clear the financial arrangements if a spouse comes—you might not charge for the spouse's share of their hotel room but would expect that the speaker would pay for the spouse's meals.

If a speaker has high enough status, you should have someone meet him at the airport or train station. It is nice to meet all speakers, but sometimes there are so many that you just do not have the staff to accomplish this. Also, some speakers will arrive during the meeting itself, when you can least spare people to greet and ferry them about. There is a tendency not to meet most speakers if the conference is being held in a large city, but to send specific instructions to speakers that will help ease their way into town. In smaller cities and resorts, where the speaker is more likely to be a first-time visitor, it is courteous to meet the speaker with a car. If the speaker is a woman, a little extra courtesy—being met, helped with luggage, and driven into town—will be especially appreciated.

No later than one month before the meeting, ascertain from the speakers if they will need any special equipment—blackboard, screen, projector (what type?), other A/V (audiovisual) equipment, operator— and order whatever will be required.

About ten days before the meeting, reconfirm all arrangements with the speakers, and tell them where to go when they arrive at the hotel. If possible, you or another committee member should be on hand near the hotel registration desk with formalities completed so that the speakers will not have to stand in line. If you are going to do this, tell them so that they will be looking for your name on a badge.

Further care of speakers at the meeting itself will be discussed in a later chapter.

Common Problems with Speakers

Most of your relations with speakers will be amiable and rewarding. There can, however, be some problems.

Delayed acceptance. Perhaps you have asked someone to talk at your conference and the potential speaker will not make a commitment. The person won't say yes and won't say no. You may want that speaker badly, but you can ask only one person at a time, and therefore you can ask no one else for that slot until you receive an answer. A week or two goes by, and you get nervous. Establish a rule for yourself before you ask anyone that anybody you invite to speak must reply within a week or you will go on to someone else. My experience is that, with rare exceptions, an answer that is longer than a week in coming is going to be no. A day before your deadline, phone the person you invited and say you are going to ask someone else. You will, perhaps, get the yes answer you have been waiting for. If not, you can go on. Delay holds up not only the formulation of your program but also the publicity dependent upon it.

Outlines and texts. Another problem—concern, perhaps, rather than problem—do you want speakers to provide outlines and advance texts? If so, get outlines, and get them early. This enables you to inform speakers when the content of their talks overlap. In addition, though you cannot tell them this, it gets them working on their talks sooner and the talks will be better as a result. You can use the outlines in workbooks for people attending the conference. Give your speakers a deadline for their texts to reach you. If you have a considerable number of speakers, make that three weeks before the meeting.

How do you get advance copies of speeches? Asking for them is all that is necessary in some cases. In others, it takes a lot more. All kinds of objections are offered: "I speak only from notes," "I never release a copy until I have delivered the speech," "I want to use the speech again."

But some meeting chairmen and managers do get all the advance talks. They accomplish this by making it clearly understood when the invitation to speak is extended that an advance text is part of the deal, and by reminding the speaker from time to time of the commitment to furnish a copy of the talk.

Why have advance texts? Because they can do the following:

■ Force the speaker to organize his thoughts and get them down on paper long before he has to deliver his talk.

■ Assure you that he has done the preparation necessary to give a successful speech.

■ Assist greatly in obtaining press and broadcast coverage of the convention.

■ Help the stenotypist or other person in preparation and early delivery of a transcript, if you are to have one.

■ Spread the speaker's ideas among those attending the conference if the text is made available to them following the talk.

■ In some instances a text is useful for other reasons—for example, where people from a number of countries will be present and translations are necessary. (In this instance, of course, extra time is necessary to allow for translation.)

Don't insist on advance texts unless you need them and will use them. But if you want advance copies, you can get them.

Briefing. Another concern is that your speaker know exactly what is expected of him or her. If the speaker does not know, it is your fault. You should define the area to be covered, as noted above, the amount of time allotted for delivery of the talk, and—very candidly—any taboos. If the talk must be strictly educational, informational, and noncommercial, with not even a mention of the name of a speaker's firm in the talk, say so—and make sure the person understands. It will be too late to stop him once he gets on the podium.

No show. The biggest speaker problem about which you can do something in advance is the speaker who does not show.

Speakers, being human, sometimes become ill, have family crises, are delayed by grounded planes—in two words, don't show.

A little prevention helps. Start each morning's program with a local speaker, if possible. This is because an out-of-town speaker who plans to arrive in plenty of time can be delayed. And if your out-of-towner never arrives, you have a little time to try to fill his slot.

From unhappy experience, I have learned to have a relief speaker on hand. Select him from your normal audience and waive his registration fee. Someone who lives in or near your convention city may be appropriate and may also save you some money. He must be available all through the meeting, ready to step in at any time. Your relief speaker, in return for being on hand, is saved some money he otherwise would have paid. He deserves a nice letter of thanks from you after the meeting, whether or not he spoke. (I had considerable success with a professional in a technical field who was also a real humorist with excellent delivery.)

A personal experience shows what can actually happen. Some years ago I was meeting manager and chairman of a two-and-a-half-day meeting in New York. The session opened at 9 A.M. of the first day, and all seemed to be going well.

At 10:30 A.M. I received a note on the dais, saying that the second speaker of the afternoon, who was to talk on hospital expense coverage, had been involved in an accident and had himself been taken to the hospital in an ambulance.

Fortunately, the first speakers of the morning had generated more questions than they had time to answer, so that I asked these speakers, plus two other knowledgeable people, to form a panel that afternoon to treat their subject in greater depth—and incidentally, of course, fill in the empty time slot.

At 10:35 a second note reached me, saying that the speaker scheduled to talk first that afternoon had arrived from the Midwest the evening before, had gone out to dinner, contracted a very upset stomach, passed a miserable night, and had taken the first plane in the morning for Indiana.

Again, help was at hand. A member of the audience prepared a short talk on his specialty during the luncheon period. It turned out to be too short for the time slot, but I put the panel discussion on early and, by the end of the second speaking period in the afternoon, the program was back on schedule.

You may never need a relief speaker, but have one on hand. It is a relief.

Is there one type of speaker who is particularly likely not to show? Yes. That is a politician in a nonelection year, especially if he is in the federal government and your conference is being held away from Washington. Some members of Congress have a good record for meeting their engagements. A few promise frequently but rarely deliver. Ask around.

Some important people are usually paid. Some who customarily get an honorarium occasionally speak free. If the speaker is going to get paid he will make a greater effort to keep his engagement. Incidentally, if a speaker agrees to talk for a fee he will probably insist that you agree to pay the fee if for any reason the conference is canceled. This is only right. It is equally fair to make him agree that if the meeting is held and he for any reason does not appear you will not pay him. No talk, no pay.

What should you do if a headliner promises to speak but finds that he cannot fulfill the promise?

Remember that you have used this person's name in promotion. He or she is probably listed in the printed program. People have indicated their intention to attend, based in part on their expectation that the headliner will speak.

If you know as much as three weeks before the meeting that your headliner won't show, you should tell everyone who has registered, and change all future—that is, last-minute—publicity. If promotion brochures are already printed, enclose a slip with each brochure telling the current situation. If you can get a replacement, do so. If the headliner was to talk on a subject that really must be covered, try to secure a speaker to talk on the same subject. The idea is to play fair with the audience.

If the speaker cancels his engagement less than three weeks before your conference, there is usually little you can do to let your audience as a whole know about the no-show. In this case, tell the meeting-goers about the program change as early in the meeting as possible. Either put a slip in the meeting kit or announce the change from the podium during the opening session. Of course, do not merely say that one speaker will not show. Tell the audience whom they will hear instead.

(One aside here—the association or other sponsor of a meeting that has said in its publicity, "So-and-so has been invited to speak," is also inviting trouble. First, this indicates that the organization is behind schedule in acquiring speakers. Second, the person named may not like having his name used in publicity when he has not agreed to speak. And third, if the invitee says no to the speaking invitation there is a likelihood of dissatisfaction on the part of those who attend the conference, even though there was no guarantee that he would appear. You have a semi-no-show situation on your hands.)

Special Situations

Before leaving the subject of securing and dealing with speakers, there are special situations, unusual, but worth looking at if they concern your meeting.

Politicians as speakers. During an election year the voice of the politico will be heard in the land. Do you want his voice heard at *your* meeting, and if so, how can you land him?

A headline political figure—representative, senator, governor, perhaps someone higher—is an asset for most conventions, especially if he is speaking on a subject in the area of interest of your organization and on the theme of your program.

Even if his topic does not deal with your field, people will come to hear him speak if he is prominent. They will want to hear his views on subjects that transcend the field of concentration of your business or specialty. The speaker may even use your meeting as a forum for an important statement.

In either case, you have a "draw" for your meeting. You should know the difference, however, between the headliner who knows your field and the one who does not.

What type of political figure is the most likely to agree to speak? In an election year, it is the politician who is running for office. This can mean all the representatives, one third of the Senators, many Governors and members of the legislatures—and candidates for those offices—and every fourth year the President. Incumbents who are not running will often be making speeches in support of candidates of their party.

It is often difficult to get members of Congress to speak outside of Washington or their own districts or states when Congress is in session. These men and women cannot predict some months ahead when an important bill will come up for a vote. They may be needed on the floor when you expect them on your dais. If you want to get a Congressman or Senator as a speaker during an election year, your best bet is to have him put your organization on his schedule during the recess that Congress declares for campaign purposes. Discuss this with the candidate's campaign committee as far ahead as possible.

A candidate is a busy person in an election year, and time is most important to him. He likes to avoid nonproductive travel and talking to audiences who cannot vote for him. He likes to talk to a second audience in a town he has to visit anyway. It's even better if he can make that talk to an audience where a majority are committed to him, but where a sizable minority can be won over.

If your prospective speaker has sponsored legislation important to your membership, your invitation to speak will have appeal for him, and if, additionally, the meeting is being held in the candidate's district your invitation will have strong appeal.

Obviously, a large audience is more attractive to a political candidate—or any other speaker—than a small one. Do not rule out important men and women as speakers, however, just because your meeting will not have a huge number attending. Winston Churchill gave his Iron Curtain speech at Fulton, Missouri.

We said earlier in this chapter that the meeting manager himself should usually contact the speaker or his agent and extend the invitation to participate in the program. In the case of a political figure it is better if the approach is made by a friend of the prospective speaker, or by someone who is a political associate. The cement of politics has as major ingredients obligations, debts, and rewards. Unless the audience you can deliver to the speaker is of overwhelming importance to him, he is more likely to agree to talk to your membership because a friend asked him than for any other reason.

Caution: Politicians sometimes do not show and commonly are late. The first problem can be countered by not choosing a speaker who is likely to be elsewhere when you need him. There is also the speaker who habitually makes promises and then does not keep them. A few of these people are well known to meeting managers. Before you invite a political figure it is well to contact other meeting chairmen who have listed your proposed speaker on their programs to find out if he actually appeared.

There is little you can do to prevent a speaker's arriving late for his engagement with your meeting. The best precaution is to have other speakers on hand so your program can move forward whether your headliner is present or not. Do not schedule him as the first or last speaker of the day. Also, try to have some warning as to when he will actually arrive. For example, if a member of your committee is meeting the politico at the airport, this person should phone you as soon as he has met the speaker, or as soon as he knows of a delay so that you can estimate their time of arrival at the meeting.

Politicians usually make good speakers. They are glad to speak in their home districts during recess from their government activities, especially during election years. If they can talk on subjects close to or within the area of interest of your audience, good, but it is often interesting and instructive to listen to them anyway. You should start extra early to secure them, and consult their convenience as well as your own in arranging dates and places.

Speakers and the traveling road show. Sometimes you may have a one-day program that is going to be run successively in a number of cities. The speakers are going to be the same at each meeting, possibly with a substitution here and there. The content of the program gets better as the schedule progresses and the speakers refine their talks, but the meeting manager has a lot of work with hotel arrangements. Everyone has a lot of traveling and gets pretty tired. How can you make it easier for the speakers, who may not all be as young and vigorous as the meeting manager?

One large organization has a staff member specializing in meetings who has devised a system of helping with travel that really works.

Prior to the meeting the hotel management has been sent a VIP list showing speakers and staff whose bills should be charged to the association's master account. One staff member (whom we can refer to as the meeting manager here) arrives at the hotel in advance of the speakers. She makes sure that the VIP list has been communicated down from the sales manager of the hotel to the front desk manager, correcting this omission where necessary.

She then goes through the formality of checking in the speakers so that when they actually arrive she is waiting in the lobby for them with their room keys.

Besides not having to stand in line to register, association speakers who are traveling from one city to another to put on the one day programs receive valuable assistance with their luggage.

Before each day's meeting is over, the meeting manager contacts the airline, telling it that she will arrive at the airport with a given number of suitcases and cartons. She tells her airline contact whether there are pieces that are particularly heavy, asks where the luggage should be taken when she arrives at the airport, and gets the name of the person she is talking to. She speaks to a supervisor where possible.

The meeting manager is, of course, ticketed on an earlier flight than the speakers and the rest of the staff.

On arriving at the airport, she looks up her contact or delivers the excess baggage to the designated area, and pays any required extra charges. The extra charge may not be very much, as the airline would be carrying the speakers and their luggage first class on a later flight, in the normal course of events, without an extra charge. By phoning ahead the meeting manager ensures that the airline expects the luggage and gives it time to prepare tags if desired. (Some airlines have different tags for suitcases from those for cartons; hence the importance in the advance phone call of designating how many of each are in the shipment.)

On arrival at the end of her flight the meeting manager collects all the luggage and takes it by cab to the conference hotel. Sometimes two cars are required, and sometimes there is so much that she has phoned ahead to have a van waiting.

If she feels that she has a good cab driver she will give him some money and send him back to the airport to meet the speakers and drive them to the hotel.

Upon arrival at the hotel, the meeting manager, signs the VIPs into their rooms. She then accompanies a bellman as he puts the luggage in the respective rooms. This gives her an opportunity to inspect each room to make sure that the rooms are all satisfactory. If any VIP has been assigned a room near an elevator or overlooking the hotel garage or a noisy area she arranges to have it changed at once. Because this is a time-consuming job, she often barely has it finished before it is time to meet the speakers in the hotel lobby and give them their keys.

This meeting manager has a particular way of handling meeting materials and food for cocktail parties. Her organization is headquartered in a suburb of a large Midwestern city. Because this association has many meetings during the year, she works with a certain day porter at the airport and a certain night one. Of course, she also has built up a relationship with individuals at the airline counters. When she has meeting materials to go out of town, she alerts the porter she knows so that he will be waiting for her when she arrives at the airport to take a given flight and informs him of the number of pieces she will have with her. Before her flight leaves she tells him when she will be returning and how many pieces she will have at that time.

This meeting manager has a few suggestions about storing food overnight for small receptions and cocktail parties. If you intend to have informal receptions for speakers, you may want to store perishable food in the hotel's refrigerators. Some of the hotel staff may give you difficulty. It is important to reach the right person to get permission, determine ahead of time what refrigerating unit you can use, and be certain that the individual in charge of the refrigerator at the time you want it opened knows that he has the authorization to open it.

Recognition. If a speaker is not paid, and you wish to give him or her a sign that you appreciate the contribution to your program, you can present a small gift immediately following the talk. You can do more. Everyone, including your speakers, likes to have his status enhanced. Before the conference takes place secure from each of your speakers a list of people, organizations, companies, and print and broadcast media that he would like to have receive a copy of his talk. Make suggestions of your own. Then duplicate the talk.

Secure from the speaker, or have made up at your own expense, a number of glossy pictures of him or her. There should be enough to send to every one of the media and have a few left over.

(In Chapter 4 we tell how to compile a list of print and broadcast media and how to write a news release.)

Convention Bureaus

What can a convention bureau do for you? There are pros and cons to working with a convention bureau. Usually, it means less flexibility for meeting managers. Some bureaus are strong in certain departments and weak in others (not necessarily the same departments in all bureaus). Most convention bureaus are good on hotel arrangements, I've discovered over the years. But on the other hand, some convention bureaus are not so good at handling your press relations.

An inexperienced meeting manager can make extensive use of a convention bureau. When he becomes more proficient he may wish to use only certain services that the bureau can perform well because it is on the spot.

A good convention bureau will make an effort to solve your particular problems and take care of your meeting's needs. By its nature, however, a convention bureau regards one conference or convention as pretty much like another of the same size and duration. It knows little of your business, and the more you can handle of your own organization's requirements, the more control you will have and the better satisfied you will be.

Hotels

If you are planning an out-of-town meeting in a city where you are not familiar with the hotels, you will wish to consult a hotel directory. Go to your local library and look at the directories available to see which supplies the information you most need.

Hotel vs. motel. Which is better for a meeting, a hotel or motel? There is no good generalized answer to this question. Much depends on the nature of the meeting.

Let us consider a hypothetical hotel and a hypothetical motel, both of high quality and able to accommodate your meeting. (Obviously a motel or motor inn cannot normally take a large convention.)

Usually the hotel will be downtown, longer established, as compared to the motel. The motel or motor inn will probably be outside the built-up area, and newer than the hotel.

As a result, the hotel will have the advantage of more spacious meeting rooms, good restaurants inside the hotel and nearby, and handy night entertainment.

In a motel it is easier to keep your meeting-goers together, as there is less for them to do in the evening and it is more effort for them to travel the greater distances to restaurants outside the motel. Food inside the motel may not be so good as in downtown hotels, or at least the motel has probably had less time in which to build a reputation for its restaurant. On the other hand, a motel that is housing no group but yours may make a greater effort to please you in all ways.

Which type of accommodation is usually quieter? Unless the meeting itself is noisy, a motel may be quieter, especially if your group virtually fills the building. A downtown hotel has street noises. Also, maids in hotels start making their rounds earlier than they do in motels. That may not be a consideration for the conscientious meeting-goer who gets up for morning sessions, but a spouse who wishes to sleep late may not like it.

Generalization, however, must be weighed against the particular facility you are considering and the needs of your conference.

Lead time. How far ahead of your meeting date should you pick a hotel? This varies a good deal. For a meeting with thousands of conventioners and special meeting room requirements, it may be necessary to schedule and reserve several years ahead. For a medium-sized meeting, say 200 to 1,000 people, a year ahead is right. Much depends on the flexibility of your requirements as to meeting rooms and site.

How do you choose a hotel? Some of the answer to this question is obvious—your geographical site may have only one hotel, as in a resort location. The size of your meeting may dictate a large hotel. You may need a certain number of guest rooms, or meeting rooms that will accommodate certain numbers of people. But I am going to pass over these important but obvious aspects to discuss some of the other considerations when you have *a choice* of hotels for a meeting. For the benefit of new meeting managers and the interest of those who are more advanced, I shall go into some detail.

In the first place, know as many hotels as you can. Hotels interest us—new ones, old ones, resort inns, city hotels, whatever. I attend a number of meetings a year, run a number myself, and travel a good deal on vacation. At every opportunity I have visited hotels. And once I leave a hotel, I make detailed notes based on my observations. You should do the same.

Visit a number of hotels in every place you go, not just the hotels that you think are the most likely for holding a meeting. This is basic education about hotels. The more hotels and motels you visit, the more you know what to expect of any hotel you may eventually choose for a meeting, and the more you know about specific hotels.

When I go into a hotel I look at the lobby, the public rooms, restaurants, and bars. If there are elevators to upstairs meeting rooms I take those elevators. What I am looking for is a general impression—of tone, capacity, efficiency, neatness. If the hotel interests me sufficiently I eat a meal in one of its dining rooms.

I look to see if this is the type of hotel the group I have in mind will like. To put it baldly and in an extreme way, is this a chrome and glass hotel, or an old hotel with grace and beauty but which may show her years? There is nothing wrong with either type of hotel, but we don't want to put the incompatible together. People who go to a meeting should enjoy their surroundings.

I never voluntarily identify myself to the sales or banquet manager in the early part of an exploratory visit. If I did so, I might get some special treatment that would fool me as to what the average convention-goer would receive.

How do you judge efficiency and neatness? Are bellhops standing ready, helping people? Quick registration of newcomers at the front desk? Fast service in the dining room? These are all good signs. Watch to see whether service is given cheerfully and in a friendly manner.

Then check the cleanliness of the lobby, carpets, meeting rooms, elevators and hallways, table silver and cups. (A friend of ours inspects kitchens before dining in restaurants.) Be sure to examine the rest rooms.

A third important consideration is food. If you are seriously considering using a certain hotel for a conference, and are visiting the hotel in the manner I have described, have a meal incognito.

I cannot imagine holding a meeting in a hotel that does not rate high in efficiency, courtesy and friendliness, cleanliness, and food.

If the hotel passes these tests with flying colors, I want to see the meeting rooms. I like to do this on my own, and can usually learn most of what I want to know without being seriously challenged. (If asked what I am doing, I say that I am considering the possibility of bringing a meeting to the hotel, and am then always left alone.) As I walk around I continue to look to see if the rooms are well maintained, tables and chairs are in good condition—if the hotel has the atmosphere of a taut ship, not a slack one.

I look at size of rooms, making a mental note of such problem areas as low ceilings and hard-to-find rooms. I also look for proximity of smaller meeting rooms to one another—in case I wish to break out our meeting into simultaneous sessions or use small rooms for an office, press room, or storage area. If we are going to divide a ballroom into separate meeting rooms I try to see if the division partitions that will be drawn through the room are substantial enough to promise that they will prevent sound from passing from one section to another. I look for the location of speakers on PA (public address) systems. I want to see if the lighting system—spots, e.g.—in the ballroom is modern. Too many posts in a meeting room constitute a negative—they may obstruct the view of the audience.

More subtle than any of these details is the feel of whether the people in this hotel know how to handle a convention. If you visit a number of hotels you will get this feeling in a good convention hotel. Often a large hotel can handle a large meeting well but will not do as good a job for the small conference as a smaller place will. It is difficult to give rules for detecting this from an inspection—indeed one off-the-record inspection may not answer all the questions I raised above. But once you have explored as much as you can on your own, you can call at the sales or banquet office. The attitude of the sales manager will tell you a lot. You can then see guest rooms and get a guided tour. Watch how the staff reacts when the sales or convention manager is showing you around. A taut ship can be a happy ship, and you want your meeting hotel to be both taut and happy.

I would like to give you what might be called an "off-beat checklist for hotels." These points are all in addition to any formal checklist you may draw up, and they are all derived from experience.

Some of the information about the following points you must get on your own, some from the hotel sales manager, and some you will pursue in the neighborhood of the hotel.

1. Is the hotel planning any construction, addition, or renovation? Is any planned for neighboring property? If so, when is the job scheduled to be finished? Nearby pile-driving, bulldozing, or demolition can drown

out your speakers, and interior painting and plastering can cause disarray with your sessions. Remember that few big jobs are completed on schedule. Allow extra time before you put your meeting in the hotel.

2. When do the hotel's union contracts come up for renewal? What are the names of the unions? What is the track record for labor relations? Rocky? If so, choose a time well away from the contract negotiation period.

3. If the hotel is at the shore, does it provide chaise longues to its guests—free? If it does not but lets a concession collect for them, look closely at other aspects and facilities of the hotel. It is probably cheap and likely to cut corners.

4. Pick up the house phone. Call the front desk and ask what the temperature is and what the weather forecast is for the day. It is surprising that a guest can often get up in the morning, wondering what to wear, ask the desk about the weather, and find that the clerk has no idea of what it is going to be. That information should be as accessible as the correct time.

5. If you are planning a one-day meeting, with lunch, what is the head chef's day off?

6. When you approached one of the hotel staff to ask directions to the office of the sales manager, did the hotel employee—

(a) Turn away when he saw you coming?

(b) Continue his conversation with a friend while you stood in front of him waiting for him to finish?

(c) Speak to you promptly, and in a friendly manner and ask you how he could help you?

(d) Go part of the way with you to show you where to go?

(e) Appear neatly dressed and well groomed?

If you get favorable answers to these questions, if the hotel seems clean and efficient, and the staff friendly and anxious to serve, it may well be worth talking business with the hotel's sales manager.

Dealing with the hotel. When you go to talk with the sales or banquet manager at the hotel you should be armed with certain information. Some of these items are the dates of your meeting, number of people you expect, the kind of meeting rooms you will need, number of people for each, whether there will be any exhibit area, what meals and receptions you plan, some idea if possible of the number of guest rooms needed, and any special equipment the speakers will need. This is the ideal information to have on hand. It is unusual to know it all early, but know as much as you can beforehand.

Meeting rooms. Usually the hotel grand ballroom, or the largest room available, will hold your entire group, or you would not have chosen this hotel or motel facility. This is basic.

Any meeting room can be set up in two ways—schoolroom style, with tables with cloth covers, or theater style, with chairs only. Theater style seats many more people, but there are no tables for people to write on.

If you have only one large room to meet in, and plan to have lunch there, you will have to break for an interval to have the room reset from schoolroom or theater style to banquet setup. For that reason, most larger meetings have two sizable rooms, one for the meeting, the other for lunch to avoid the conversions. It is best if these rooms are close together.

You should give thought to smaller rooms for seminars, table brainstorming sessions, and the like. You will have to make some estimates as to the number of people who will attend each of these small-group sessions. This is not easy at an early stage, and accuracy is not too important, as long as your estimates are not too far off. When you send out your registration material to prospective meeting-goers you can ask for preferences for the small sessions. If one room is too small for the group that has signed up, you can switch locations with a group that is underenrolled. You can also stretch a meeting room, by having it part schoolroom (perhaps the front half or two-thirds) and part theater style (the back half or one-third).

As you look at small meeting rooms, ask yourself if the ceiling is high enough for the use of screens, projectors, lighting if they should be needed.

If the meeting is a small one and you are going to use only one room in the hotel, it is wise to take a good look at the room next to yours. Is it a room that can be used for dancing, with an orchestra? Is it a room separated from yours only by the type of partition that unfolds from a wall? If either of these is the case, your meeting might have a noise problem caused by the activity in the next room, perhaps a party or a loud public address system.

"What's going to be next door?" is a legitimate question to ask your hotel contact. If he does not know, or the room next to yours has not been engaged yet, try to protect your own meeting. This does not necessarily mean moving your conference to another hotel. You can frequently get other accommodations in the same building. One thing is certain, if you wait till the meeting is in progress and you have a noise problem, virtually nothing can be done.

Discuss with the hotel representatives other rooms you may need—press room, office, storage room, committee rooms. You may get some of these free—as indicated below.

Meals. When you discuss meals with the banquet manager, you will be offered a choice of menus, each with a price attached. Ever wonder why we eat so much chicken at meetings? Because it's cheap! It comes in various fancy names, but whether it is called chicken or grand poulet en Tuxedo, it is pretty much the same thing. If you are going to keep costs down for your members or other people attending your conferences, you must have chicken some of the time. An occasional alternative—perhaps London broil—is available sometimes. (But it's not always cheap now.) Try to be different. You should know your audience, too. Some people would rather pay a higher registration fee for the conference and eat better. For small or medium-sized meetings, hotels will sometimes offer several choices for a main dish.

Bear in mind that there may be some people who are restricted in their diet by doctor's orders or for religious reasons. Ask the hotel representative how much advance notice he needs for these special orders.

Even with a meeting of several days, the organization, company, or other sponsor of the conference rarely provides dinner every night, except sometimes in the case of a very cohesive group at a small resort. It is not necessary to have a formal dinner *any* night. Frequently, however, there is one large banquet evening, quite often the night before the meeting closes.

Serious meetings for educational purposes that start their sessions early in the morning often have a buffet breakfast set up in a large room. Many other groups meeting for the same educational purposes leave those attending the meeting on their own for breakfast.

If you are running a proper meeting, you should provide lunch, and this is where the chicken comes in.

If you are considering having no meals at all, think again. You may be surcharged on meeting rooms, wiping out any savings you would have. You also reduce meeting solidarity and intermember conversation, and lessen opportunity for programmed events such as luncheon speakers.

Receptions. If you are running a two- or three-day meeting, with the formal program starting at, say, 9 o'clock the first day, you will want to provide something for those people to do who arrive the afternoon or evening before. You can bill this as a get-acquainted cocktail party, and it is frequently "no host" (that is, cash bar). If you have not planned to entertain early arriving speakers in your own room or suite, make sure that you and members of your committee are on hand at the no-host party to make the speakers feel at home and to see that they do not pay for their drinks. It is not customary to have hors d'oeuvres at the no-host party, though frequently there are peanuts, potato chips, or pretzels.

With the true cocktail party, you can go as far as you wish and your budget will allow—from hors d'oeuvres all the way to ice sculpture and an orchestra. If you have hors d'oeuvres, they will be fairly moderate in cost if they are cold and expensive if they are hot.

Cocktail parties are a serious matter to hotels. This is where they make considerable money. You can certainly save if you buy your bottles outside and bring them in. Sometimes the hotel will let you do this; in this case if you have a hotel bartender you will pay corkage on each bottle, which eats away at your saving. Frequently the hotel will insist on selling you the liquor. (Don't think you can bring in your own liquor without the hotel's knowing. You will have to buy setups and soft drinks in any case.)

You will very likely have a choice of buying liquor from the hotel by the drink or by the bottle. Which you do depends chiefly on the amount of liquor that will be consumed—if the amount is small, buying by the drink may be worthwhile; otherwise, buy by the bottle. How much liquor will be used depends on how many people will drink, and how heavily they will drink.

To estimate the amount of liquor you will need, take the total number of people you expect to come to the party, and decide how many of them are likely to drink (you know your group). Then multiply by the average number of drinks you think they will have. (The length of the cocktail party can affect this.) The total number of drinks to be consumed should be multiplied by the price per drink to determine what the charge will be if you pay on a per-drink basis.

To get the bottle figure, divide the total number of drinks by 17 (the number of average drinks in a fifth or the new 750 milliliter bottle) to get the total number of bottles. It is then a simple matter to compare costs.

I confess to a preference for the bottle approach. It fosters a more relaxed and less structured atmosphere at a cocktail party. I also prefer the bottle standing up on the bar—I am put off by seeing bottles suspended upside down from an overhead rack.

Whichever route you use, insist on name brands of liquor. The house brands are awful.

If you buy the liquor by the bottle, you are entitled to any left over in the bottles you purchased. Tell the hotel you expect this (and be on hand to collect the bottles when the bar closes).

One problem that sometimes arises is that you wish to hold a cocktail party on a Sunday before your meeting starts, and the town is dry. The best solution is to hold your party at a private club. At one meeting I attended (I won't say where), people arriving at the cocktail party in a hotel found that they had become "members" of a new club for that evening only. I suspect that this impromptu organization folded at the end of the evening. If the weather is good, the crowd small, and the host's house large, you might hold a cocktail party on the lawn of a private house, with the possibility of moving the party inside if it rains.

Coffee breaks. Coffee and soft drinks are charged by the hotel at so much per head, in most cases.

Guarantees. The hotel will expect approximate numbers from you in your preliminary discussions, as to meals, receptions, and number at sessions. In estimating the number of people you expect, be realistic. It is easy to be over-optimistic as to the number of people your meeting will attract, especially if this is the first meeting of the group. Do not forget to include the speakers and your staff and any invited guests in your estimates. Actual guarantees to the hotel, however, are not necessary at this point. The hotel will tell you when you must give guarantees, the deadline on signing a contract, and similar matters.

Guest rooms. If a good part of your attendance is from far enough away so that they will be staying overnight, you should go to your conference with the hotel business people with an estimate of how many guest rooms the hotel should block out for your convention. If you have taken over a meeting that has run regularly in the past, any past records will be a big help to you. If the meeting is new, your task is somewhat harder.

Nowadays convention hotels are interested in knowing just the total number of rooms you need. It is useful for you to know how many rooms with single beds, twin beds, and double beds (or queens) the hotel can block off for you. This helps you meet the preferences of your membership when they return their registration forms. If the hotel has only twin-bedded rooms you should know it now so that you can tell the membership. Guests who request a double bed and get twins will be unhappy and blame you. In fact, with the Hollywood-inspired, twin-bed fad pretty well past, if two hotels were equally attractive and one had only twin beds and the other a variety of accommodation, I would be inclined to put a meeting into the second. Modern motels frequently solve the problem by having two queen-size beds in each room. Be sure to look at a good sampling of the rooms the hotel will make available to you.

Free space. Do hotels give away space free? Yes, Virginia, hotels do let you have space free. It's free, that is, provided you are bringing them enough other business. The more people you have attending your meeting, the more leverage you have. If you can fill many of the hotel's sleeping rooms, it may, on request, let you use its meeting rooms free. Perhaps, also, small rooms for an office, press room, or speakers' waiting room. Provide enough business for the hotel, and you will very likely get free sleeping rooms, and perhaps suites, for your staff. You do have to ask, and there is some bargaining possible within the limits of the hotel's policy. Some hotels have a policy of providing one free bedroom for every 40 or 50 sleeping rooms blocked off and used.

Material, equipment, supplies. In some cities only one company can move material into a hotel. The sales manager of the hotel can tell you if this is the case. Not only do you need to know, but you should also inform any companies that will have exhibits at your meeting.

Schedule for hotel. You should make up a schedule for the hotel, and for you and your staff, that shows just what happens when, who is responsible, and what equipment or supplies are needed. This is one schedule that everybody gets. It is very detailed and, for meeting sessions or meals, will be tied down to the minute. For a small organization having a luncheon, the schedule may be as simple as the one on page 37.

The schedule for a large convention of several days may be a real book.

There must be enough copies of the schedule so that everyone concerned can have a copy of the part that applies to him. You should go over the schedule with the sales and banquet office people before putting it in final form. Establish rapport with each person on the hotel staff who will supervise a room and its event and go over the schedule with him or her, to see if there are omissions or problems and to be certain that the schedule is fully understood. Each member of your staff will need a complete copy of the schedule, and parts of it may be useful for your speakers.

It is evident that the schedule is not something accomplished at your first meeting with hotel people. It is something that you begin working

Luncheon for Conavest Company

Midway Room, Demar Hotel — May 14, 1983

12:00 NOON	Cocktails. Open bar.
12:30 P.M.	Lunch. Appetizers on table.
12:40	Serving begins.
1:05	Waiters clear, serve dessert, coffee.
1:13	Waiters complete serving.
1:15	President Smith welcomes audience.
1:17	President Smith introduces head table.
1:20	President Smith introduces Senator Hoskins.
1:40	Senator Hoskins finishes, answers questions.
1:50	Senator Hoskins finishes questions. President Smith thanks him.
1:53	Adjournment.

U-shaped main table, head table to seat 10 at north side of room.
  Total at lunch 40.
Equipment: table lectern with microphone; one blackboard.
Tickets: none to be collected.
Menu: attached.
Liquor: 2 fifths each, ____brand scotch, ____brand vodka,
  ____brand gin; 1 fifth each, ____brand bourbon, ____brand rye.
Assorted soft drinks.
1 bartender, furnished by hotel.

on after this initial meeting and complete and deliver a week or ten days before your conference. It is also evident that all the bugs should be out of it before you put it in final form and distribute it.

Parallel with your schedule in time is the development of a tickler file that tells you when to accomplish each job you and your staff have to do and keeps you on the track.

Special Situations

Speaker breakfast. Some meeting managers and chairmen have a breakfast for speakers on the day these people are scheduled to talk. The meeting manager can bring his speakers up to date on developments connected with the meeting, tell how the program will be conducted, and explain to those present what he expects of them. A speaker breakfast also gives a valued opportunity for the speakers to get acquainted with one another.

Some chairmen and meeting managers feel that the speaker breakfast is too "structured" and have a coffee room near the meeting hall where speakers are encouraged to drop in and socialize. In this case, the meeting manager will be able to talk with the speakers only on an individual basis, as they will come in at varying times. His main communication therefore has to be by letter prior to the meeting.

Both the speaker breakfast and the coffee room are good ideas. You must arrange with the hotel if you wish to implement one of them.

No-smoking guest rooms. The hotels do not now have rooms for people who do not smoke and who do not wish to breathe the dank, heavy air of long-dead cigars. We have some precedent—no-smoking sections of meeting rooms and even restaurants. No-smoking guest rooms are possible and we can hope that we can have them some day.

Tips for the Smaller Association

The large associations, with giant conventions, have to work years in advance. The big meeting has much less flexibility than the small one. It can afford to make no mistakes in meeting site or date. Some of its methods, however, can well be borrowed by the smaller association.

It is entirely possible for the small organization to plan more than one or two years ahead. Sometimes the officer structure in the association helps this. If your organization is a relatively small national one, and if the person elected treasurer this year becomes secretary next year, vice-president the year after that, and finally president, there is a good chance that you elect the treasurer from a different part of the country each year. In such an organization it is often customary to hold the annual meeting in the region where the president is located and make him responsible for it. Both the meeting manager and the current officers are certain to give some advance thought and planning to meetings they will be responsible for. Sites will be considered, hotels researched and discussed, and even some thought given to the substance of the coming meetings. No need to wait till a few months before the meeting.

Certainly, advance selection of places and dates has a favorable effect on attendance. People are impressed by an organization that knows "where it is going" some time ahead. People will avoid making travel and other plans that could conflict with the meeting dates if they are aware of them. And the longer promotion time has a positive effect.

Most of the intensive work for a conference has to be done in the year preceding the meeting, but it is made easier by the firm base of advance planning.

Alternatives to Hotels

Conference centers. These are meeting places within driving distance of a large city, especially New York, but also Chicago and Washington, that provide amenities and isolation for executives. Sometimes they are an inn, a converted mansion, or a motor hotel. It appears that some motels are calling themselves conference centers to attract meeting business. As a rule, holding a meeting at a conference center is more expensive than doing so at a motel. If the outside, routine business world is truly shut out, and you do not mind paying somewhat more, you may wish to consider a conference center.

Colleges and universities. Startling bargains are available if you wish to hold your meeting at a college or university. Residence halls, meeting rooms, and dining service come cheap and often the surroundings are beautiful. All of us like to become students again, on a temporary basis of course. Sometimes institutions give preference to professional societies and other nonprofit, tax-exempt groups, but educational meetings of for-profit organizations will usually be considered. Even if your conference does not meet these requirements you may find it worthwhile to check with colleges or universities in the area where you wish to hold your meeting.

3

Planning, Part II

Besides the areas of planning discussed in Chapter 2, planning involves advance registration, badges and signs, kits, spouses' program planning, the later stages of arrangements with the hotel, and provision for the press. Promotion and publicity are so important that they will be dealt with at length in the next chapter.

Advance Registration

Most meetings of two or three days or longer require most of those attending to use hotel rooms. (In a city the local people will probably go home each night.) Therefore, in a sense, anyone who needs a hotel room will register in advance of the meeting. What I really mean by "advance registration," however, is registration well in advance of the deadline you set for signing up for the conference or convention.

Advance registrations pay off for any meeting. They bring more people to your meeting and make your job easier in a number of ways. This is so well known that we need touch only the highlights:

- Advance registrations tell you how many people to expect.
- They bring in money to work with, if this is a factor.
- They help you get much of your work out of the way before the crush of registration day itself.

■ Publicizing advance registration helps build your ultimate attendance.

Encouraging it. To get people to register in advance, start several months before your meeting. Urge registration with each mailing, and enclose forms. Once someone has registered, however, maintain his interest with more mailings, but do not solicit his registration. You don't want duplicate registrations.

The greatest inducement to advance registration is the almighty dollar—offer a discount for early birds. This has consistently been the most successful device I have seen to get early commitment.

A secondary inducement is helpful where you have a very large meeting that spills over into several hotels other than the headquarters hotel. Give convention-goers their choice of hotel on a first-come-first-served basis.

The system. Setting up a good system for pre-registration is important. Cards are the way. They are much better than sheets of paper, which slide around, get caught on clips for other files, and tear. Use a good-sized card—5 in. × 7 in. is best.

How about color? Do you want to distinguish early registrants from later ones by a different color? Is status in the organization or geographical location important? A different color can help. Different colors can make classification easy. Use enough colors so that if someone inadvertently spills all the cards on the floor it will be easy to sort them out.

If you will want to include considerable information, print your form text on the card by some inexpensive process. The card shown in Figure 1 follows the form used at one convention. Although it contains more information than I believe necessary, the meeting manager who used it found this information important for him. You may want more, or less, or different information. Note that this card was used from the initial registration right through the meeting. (Hotel rooms were assigned before registrants arrived, and the cards served as a directory during the meeting.) A feature we particularly like is the "BE" in the right-hand corner—making it easy to file and locate Mr. Benson's card. The card does not have details about Benson's room reservation. This was handled by a separate blank.

■ The cards go into boxes or trays, of course with alphabetical dividers. Have a small envelope made up with the registrant's name written on it, to be paper clipped to the card. This envelope will contain the registrant's badge, tickets, and spouse's tickets and badge. (Put bulky things that are not personal or of value in kits.)

Acknowledge receipt of the conventioner's registration and fee on the same form as if he registered later. Be sure the receipt indicates the amount paid. Use the occasion of the acknowledgment to include information on nonmeeting items—clothes to wear, the golf tournament if there is one, sightseeing, and similar matters.

Typing addresses can become a chore for a secretary. Most meeting

```
                                                                    | BE |
                    10th Annual Convention, JKL Association

John J. Benson                                          Room No.  627
Vice President
Grand Corporation
101 Main St.
Histown, Calif. 90000

Officer of JKL?  Yes_____   No  X   Office_____

Paid:    Early Registration $240 ___X___      Bill company _____
         Regular Registration $300 _____  Bill registrant _____

Spouse attending?  Yes  X    No_____     Paid?   Yes  X    No____

Spouse's name for badge:  Martha_____

Room reservation rec'd?     Yes  X       No _____

Special remarks:  First meeting attended._____
```

Figure 1. Sample pre-registration card.

managers have access to some kind of duplicating process that will lighten this load. Of course if you maintain stencils of potential meeting-goers you will move the stencil of the person who registers from the solicitation file to the registered file.

■ A large meeting may have its registration process computerized.

■ Consult the hotel to see if its convention manager wants word on early registrants. Probably the hotel will want to wait until near the time of the meeting. If you can have the pre-registration process include final hotel registration, your conventioners will be very grateful. In this case include the hotel key in the registrant's envelope when the key becomes available.

When the time for the meeting comes, there will be two sections at the registration desk, one for pre-registrations and one for those not previously registered. As each pre-registrant gives his name he will receive his small envelope and a kit. Nothing more is needed. His card in file, without the envelope, is a sign that he has registered and picked up his material.

Hotel information. Now let us retrace and look at the hotel information you need to secure from the pre-registrant.

Your promotion will tell the prospective meeting-goer the hotel or hotels being used. But if more than one hotel is involved, indicate which is being used as headquarters.

Include in your form the appropriate nights so that your meeting attender can check off those for which he or she will need a room. Some meeting managers prefer to have the registrant fill in arrival and departure dates. If the hotel requires check-in before a certain time in the afternoon or evening, show this.

Determine what types of sleeping rooms your meeting hotel or motel has, and be specific in what you offer your members. Hotels have the following types of rooms:

- Single (one bed for one person).
- Double (with double bed, or sometimes queen or king, for two people).
- Twin (two beds, for two people).
- Adjoining (two rooms, with any bed arrangement, which open onto a common corridor and are next to each other, but do not connect).
- Connecting (two rooms whose occupants may pass from one room to the other without going into the corridor).
- Suite (a living room plus one or more bedrooms).

Motels often have two double or queen-size beds in a twin room.
Never call a twin room a double room. It only causes confusion.

One potential problem—the registrant wants a doubled-bedded room but the hotel has only twins. Spouses at conventions are here to stay, and not everybody who wants a double bed is a honeymooner. Your preliminary discussion with the hotel should include the subject of whether it has double-bedded rooms and, if there are few of this kind, how many they have. In all cases where there is a choice, your registration form should offer the choice. If only twin beds are available, say so on the registration form. Then the hotel, not you, is recognized as the culprit in case of disappointed expectations.

If the hotel requires a deposit, mention this on the registration form you send to potential meeting-goers.

A major difference in processing depends upon whether you or the hotel is handling room reservations. If they come to you, whether you pass them on or not, you have the opportunity to mark the registrant's card so you know that he has taken care of his lodging. If you are not going to see room reservations, that is if they go direct to the hotel, you have to let the registrants fly by themselves. Some meeting managers prefer to stay out of the room business completely, limiting their concern to sending out the hotel's registration form with promotion.

Some of the best-run meetings I have attended, however, have been those where the meeting manager had arranged with the hotel to assign rooms ahead of time and give the keys to the meeting committee. These are then placed in the small envelopes and clipped to the registrants' cards. People, upon arrival at the hotel, get into their rooms faster and usually accept their room assignments without question.

As can be surmised, the procedure described for early advance registration (except for the discount allowed for early sign-up) is followed for all other registrations right up to the meeting itself. There is more pressure, however, as time goes on.

Related Matters and Problems

Discount for multiple meeting reservations. You are frequently asked for a discount where more than one person from a firm wishes to attend your conference. You should have a policy on this, and here is what I suggest.

Your first principle should be that the first person to register pays the full fee. Any additional people get a reduction. If there is a cancellation, the cancellation applies only to the most recent registration made as far as the fee is concerned, no matter what individual cancels. Make this clear and you will avoid possible disagreements later.

Next, any reduction should apply only to additional registrations from the same firm, association, local, or whatever. Otherwise you will be giving discounts where you are truly entitled to get the full fee, and could get it.

Consider carefully the percentage reduction you can afford for the second and succeeding registrations. If your meeting is intended to make a profit you can afford a larger proportional discount than you could if you were running a meeting for a small nonprofit organization and you did not intend to make money on the conference. Furthermore, in the latter case if most of the registration fee is to pay for meals your discount can be only minimal.

In many cases, especially where meals are not the major cost of the conference, a 25 percent reduction for the second person and succeeding people who attend is reasonable, and attractive. You may, of course, have reasons for making it more or less.

One registration—several users. Another question that arises concerns what to do about a firm or association that pays registration for one person but wants different people to use that registration in parts. To the firm this seems to be a reasonable request, since only one person is at the meeting at any particular time. From the meeting manager's standpoint, this can cause a little extra work with badges, but I cannot see making a fuss about it. I would honor requests for this, but would not announce that I am doing it.

Sometimes an association or firm will pay for one person to attend, but will then ask if other people can listen in for a portion of the meeting without charge. I have allowed this where a speaker wanted one or two of his firm's employees to hear him speak. I have permitted other exceptions from time to time, even where there was no relationship between the speakers on the program and the free riders. I would not, however, let people in free to hear a headliner, especially if my firm or association had paid a good deal of money to get such a speaker, or for free meals, or in any considerable numbers. We are not, or course, talking about press, who are rarely charged.

Part-time attendance. If you are running a meeting for two or three days, and you have a number of requests to attend only a half day, you may wish to reply to such requests by quoting a fee somewhat larger than the proportionate amount of the total. For example, for one half-day of a full three-day conference you might ask one-fifth of the total conference charge instead of one-sixth. You would have an additional fee for a lunch or cocktail party. This gets complicated, however. You have to rely on your part-time registrant's honesty not to attend other parts of the conference (unless you make him a second-class citizen with a distinctive badge). I think it best not to bother with charging for fractional parts of a conference. I suggest that you have a general policy of not allowing people to attend only part of the meeting; then make exceptions, without charge, where you wish to do so. Grant the privilege rarely.

I should say, however, that some large associations, especially in technical fields, have had success in splitting, say, a two-day conference, so that a person can attend the whole meeting period or, if he wishes, register for one day at a rate about 60 percent of the fee for the two days. Different color badges are used to keep straight who paid for what.

Multiple sessions—estimating attendance. Some meeting managers and meeting chairmen need to know ahead of time how many people to expect at small, simultaneous sessions in the hotel's smaller rooms. This is so the meeting manager can plan in what room to put which session. If this is your situation, ask for a sign-up on your meeting registration form. If you do not need to know until the meeting itself, but must know before the sessions in the small rooms start, ask the audience at the opening session of the meeting, "By a show of hands, how many wish to attend the session this afternoon . . . ? How many wish to attend the session on . . . ?" etc.

Room directory. I have said that if you get the registrant's hotel room number on his registration record card, you have a hotel room directory ready made. This can be very useful to you, to your speakers, and to others who wish to confer with one another. This would be minimal use of the information.

At the other extreme would be a typed list showing all names, affiliations, and hotel room numbers. If your meeting is at a small resort, fairly isolated from a big city with its problems, you might wish to do this, once everyone has registered. On no account should you put in street addresses or zip codes (the city of the registrant is all right). Your members will not enjoy being put on someone's mailing list.

Use care in how you give out room information. There is a danger in linking a hotel room number with a person's name. It gives undesired people an easy way of contacting a potential victim. If a person with your association's meeting badge on his chest approaches the registration desk and asks if Joe Doaks has registered yet, there is no harm in telling him yes or no. If he asks for his room number I would not give out that information unless I knew the person making the inquiry. I would tell him to ask for the person over the hotel's house phone. We did not always have to be so careful.

I see no point in making a list of names and complete addresses of people attending a meeting, for distribution or to be furnished to people on request. At times other than a meeting, if a member wishes to get in touch with another member he can do so through your association's headquarters or secretary. Or, if you believe intercommunication among members is really important, print a complete list of members for your organization. Be aware that if you have a printed list, it will probably become available to mailing houses if they consider it valuable enough. It will, however, be of real service to your members, as compared to the limited service of a partial list comprising only those who attended a meeting.

Cancellations. If you allow cancellation of advance registrations, plus refund of part of the fee—or all of it—your policy must be spelled out in your advance registration material. Require that cancellations, in writing, actually reach you by a certain date (a phone call followed by a letter will do). Some meeting managers allow cancellation beyond the usual cancellation deadline, with a partial refund. Sometimes they have a sliding scale—the later the cancellation the less the refund. If there is really a good reason for a schedule, then do it. But keep the process as simple as possible. You don't want cancellations to interfere with service to paying customers.

With prepayment *you* have the leverage. Be fair with your cancellation policy, but be firm. The type of meeting can make a difference in the policy you adopt. If a large corporation is sending a person to your meeting and the person who registered cannot attend, it may be easy for the company to send a substitute. A small association may not be able to substitute so easily. Once in a great while, too, it becomes necessary to refund a registration fee to someone who discovers just before the meeting that he cannot attend for a reason he could not foresee, such as family illness, and you cannot refuse the refund.

When the registrant has not prepaid, *he* has the leverage. Consider this when you formulate your cancellation policy.

An approach used by some meeting managers is to charge everyone a nonrefundable $45 or $50, payable in advance, as part of registration.

Chapter 7 discusses what to do with registrants who do not show up at the meeting.

Honoring the loyal. People who attend your meetings regularly, especially annual meetings, deserve special recognition. (See Chapter 5.) Keeping a record, so that you know whom to honor, can be done in tandem with your advance registration procedure. You will not want to give public recognition to faithful attenders until your organization is at least five or ten years old. Then you may devote three minutes or so at a luncheon session to reading the names, or, if there are too many to mention, you may list them in the program. (Printing the names in the program requires advance work.) While the organization is still new, keep good, typewritten records of people who attend the meetings. Then compile your list of the loyal on 5 in. × 7 in. cards. A suggested card is shown in Figure 2.

The form of the card is largely self-explanatory. The upper part is for name and address, with the right-hand part available for changes. In the lower part, you keep the year-to-year record of attendance.

Many organizations recruit some speakers from their membership. For this reason a place is left on the sample card to record them as present and speaking.

When a card is filled, staple a new card on top of the old one and fill in the name, address, etc. How these cards are used will be told in appropriate places in the chapters to come.

Registrant wants to bring a girl friend or boy friend. These are liberal times, and this may happen. If the registrant makes the hotel reservation independently there is little you can do except to tell the member that the friend may not be very comfortable at the meeting, if that is the case, and that it will do the organization no good. If the reservation is

Annual Meeting						(Space for changes in title, address, affiliation)		
Last name First name Initial								
Title:								
Firm:								
Address:								
Year	Attended	Spoke	Year	Attended	Spoke	Year	Attended	Spoke
1981			1986			1991		
1982			1987			1992		
1983			1988			1993		
1984			1989			1994		
1985			1990			1995		

Figure 2. Sample "loyalty list" card.

made through you, in the usual way, you may wish to suggest that the person make it himself or herself, at another hotel.

Badges

Badges are important. But they are the most consistently mismanaged aspect of all meetings, large and small.

Do you want a badge to be an ornament or to communicate quickly and visibly the name and affiliation of the wearer? You can have it do both, but is not communication more important?

Badges are too often an absent-minded decision of the busy meeting manager. Actually, the size, color, type, and lettering are all important. Also, where the badges are worn, when, and their disposition after they have served their usefulness are important. You can save money on badges, make them do double duty, if you wish.

Size. Use large badges; 2½ in. × 4 in. is much better than 2 in. × 3 in. You need the additional space for lettering.

Color. Almost any light shade is all right (for contrast with lettering). Badges need not be white. Color becomes significant only when a different color is used for officers, speakers, regular registrants, different disciplines, and guests. What the colors mean should be explained in the program.

Legibility. Can people really read the badges you give your registrants? We don't mean of course that anyone outside Greece or China deliberately letters badges in Greek or Chinese. But we do wonder how many meeting managers have any idea how difficult it is to read many of the badges distributed to their convention-goers.

Compare

BOB LORD

And. . . .

To test legibility, prop this book up against a wall and move away until you can just read the typewritten name. Note that place, and then move back until you can just read the hand-lettered name. Quite a difference, isn't there?

What makes the difference? Several things. First, the hand-lettered badge is obviously much darker. The letters are larger, and they are farther apart. But nearly as important as these other factors is the fact that the hand-lettered name is in upper and lower case (capital and small letters). Practically everything we read is printed this way, and the eye can read upper and lower case material better and faster than it can material which is entirely in capital letters. Yet an estimated 95 percent of badges are typed in capitals only.

Since the purpose of a badge is to tell people the name of the wearer, communication should be fast and painless. Which of the badges above does the better job?

Badge economy. Some meeting managers may object that they cannot afford hand-lettered badges, no matter how attractive and effective they are. One solution to the cost problem is to have the badges hand-lettered, but use them meeting after meeting—asking the members to return them each time. There are also ways of making badges at moderate cost.

One way is to have the badges typed on a typewriter with jumbo type. This is big, dark type designed especially for work like this. If you do not have easy access to such a machine, you can find a shop that will type the badges for you in all but the very smallest cities. Be sure, however, that the badges are typed upper and lower case. Some jumbo machines can do this.

If you are reduced to using the ordinary office typewriter, do the best you can. Have a dark ribbon in the machine, and type upper and lower case. And, of course, use a typewriter with large type—pica rather than elite.

The "right" way. Having legible type on badges is only part of the battle. For a badge to be easily read, the conventioner must wear it on the *right* side of his chest. This is because when people shake hands they do so with the right hand. The "sideways shuffle" to get a look at a badge that is worn on the left is both awkward and embarrassing. A badge is communication, not battlefield decoration.

The two most common faults of badges are that they are made with lettering too small to be read and are too often worn on the left side. You can do something about the first. You will have to tell your meeting-goers about the second. Tell them in the meeting program or instruction sheet in their kit. Put up a small sign at the registration desk:

> Badges worn on your right
> Are easier to sight!

Wearing a badge on the left is only a habit. Like other bad habits, it can be broken.

Types of badges. Badges worn on the right have to be pressure-sensitive badges, or be backed with a clip or a pin. Pressure-sensitive badges lack durability, but are not bad for a one-day meeting. I prefer badges in a plastic holder backed by a pin. Some people object that a pin makes a hole in clothing. It does, but it does not *leave* a hole in most fabrics. A day after attending a meeting I cannot find a hole in any of my jackets, no matter what the material. Badges that clip are hard on clothes. How about the badges that slip into a man's breast pocket? The best that can be said for these is that they are cheap. But they have to be worn on the left and the holder is sometimes too large to fit into a man's jacket pocket. They are entirely unsuitable for women's clothing. Avoid them.

Wording—Names on badges should read the way the wearer wishes to be addressed when called by his first name. For example, R. T. Smith is not very helpful to people who shake Smith's hand, even though Smith may mumble something more explicit. R. Thomas Smith, or Tom Smith means much more.

Affiliations, if used, should be kept short. Abbreviate all you can. Save most of the space for the wearer's name.

Keep the identification of your organization or company small. Just a symbol or logotype in the corner is fine.

Use and misuse—a few words about how the meeting manager can use badges and control their misuse.

Badges sometimes make it possible to dispense with meal tickets. This will work in a controlled area, like a company sales training school. It will not work in a large hotel open to the public, where freeloaders can come into the area, pick up a badge from a table, and mooch a meal, or do worse.

If you make wearing a badge a requirement for entrance to a meeting, station guards at the door of your meeting room to enforce it. Be sure there are no unguarded doors. If anyone reports a lost or stolen badge, immediately notify the guards at the door of the person's name so they can watch for that badge. (Badges that can be read at a distance pay off here.)

Control of badges is important to frustrate thieves. We live in times when many people in big cities are not as honest as they should be. Some professional crooks haunt convention hotels, looking for purses, attaché cases, tape recorders, anything of value they can pick up. Often these thieves are well-dressed people who mingle with the convention crowd.

Because badge control is essential, badges should not be spread out on a table for registrants to pick up on their own. Keep them in boxes in alphabetical order, with good alphabetical dividers, and pass them out to individual registrants as they identify themselves. The same objection to placing badges with names on a table applies to blank pressure badges— those where the registrants write their own name on the badge. Badges should be handed out individually to the people as they check in.

Using badges again. Reusing badges saves money and work. If you expect many of your registrants to appear at the next meeting, put each badge in an envelope (as mentioned in the section about registration). The badges do not get tangled that way. Put the member's name on the outside, and file it in a box. As the next function approaches and advance registrations come in, badges again go into "registered" boxes.

When badges are reused, you will need to catch members who have not registered at the door, so they can pay for their registration and you can reach into the "not registered" box and get their badge. You should also have meal tickets, printed with the name of your organization or company and "Luncheon" or "Dinner." These, too, can be reused if you have the hotel or restaurant return them to you.

One more word about security—people should, of course, remove their badges when leaving the hotel or other building where the meeting is being held.

Signs

In this chapter we will tell you what signs you will need for a sizable meeting and what they should say. Chapters 5 and 6 explain how to use them.

Color coordination. First, let us suggest that you choose the same color cardboard for all your signs. Instead of white, use a light pastel that will contrast with the dark lettering. That one color will then be identified with your meeting, and serve as a subtle aid to your membership. If you can afford it, you can have your organization or company logo on the upper part of the sign.

Where to go. The first signs you need are those telling people where to go to find your meeting, or parts of it: XYZ Association, Lunch, Press Room, Registration, Credentials Committee, Speakers' Breakfast, Reception. Don't forget direction signs in the hotel lobby and in corridors where necessary. If the sign requires an arrow, cut it out of another piece of cardboard and attach it to the main part of the sign with a pin. In this way you can turn the arrow to point in either direction and reuse it at another meeting. A wrinkle—some meeting managers use lettering on a sign giving directions that make it look like a street sign.

Speakers' signs. Next you need speakers' signs. These should be made with letters as large as possible. Why? Most speakers' signs have letters about three inches high, are all capitals, and some of them show the speaker's entire name. At the next meeting you attend, try reading the signs from the back of the room, or even half-way toward the back. I'm willing to bet that you can't make out what the sign says.

Make all letters on a speaker's sign at least five or six inches high. No harm in making them seven inches if you reduce slightly the white space above and below the name.

Next—and this is important—insist that the name be printed in small letters except for the first letter. This is, again, upper and lower case.

Third, use only the last name of the speaker. This makes possible large letters on signs of conventional size.

By insisting on signs like this you may raise the hackles of your artist, but you are striving for communication, not art. And a sign drawn as we have described does look clean and uncluttered and is legible.

A further hint—have three or four blank signs, with the back easels all glued on, for possible last-minute program changes. Have a brush or grease pencil on hand at the meeting for emergency lettering.

I think a lectern sign is a good idea. Long ago hotels found that they could get free advertising by inscribing their name on the front of their lecterns. This has seemed to us an understandable commercial practice. Every time a photograph of a speaker is printed there is a good chance that the name of the Super Majestic Convention Hotel will be out there, bold and clear.

But lecterns get old. They get scratched and battered. Hotels do not throw them out or even refinish them. Photographs begin to show speakers' faces peering from above tired old lecterns advertising the S. M. C. Hotel.

A number of organizations wisely decided that it made sense to hide both scratches and hotel names with signs saying State Artists' Society or F.P.C. Sales Caravan. This was a welcome advance over the S. M. C. Hotel. I suggest you do the same.

You can go further and give the speaker himself an extra plug. Use the organization or meeting sign, of course, but for each speaker have his or her name printed on a card and place the card on the large sign on the front of the lectern when the speaker is about to talk. Use last name only, all upper and lower case, just like the sign at his seat on the dais.

Registration. If your meeting is large, you need several signs for your registration area, but even the smallest meeting should have at least one sign or banner to tell the meeting-goer that he has finally reached the place where he should be for the meeting. A large registration area should have large signs on the wall to designate "Pre-registered" and "New Registrations." You may need alphabetical signs to split your crowd into manageable groups, "A–L," "M–R," "S–Z." You may want a separate area, and therefore a separate sign, for VIPs—officers, former officers, speakers, guests, press. Other frequent signs are to identify the "Problem" desk, "Sightseeing" table, and similar service areas.

You may wish to put up signs in conspicuous areas saying when certain committees will meet, and where. Posters advertising next year's convention will tell when, where, and show scenes of the host city.

Where signs stand free, away from walls, they require easels. Borrow them from the hotel.

Registrants' tents. If your main meeting room is to be set up school-room style, I recommend "tents" for the names of the meeting-goers. Go to your printer and have him take light cardboard which, when printed and trimmed, will be about 7 in. × 10 in., with a light score 10 in. long down the middle the long way. The printed copy (one side of card only) will be Name and City (or Council, Company, or whatever you wish for identification). This copy will appear on each half, so that when the card is folded and stood up on the table it will be readable from either side. The card looks like the illustration, before folding.

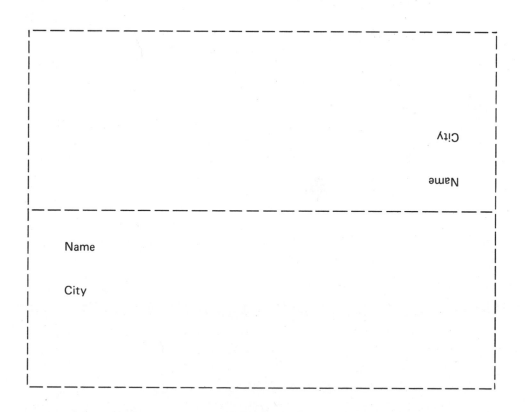

Furnish three grease pencils for each table, and see that each meeting-goer gets a card in his kit, or else put one at each place at the table. Ask people to print their name and identification, large, on their "tents" and put them up. Best get-acquainted device you ever saw. It is easy to locate someone you want to see. Once you try it you will use it for every meeting. It has been a practice at meetings of the American Management Associations for years.

Kits

The small organization, or the simple meeting, does not need to furnish those attending with anything more than a program. After a year or two, however, as the size of the membership or attendance grows, a program alone is not enough. The association needs more prestige than a single piece of paper or small booklet affords, and the kit is born.

The cost mainly depends on how much printing you are willing to pay for, because that is the major variable.

Types. Two usual types of containers are available, the envelope and the binder. A zippered envelope of legal size at this time costs about half what the snap-open type costs. A ring binder costs about the same as a snap-open container. An imprint costs extra.

One way to save money on imprinting is to buy a binder without an imprint, but with a small embossed panel on the cover. Make a label of the name of the organization and press it down in the embossed area. Convention materials should be punched to conform to the ring binder before they go into the kit.

I prefer the zippered or snap-open envelope to hold kit materials. One advantage of the good binder, however, is that the convention-goer can put the binder on his book shelf as a permanent record.

Midway between the envelope and the ring binder, in that it has some advantages of each, is the memorandum folder. This is really a pad with a cover. It opens like a book and contains a pad and a pencil or pen, giving the meeting-goer a hard surface on which to write.

Imprinting. If you imprint, should you use the date, or specify which conference this is in the series being held? I think not. Say, "Annual Conference of Steel Processors," or, simply, "Baker Company," but not "1981 Annual Conference of _____," or "23rd Annual Convention of _____." By omitting mention of dates, you can order binders or containers for several years at a time and secure a better price than you could otherwise.

Sometimes a commercial firm will provide envelopes or ring binders, if you will include the firm's imprint or give it a mention somewhere in your printed program. Sometimes, too, such a company will supply pens—of course with the company name on them. So much the better, if you do not mind the commercialism.

What goes in. Here are some of the materials which should go into a kit:

1. The program for the meeting.
2. Pictures and biographies of the speakers, if these pictures and bios are not in the program.
3. Spouses' program (again, if this is not in the main program).
4. Schedule of leisure-time activities.
5. Plan of the hotel if it is large or confusing.
6. Map of the city where the meeting is being held with information about entertainment, transportation, and restaurants. Frequently the hotel, convention and visitors bureau, or chamber of commerce can furnish free publications that contain information about entertainment for the week and advertisements for restaurants. (Many meeting managers prefer to place this material on tables for the registrants to pick up rather than place it in the kit.)
7. A critique sheet, for feedback from the convention-goers to you. Ask them how they reacted to hotel, meals, and site as well as how they liked the topics and speakers.

The following are optional:

8. List of registrants.
9. Outlines of the talks.
10. List of hospitality rooms.
11. List of members present who have a long history of attendance, with number of meetings attended.
12. List of present officers.
13. List of past presidents.
14. Locations of past meetings.

Some meeting managers put badges in kits. Unless your meeting is very small, this unnecessarily complicates registration, as each kit has to be marked to indicate who is to receive it. It is better to have all kits the same and hand out the badges from boxes. Meal tickets can either be placed in the kit or given out separately.

Exhibits

Exhibits usually mean booths, but often there are large pieces of artwork, e.g. graphs, to be exhibited on easels during a talk, as well as other kinds of exhibits. Artwork can be handled in the same way as you would signs. Slides and booths will be discussed in detail in Chapter 10. Many meetings do not have slides or booths, and it is appropriate to omit them from the current chapter which deals with preparation for the usual meeting.

If your meeting will have booths, slides, or other exhibits, you *must* make advance preparation for them. (See Chapter 10.)

Spouses' Programs

We used to call them wives' programs, but they are now more often called spouses' programs. Let's make clear in the beginning, lest there be misunderstanding, what spouses' programs have been, and then we can discuss what they can be.

Traditionally, a spouses' program is designed for the entertainment or educational interest of the wives of men who come to participate in a predominantly male group at a convention or other meeting. Spouses are not expected to attend the formal program. They are present because their husbands are there, not because they themselves have an interest in the program that is the business of the meeting. A spouse registration fee must be paid. From the meeting manager's standpoint, they are not guests.

A spouses' program could theoretically be designed for the husbands of women who have come to a predominantly female group, but probably many fewer husbands accompany wives to the wives' meetings than vice versa. Some women's organizations discourage husbands from coming to their conventions. A spokeswoman for a large women's association said, "We don't want husbands. They only take up beds." On the other hand, many organizations whose memberships are mostly male do not encourage spouses' presence. One way to discourage them is not to arrange special spouses' programs.

When husbands do come with their wives to a women's meeting, they usually find things to do on their own. They may wander by themselves, play golf, or swim, depending on the locale. Even if a program for husbands were organized, it is unlikely that you would get enough of them together to make it viable.

In view of this, we can address ourselves to the question of putting together a program for women. Creating a good program is not easy. Here are some of the problems:

- Most of the wives do not know one another and usually have little in common.
- Some of the traditional fare can be expensive—tours and meals in fancy restaurants, for example. (But a golf or tennis tournament may be only moderate in cost and be well received.)
- If you plan too attractive a program—sightseeing in a major city, for example—you may find that some of the men who have come

to participate in the program may want to join their wives. This does not happen very often, but it can drain attendance and have an adverse effect on the meeting.

■ It is difficult to think of new ways, year after year, for the women to spend their time.

The best programs are invented by the wives themselves. Although the meeting manager cannot let control of this part of his responsibility get away from him, an innovative, outgoing woman can usually be more effective as chairman of the spouses' program than he can. She should be in on the planning as well as the execution. The right chairman can break down walls between women who do not know each other, she will know how to improvise when hitches appear, and she will keep the program on schedule.

The program should be really good. Fashion shows, tours, and shopping trips may be fine—perhaps the women in your group want nothing else—but it is a mistake to underestimate their tastes. The tours should be related as much as possible to the interests of the group. Why not take a straw vote some months in advance of the meeting by sending to a number of wives a list of the attractions at the site location, asking them to indicate—1, 2, 3, 4 (decreasing order of interest)—those activities they prefer?

Include in the program at least one time slot for the women to be told about their husbands' business—what it is about and how they can assist their husbands.

Women increasingly want the opportunity to acquire new knowledge in areas so far considered off limits to them. The following are some examples of how lectures or field trips for wives can be linked to the areas of specialization of the meeting:

■ A metallurgical meeting in a steel city—tour of a steel plant.
■ Financial type of meeting in New York—visit to the New York Stock Exchange or a large bank.
■ Nurserymen's convention—tour of gardens if the site city has them, or lecture on gardening.
■ A doctor's meeting—visit to a hospital or health maintenance organization.
■ Educational meeting—a visit to an important library or art museum, a lecture on fine books by an expert.
■ Religious meeting—tour of famous and beautiful houses of worship in the host city.

These are just some ideas to start your thought processes associating the purpose of the convention with allied activities of interest to the wives.

Often, by raising the sights on the quality of the field visits or talks incorporated in the wives' program, the meeting committee can increase the information feedback to the husbands who are attending business sessions at the conference. After all, no one can be in two places at once, and a good wives' program can increase not only the information that they take away from the meeting, but the information their husbands do as well.

A further note—when planning for the wives, remember that it is important for them to know, a number of weeks in advance, what clothes to bring. Tell them how many social events, at what time of day, how formal or casual these events will be, what specifically "people are wearing" at parties in that area (for example, skirts to the floor), and likely daytime and nighttime temperatures.

Some specific programs. Here are programs for spouses that meeting managers have arranged recently that actually worked. Note that the members themselves can take part in these programs.

In Washington, D.C., the meeting manager combined a cocktail party, theater program, and dinner for a successful program. There was a cocktail party at Kennedy Center (6 P.M. to 7 P.M.), then a play at one of the three theaters in the Center. Following the play was a banquet dinner (beginning approximately at 10:30 P.M.) at the roof restaurant. About 400 conventioners attended the evening program. (Other possibilities in Washington include going to sports events instead of the theater and holding cocktails, a banquet, or both in the big hall of a large museum, which provides a grand setting.)

In Honolulu, at a meeting of 2,000 plus spouses, a full program was arranged for leisure hours, but conference-goers and their wives could pick and choose—Pearl Harbor cruise, how to make leis and hors d'oeuvres, lessons in Hawaiian dancing, a fashion show, talks by speakers of stature.

The meeting manager for the Washington meeting just described showed his consideration for spouses when he included a letter for them in the kit that registrants received. The letter did the following:

1. Welcomed the spouses.
2. Invited those receiving the letter to a special meeting during the convention that would help plan the next year's annual convention.
3. Promised a packet of information on this year's convention city, to be distributed at the special meeting.
4. Announced a film on the convention city selected for next year's meeting.
5. Invited all spouses to hear the keynote address at the current convention and to attend any panels they desired.

A section of the printed program was devoted to convention information for the spouse.

Badges for spouses (included in the registrants' kits) admitted spouses to all sessions.

Advance promotion for the Honolulu meeting was extensive. In advance of the convention the organization sent out a complete, typed spouses' program schedule. Preceding another meeting a full page in the association's magazine was devoted to spouses' activities at the upcoming convention. At the annual meeting itself the spouses got a program brochure detailing their own program.

I have indicated that it is a good idea to welcome spouses at business meetings of the organization. Not all meeting managers agree. A few feel that planning becomes too difficult if you encourage spouses to attend a large meeting. You may think you will have 2,000 in the Grand Ballroom when suddenly 600 or 700 more wish to attend. You may feel the same way for your conventions. In such a case you might not turn anyone away, but not encourage spouses to attend regular members' sessions.

What Will the Kids Do?

How often do we think of programming activities for the children who come to a convention with their parents? There are any number of spouses' activities, but the children are largely forgotten. Somebody may say, "But they vary so much in age, what can we do?" Well, let's try.

Except in big cities there will usually be swimming, and the aquatic-minded will make their own way to the pool. Let's assume that there is tennis as well. How about a tennis tourney for the teen-agers, to be run while the members are at the meetings? If the facilities are not crowded perhaps they can have their time on the golf course.

For the younger children, some of the women who enjoy working with young children could plan a party for an afternoon when most of the mothers will be on tour or watching a fashion show. If the meeting is at a resort, the party can be held outdoors (weather permitting), perhaps with games and some competitive activity. If the conference is in a large city the party can be in a hotel suite or in one of the smaller meeting rooms.

A big city often has cultural opportunities—concerts, plays, museums, music halls—where groups of children are welcomed when accompanied by adults. Do some advance planning with members or their spouses who live in the host city.

At one convention some enterprising teen-agers got together and put out a daily paper about events and people during the meeting. Yes, an actual daily paper. At another the children drew and painted pictures and put on an art show of their own as a feature of the meeting.

Also, use a little ingenuity to find out what local children do in the place where the meeting is held and adapt the ideas to your own use. This way, the children will remember the meeting with pleasure, and not as just another hotel where they watched television. They could do that at home!

Sightseeing, Where to Eat, How to Go?

*Seeing the town.*The meeting manager can enhance the enjoyment of the conferees and spouses by sending in advance of the meeting a map of the site city and a list of worthwhile things to do and see. Because of the special interests of the convention-goers, not all places of interest to them may be on the usual "points of interest" list on the usual tourist map. You may wish to make a list headed "71 Things to See and Do in Washington, D.C.," "52 Things to Do and See in San Francisco," "73 Things to Do and See in New York," or "29 Sights to See in Atlanta and Nearby." Your list will be more work to compile, but more useful to the recipient, if you include addresses, phone numbers, and days and times the attractions are open. A word of warning—these lists become out of date very quickly, especially as regards information about when the sights are open to the public. Warn your members that if they are planning a long trip from their hotel to a point of interest they should phone first. Sources for your list—your local people, convention and visitors' bureau, chamber of commerce.

Meals. Most conventions do not provide all meals for their registrants and spouses. Some meals have to be eaten off the program, so to speak. Prices of meals in hotels have skyrocketed. The usual meeting-goer and his spouse do not know where they can go for meals attuned to what they want to pay.

Why not have a local leg-man, or two or three leg-men, in the site city check out coffee shops, snack bars, diners, and restaurants in the vicinity of the convention hotel, for breakfasts and lunches? Your investigator should get a list of prices for typical meals—specific dishes and beverages, not just a range of what the eating place charges. He should also note cleanliness and atmosphere.

Publish the prices on a sheet for your conventioners. It will be a boon, especially to those people who are on a per-diem allowance, such as government employees.

Of more importance to the convention-goer than knowledge of places to eat breakfast and lunch, is good, advance information about places to dine. Among the members of your organization who reside in the convention city there are certain to be at least a few who appreciate good food and know where to find it and how much it costs. Get them to compile a list for you that you can provide the registrants. This list of restaurants should give the usual vital statistics—name of restaurant, type of cuisine, atmosphere, times closed, whether reservations are required or desirable, required dress (jackets, ties), approximate cost (inexpensive, moderate, expensive, very expensive, with these terms defined somewhere in your list), address, phone number, and approximate taxi fare and time from convention hotel.

Some of the best leisure-time information for convention-goers can be furnished by local members of the organization, when this is possible. The small association, if too short-staffed to do something of this kind, can still provide its meeting-goers with helpful advance information. Ask the chamber of commerce to send you, well in advance of your meeting, enough copies of tourist and other printed material so you can send it to all the prospective convention-goers? This helps you build attendance, helps your meeting-goers plan ahead, and helps the convention city publicize its attractions.

Taxis. Almost no meeting managers give their people attending a convention information about taxis. This is too bad. Yet most convention-goers who do not drive their own cars to a meeting or rent one there have to rely on taxis to get around town during their free time. Public transportation rarely fits the needs of people attending conferences. It behooves meeting managers to include a sheet about taxis in pre-convention mailings, or in the convention kit, to enlighten people as to local customs and rates. Some of the following may sound elemental, but you can adjust it to the street-sophistication of your membership.

First, how do you get a taxi? If you are leaving from a major hotel the doorman will do it for you. But how about getting a cab coming back? The driver who took you there may pick you up on request, you may be able to phone for a cab when you are finished at your destination, or you may have to try in the street.

How do you hail a taxi completely on your own? In New York City, all regular cabs are yellow, no matter what the cab company, and a free cab has the center part of its roof light lit. If the roof lights say "Off Duty," the driver is probably on his way home. If you indicate by gestures that you are going in the direction he is, he may pick you up. In that case you pay the regular passenger fare.

In some other cities, a lit roof light means nothing. In some cities, or parts of cities, there are cab stands where you can get a cab. In others you can only secure a cab by telephone. Indicate how to get cabs, and include phone numbers.

Does it make a difference what cab you flag down? Sometimes it does. Certain cabs in some places will not go out of city limits, while others will. Some cities allow the sharing of cabs by separate parties. If there are five of you in a group in New York there is no use stopping a taxi that is the same size as a medium-size regular passenger car. Only a large cab with jump seats will be allowed to carry all of you. In some cities taxis charge extra for additional passengers after the first; in New York, on the other hand, they do not. In some places there is an extra charge for luggage.

Then, rates. This is where the most trouble comes for unwary travelers. Most cabs are metered, but some (in Washington, D.C., for example) operate on a zone system. While a cab may have its rates on the side door, if metered (x cents for first ¼ mile, x cents per mile thereafter) this does not mean much to the stranger in town, who does not know how far the destination may be.

In Washington, D.C., cabs have a map inside for the passenger's benefit, explaining where zones are located. Only the major streets are shown, however, so the map is not much help if you do not know the city.

What your convention-goer really needs to be told, in addition to how to get a cab, and certain other local customs, is the average fares to get from his hotel or the convention center to certain popular sightseeing places and restaurants he is likely to want to reach. It is also useful to tell the member what route he should specify to the cab driver to get to and from the airport. Some cab drivers overcharge by taking the long way.

Taxis in some convention cities will perform special services, like carrying small parcels for you. Enlighten your convention-goers as to these wrinkles.

Finally, on your taxi information sheet, list the phone number of the local hack bureau so that a person with a complaint can report the name and number of a driver who is out of line.

Hotel Arrangements, Later Stages

Ever since you first made the decision as to what hotel would host your meeting, you have no doubt had contact with the hotel people. There is no set date when all arrangements are complete and nothing more happens. The law that says that the only things certain in life are death and taxes is incomplete; a third thing certain is that something will go wrong during a meeting.

If, however, you have conscientiously made all the arrangements described in Chapter 2, kept in close contact with the hotel on significant matters, and have been working on your physical arrangements program you should be in good shape 30 days before your meeting.

In this period of 30 days to ten days or a week before the meeting, you go over all past understandings with the hotel people, be sure everything is in writing, and be certain each hotel supervisory person knows just what is expected.

In addition, during this period you should take care of nitty-gritty, last-chance details. How many mikes should be in each room? What kind do you need—lectern or floor? Where should they be placed? At what exact times? What AV equipment will you need? Where? When? What about blackboards, easels, screens, lighting. Are your meals programmed as far as the hotel is concerned? If you want to start your business program just after the waiters put dessert down, and you schedule the business program kick-off for 12:43 P.M., you want the main course cleared and the dessert down by 12:43, not 12:48, and this must be in your schedule. It is now that you watch and check to be sure that the oral assurances you got earlier that no loud program will go on in rooms adjoining your conference are really to be carried out. You can do this by incorporating these assurances into a letter and asking for a reply corroborating them.

From the ''30 days before meeting'' time onward you will be watching numbers closely so as to give fairly accurate guarantees to the hotel. Do not give these before the hotel requires them—you will only have to change the figures. On meal guarantees many meeting managers like to guarantee about 10 percent fewer than are expected. If you have a large, last-minute surge for a meal, however, let the hotel know immediately so that it can set more tables and check its food supply.

The number of last-month—and last-minute—matters to check with your hotel cannot be predicted. There will be many. But early, good groundwork helps make for a smooth ride.

Printing and Shipping

The efficient meeting manager will have every possible piece of printed material in hand *more than* 30 days before the meeting. Some inevitably will be later, but the less that has to be done in the last month, the less panic there will be. Printers frequently have trouble with deadlines. Here are some things that, with a sizable meeting, may need to be printed—programs, outlines of talks, speakers' texts, tickets, spouses' programs, places to go, list of restaurants, taxi information, list of registrants, handouts. You may add other material for your own meeting.

Handout quantities. Be sure there are enough handouts for everyone. Take more than you think you will need. Remember that some of those attending will pick up copies for their friends. It is an evidence of bad planning to run out of handouts. The dissatisfaction of part of your audience is not worth the slight extra cost.

Plan to ship everything at least a week earlier than you need to. Know the exact number of cartons, and keep all bills of lading handy. I like to have a carton addressed like this:

HOLD FOR ARRIVAL

John Jones, Exec. Dir.
Nat. Assn. of Widget Mfrs.
Paradise Hotel
535 Eden Blvd.
Parnassus, Ohio 00000

For Grand Ballroom use
June 25, A.M.
Rogers handout

This tells your carrier where the carton goes; it tells the hotel whom it's for, and it tells your staff where and when you will need it and what it is.

If you are shipping across an international border, certain formalities must be observed, required papers must be completed and it is likely that you, or one of your associates, will have to appear at the customs office to get your material released.

Remember to ship displays and other material you will need for your staff and the press room. Don't forget such mundane things as stationery, plain paper, carbon paper, envelopes, clips, scotch tape, string, broad-point pens and grease pencils, staplers, and of course office machines if you carry them instead of renting locally. A screwdriver and pair of pliers will come in handy. If you have banners, how will you hang them—from standards or with string from a balcony? If they go against a wall you will need masking tape.

The Press, Office Machines

How to deal with the press will be discussed in the next chapter. Part of your planning activity, however, is to provide a press room, if your meeting is large enough. You will also need typewriters, paper, other office supplies. It is customary to rent typewriters locally. The large meeting should have one or more typewriters for the exclusive use of the press, plus one or more telephone extensions in the press room. You will want a typewriter for a secretary from your own staff, to type news releases and last-minute texts.

You will also, probably, want a typewriter (jumbo type, upper and lower case if available) at your registration desk to type badges for late registrants. All these typewriters can be ordered at one time.

You will also want to rent a duplicating machine, or make arrangements to have access to one on a basis of reasonable cost. This is to furnish material to the press and for other purposes.

4

Promotion and Publicity

Promotion and publicity are not precisely the same things, though there can be considerable overlap. To see the difference, compare an advertising flyer for your conference, which you control and mail out to lists, with a newspaper story that may arise from your news release but is truly in the hands of the reporter and his editors.

You can do your own promotion and public relations, but if you can afford a professional public relations person to handle these functions, we strongly recommend one.

Promotion

Direct mail. The main principles in using direct mail to promote your meeting are:

1. Be sure your promotion is good.
2. Start early, and repeat.
3. Use every list that may be effective.
4. Watch your timing.
5. Scale your costs to what you can spend.

Be sure your promotion is good. Facts are more important than puff. Aim at your readers—their interests and desires. Tell as much as you can. Be enthusiastic. Make your readers anxious to attend and sorry if they do not. If there are professional PR services available to you, use them. Get the PR person involved early in the planning for the meeting. Use good taste in your material. If you want art work, be sure it is appropriate to the form of printing you are using—don't try for effects in black and white that can only be accomplished with four-color printing.

Start early with your promotion. Three mailings are better than two. Two are better than one. Allow three weeks for nationwide mailings to return major results to you. Don't bother people for two weeks before Christmas.

Watch your timing. Figure back from the date of your meeting to construct your promotion schedule. Let's assume that your meeting is the 15th of May. You want reservations in by a week before that, or May 8. Three to four weeks before that, April 10 to April 17, your last major mailing should go out, and four weeks before *that* (March 10 to March 17) you should get your mailing piece written and illustrated. This allows time for copy preparation, making of the mechanical (finished art work), printing, collating, trucking. In other words, for a major mailing for a meeting to be held May 15 you should start preparing your mailing piece no later than March 15. More informal mailings need less lead time.

Here are some tips on saving money: Each different promotion piece you prepare costs you money—for copywriting and art work if the job is done outside your firm or organization and for time if performed internally—and for printing. Obviously, one brochure will cost you less for copy and art work than two. If you are going to have only one brochure, to be used in several mailings, calculate the total number you will need and have the printer run that quantity at one time. If you wish some variety with the one piece, have some printed on a different stock or with different colored inks—the additional cost is small. (But be sure ink and color of stock make an effective combination for all your copies.)

Suppose you plan to use two different brochures, each in, say, three colors, and the colors are the same. With most printers you can save money by running them at the same time, provided the quantity is the same. Talk with your printer.

Should you use first class mail or third? I prefer first class. But watch the weight. The minimum you must send out is a #10 envelope that carries a piece to "sell" your meeting (frequently a brochure) and a means of reply (a coupon, part of the brochure or separate, or a postcard), and, usually, a business reply envelope.

A good job of selling a meeting can be done with a packet that weighs slightly less than an ounce. Paraphrasing Ben Franklin on thrift, nine-tenths of an ounce—happiness, eleven-tenths of an ounce—unthrifty disaster.

Often hotels will furnish mailing material that can be helpful. Figure it in your weight.

There are further ways to save money. Use piggy-back solicitation—put a promotion stuffer in every mailing to your membership of whatever nature.

Watch your costs on paying return postage in connection with reservations. Some organizations still send out stamped envelopes. This is expensive and every nonreply, moreover, wastes a stamp. The customary business reply envelope is preferable, but even this is probably unnecessary. You can print a reply envelope that requires the registrant to pay the postage and send that.

Repeated dignified mailings are much better than one big, expensive splash. It is the repetition that sells the idea. The small organization may wish to gain some repetition at low cost by using postcards for a part of the promotion. Be sure they are not oversize, so that you do not pay extra postage.

A word to nonprofit organizations—make each of your mailings much earlier than required for first class, if you are taking advantage of a nonprofit mailing privilege. Our beleaguered postal system gives a low priority to nonprofit organization mail.

Much of what I have said in this chapter applies more to a large or medium-size meeting than to the small. The meeting manager will apply his experience and common sense to his own meeting. For example, with timing of direct mail. I know one very large organization that makes the first mailing for its next annual convention a very few weeks after the preceding meeting closes. Each year it must use several large hotels in the host city. Naturally, the members wish to be in one of the headquarters hotels. Rooms are assigned on a first-come, first-served basis, and the convention staff could not handle thousands of early room-reservation requests over the phone. It has to have formal reservations. Early mailings bring these in.

On the far other end of the meeting spectrum, ten days to two weeks is a long enough lead time for notice of an organization's regular monthly dinner meeting.

A note on quoting prices for your meetings—in direct mail, advertising, anywhere. If the price is in even dollars, leave off .00. Use $345, not $345.00. Why make prices look bigger than they are, with "boxcars"?

Mailing lists. When promoting meetings, meeting managers often rely on their own lists of potential registrants. Sometimes they use lists from commercial list houses. Can list houses help? How much?

When you rent a commercial list you get the one-time use of some thousands of names. The major benefit is that you probably do not have most of these names on your own lists. (Some organizations are so large that their own lists are better than any others available, but this is unusual.) To get success with purchased lists, however, use discretion in what you buy.

Suppose you are running a meeting for engineers interested in city planning. You consult a list house and find that it does not have any category such as this. It does, however, have lists of engineers separated into over two dozen categories. You might buy lists of civil, environmental, and executive engineers, but pass up the classifications of agricultural, ceramic, lubrication, and marine and naval engineers.

This is a meeting for engineers. Are there other professions that could be interested? How about municipal officials? Your list house will have them in its computer. Contractors, architects, perhaps port authorities and their officials, public utilities. One can go on. With all of the lists it is necessary to pick and choose so that you buy the lists that will have the highest receptiveness to your message. Often this is not easy.

If you buy several lists, concentrate your money and efforts on the best list for your organization or area of interest. Some people will send to this "best" list by first-class mail, and to other lists by bulk mail. You can test to determine which kind of postage gives you better results (a one to two percent return is good for any purchased list) by mailing to part of a list. You can, in fact, test your promotion copy, postage rate used, and the list itself by mailing samplings of the list in advance of your regular mailings. This is practicable, however, only if you project large mailings.

It is not necessary to buy a complete list—there may be thousands more names than you wish to mail to. You can use a portion of the list across the board, or names in just certain areas (selected by zip code). You will be required, however, to buy a minimum number of names.

List houses stand prepared to perform a number of services for you. They will run the names you want on labels or envelopes and in most cases mail for you. If you wish the labels or envelopes sent elsewhere for mailing, the owner of the list (list house) will do so.

If you wish the names on what mailing houses call dick strips, index cards, or magnetic tape, you may have them. The charges vary, with the basic price usually being charged for what are called "cheshire labels." I won't go into definitions of some of these technical terms, but your list house will be glad to explain them.

A reputable commercial list house will tell you how old a list is and whether it has been kept up to date. A list compiled more than two years ago that is not up to date will contain many names and addresses that are useless. A good list house will guarantee a high degree of accuracy—often 95 to 98 percent, refunding postage for "nixies" returned. Talk this over with the people at the list house.

Commercial list houses buy lists for their inventory, but they also compile them, too, using phone directories, trade and association reference books, and other sources. They then endeavor to keep their lists up to date with address changes, removals of names, and additions. They also try continually to enlarge their lists. This is all a great deal of work.

Because so much effort is involved to maintain lists, a commercial house will maintain lists for its customers that the customers own, if this is desired. If you find that keeping your membership list up to date is difficult, you may wish to consider having a list house do it for you.

Some list houses have their own printing equipment. Others work closely with printing plants, and can give you advice that can be helpful. Some economies may be obtained by working with a firm that has printing, lists, and mailing facilities under the same roof. For best results in the appearance of the promotion piece itself, it is best to consult a good commercial artist and the printer.

Advertising. There is a temptation to say very little about advertising, because it is difficult to get people to use it correctly, but when used properly, advertising can truly help to build attendance at your meeting.

In most cases, advertising alone is the worst way to promote a meeting. Direct mail is much better.

As reinforcement of direct mail, advertising can be very helpful. If you are promoting an industry-wide meeting, you certainly should advertise in the trade press. Repeated, small ads are much more cost effective than the big, single-time splash. Because one cannot say much in a small ad, some meeting managers prefer to give the facts, try to awaken enthusiasm, and tell the reader to send for more information. When the inquiry comes in, they answer it with a direct-mail packet with the words "Sent in answer to your inquiry." printed on the outside of the envelope. Other meeting managers prefer to pay for enough space to include a registration coupon. When advertising can be coordinated with specific direct-mail effort it is very worthwhile, but magazine distribution is so chancy that coordination is difficult to achieve.

Too many people become disillusioned with advertising because they make one of several mistakes.

They run one big ad in the business section of a daily paper or a business paper and expect great results. They may have reached a large number of people in other businesses or professions who have no interest in their meeting. They have spent a lot of money that could be better used some other way.

Or, they run only one ad in any case. This is a mistake for any advertising medium.

Another mistake is to fail to concentrate advertising in the media that reach the greatest concentration of most likely registrants. Work on the best markets, not the marginal ones.

People get disillusioned because their expectations are too great. If you run a coupon ad for your meeting the results of the ad are not to be reckoned by the number of coupon registrations you get back. Advertising is a reminder, a reinforcer, and the chief function is to tell your prospective registrant, again, that your conference is coming up, on such and such a date and at such and such a place. If you recognize that the main purpose of the ad is not to pull coupon registration, and you *must* nevertheless have a coupon count, you can key the coupon some way so you know which medium you advertised in produced the best coupon results. You can also key the coupon you put in direct-mail type packets you send out in response to requests from people who read your ads.

Most ads you place simply cannot tell your whole story, the way direct mail can. One way to maximize your advertising effort is to print extra quantities of your brochure or brochures and have them bound into magazines—both trade publications and your own house organs. If the brochure contains no coupon, you will have to run a coupon ad facing the brochure in the magazine. If the brochure has a coupon, no other ad is absolutely necessary. Using this method—paying for an insert in a magazine—is much less expensive than buying four pages of advertising. So much less that you will be very surprised. Because of the difference in paper stock on which it is printed, your brochure stands out, and its color and artwork often enhance the appearance of the magazine.

I repeat, however, do not depend on advertising alone to build attendance.

Publications. Newspapers and magazines consist of both advertising and editorial matter. We have already discussed advertising as a means of building attendance at meetings. Print and broadcast journalism, too, is an important means of informing and so building interest in your meeting. The press and broadcasting are so important, in fact, that they deserve separate treatment. There remain the company or organization's own publications—interior and exterior house organs. (An interior organ, as you know, is one that goes to your own membership or company. An exterior house organ circulates outside your organization or firm, usually to customers and potential customers.) Every issue of a house organ should promote the meetings its parent is projecting.

Probably the best way to indicate the possibilities in editorial treatment of an upcoming meeting in a house organ is to cite an example. To build interest in a recent annual meeting, an organization of professional journalists devoted five pages of its October issue to the coming November convention.

The association had provided information from time to time, for some months in advance. Then came its five-page section in the magazine. The first page pictured and described the speakers, who are the top attraction at most conventions. Most of the society's speakers are better known among journalists than among the general public, but you would recognize the names of several of the speakers.

The magazine then ran proposed amendments to the bylaws, to be voted on during the business sessions, a list of the new geographical areas into which the organization was dividing its membership territory, and a story on committee chairmen for the convention. A separate, small story reminded readers of the deadline for resolutions.

The second spread (pages four and five) opened with pictures and biographies of candidates for national office of the organization and contained a meeting reservation form as well as a hotel reservation form.

More than half the fourth page was devoted to telling the reader what he or she could do during leisure hours in the convention city.

On the fifth page of the convention section, the magazine ran four stories. One told how to get to the convention, another what activities would be available for spouses, a third what weather to expect and what clothes to wear, and the fourth a fairly long story on newspapers and broadcast media in the convention city area.

There is no need to follow anyone else's format slavishly. But note that professional journalists, in their own publication, told potential convention-goers—

- Whom they were going to hear.
- What the business of the meeting would be.
- What they could do during their leisure time.
- About planned and other activities for spouses.
- How to get to the convention city and what to wear.
- About installations or businesses, if you will, in their professional field that they might wish to investigate further while at the convention.
- And the organization asked for the order—enclosed a registration form.

Working closely with the editor of your house organ can help greatly in promoting your meeting. Any house organ or association magazine editor is glad to have suggestions for good material for his publication. So you can help him and he can help your meeting.

Publicity

For our purposes, publicity means editorial material in publications in general circulation or devoted to your particular business, discipline, or other type of interest, and broadcast journalism. We include newspapers, magazines, sometimes newsletters, and both radio and television. These are often collectively referred to as "the press." Press coverage is the strongest "third-party" influence you can have to induce people to attend your conference.

Most of what needs to be said about dealing with the press applies to all the above media.

Press coverage is very valuable. The conference that is reported by print and broadcast media is an important one. A news story provides a permanent record. Judicious use of such clippings as third-party influence helps you promote the next meeting. Then, too, good coverage does not hurt the status of the meeting manager. And not a cent comes out of his advertising budget.

To help you deal with reporters and editors I am setting down Ten Commandments, which I prefer to present positively, rather than as Thou Shalt Nots.

1. You shall determine where your meeting has the best chance of being reported. Most meetings, even small, company meetings, are newsworthy. Your meeting deserves coverage by at least some medium.

2. You shall use a professional public relations person if at all possible. Hire one knowledgeable about your industry or organization. Have him attend every meeting where your conference is discussed. Listen to him. Have him do advance work, run a press room during the meeting, and conduct post-meeting follow-up. (Some criteria for choosing a PR person are given later in this chapter.)

If your meeting is too small for a PR professional, these ''commandments'' apply equally to the person in your organization charged with the job of publicity and press relations.

3. You shall start early with all information to be furnished to the press. You should ascertain and observe requirements and deadlines for the publications and the broadcast media. Your news releases should tell what, when, where, who, and why, in good journalistic style, and should be a recital of facts, not be advertising. (Advertising releases fill circular files.) A steady flow of releases should reflect further developments in your plans and program as they occur. (Instructions on how to write a news release appear later in this chapter.)

4. You shall remember that reporters and editors may be completely ignorant about your business, your organization, and the particular problems and matters under consideration at your meeting. Furnish the press with background material, fact sheets describing your business and organization, pictures and biographical information about officers and speakers, and advance copies of talks to be given. Of course, include a program and other material you may give out at the meeting itself. Reporters like to have these ahead of time.

5. You shall contact every publication and broadcasting medium you hope will cover your meeting. Of course, keep things in proportion. Network television is not going to cover a company sales meeting unless its great size carries some special importance or unless an announcement will be made that affects a large portion of the public. But send advance releases, background material, and program information to most newspapers, to trade and association magazines, hobby and sports publications if appropriate, and broadcast media. If you invite coverage, ask all the media you contact to send reporters, without discrimination. In any case, provide a contact in your organization (or your public relations person) by name, address, and phone number—business and home.

Compile your list of publications and radio and television stations that could be interested with real care. (Your library can help.) This is important for you. The list will be longer than you had thought. Don't forget the local newspapers and radio stations and television channels where your meeting is to be held.

6. You shall, at the meeting itself, provide every possible facility for the press. Provide a press kit for any meeting, even a short press conference. This press kit will contain copies of all material previously mailed, plus any additions. Have a kit for every reporter, for no one but reporters, and you should see that the reporter receives each additional release that you produce after he has received his kit.

If your meeting is large enough, you should have a press room where the reporters can use typewriters and telephone. The press room will have duplicating facilities (or its staff will have access to them). Coffee and buns in the morning are appreciated. (The press room will be treated in greater depth later in this chapter.)

If your meeting is too small for a press room, you will provide as many press-room facilities as possible—in your headquarters hotel suite, at a table near the registration desk, or in the case of a press conference or lunch at the reception desk for the meeting. A little ingenuity will suggest ways to give service tailored to the size and capabilities of your conference. The manager of the small meeting will have to send out most material in advance and make someone, preferably an assistant rather than himself, responsible for helping the press at the meeting.

7. You shall realize the independence of the press. Do not expect a story or broadcast coverage because you dined reporters and a television news editor. There is no *quid pro quo* in a free press. Most media are overwhelmed with material and have to pick and choose. Don't annoy editors by asking at any time whether they will use or have used a story. It is unfortunate, but doing so can put your company or organization on an editor's personal blacklist.

How about freebies? What does custom entitle a reporter to receive free, and what should the meeting manager offer? The subject is sensitive, but few reporters feel compromised by a free lunch or cocktails in connection with a press conference. The same is true of a lunch where a reporter or editor sits down with a representative of a company or organization to gather material for a potential story. A reporter who attends a convention expects to receive a complimentary registration and tickets to meals and other events which are part of the program. If your meeting is quite small and cannot afford this load, tell your press invitees ahead of time, and they will understand.

You should not give free transportation or hotel lodging, but press attending the meeting should get the convention rate that members pay. Send meeting registration forms—marked "complimentary"—and hotel forms to the press at the same time you send them to members. The press should pay for meals that are not part of the program.

If spouses of registrants are admitted to meeting functions without extra charge, spouses of press and broadcast people should get in free, too. But if you charge members' husbands or wives, and the charge is substantial, you should ask a member of the press to pay part or all of the spouse's charge.

There is no absolute bar to gifts of very small value to the press, but a thoughtful note thanking a reporter, editor, or broadcaster for his coverage may be wiser.

8. You shall remember that no reputable publication requires advertising as bait for publishing a story. Don't mention it when discussing editorial matter. If you encounter a request for a trade-off, have no further dealings with the publication unless you have to. If you deal with it you're in bad company.

9. You shall be imaginative in seeking news angles the press can sink their teeth into. For example, press and broadcast reporters like press interviews with personalities. Do you have a speaker or a member of your organization who has something to say of interest, or is himself or herself of interest, to the public? Think hard, let the local media and

trade or professional press know, and do advance planning—prepared statement, likely questions, and answers checked out ahead with the personality and the room for conference reserved.

10. This above all: you shall make it easy for the editor to carry news stories about your meeting. You will give him information early; it will be full, presented as impartial facts. You will meet his deadlines and deliver all you promise to give him. You will cater to his needs for information and answer his questions frankly, refusing information only when you have to. You will not give one reporter material or information you deny to another. Treating the press equally is important. One national organization was virtually boycotted in the trade press of its profession for many years because of thoughtless discrimination at some of its meetings.

Follow these ten commandments, and you will get good press coverage for your meeting and make worthwhile contacts for future good relations with the press and broadcast people.

Some How-to's

How to choose a public relations/promotion person. Try if possible to get a PR person who knows your business or the common field of interest that draws your members to your meeting.

Choose someone who knows the media people in the locality where the meeting will be held. You can get suggestions from the chamber of commerce and members of your organization in that locality. If you prefer to have a person known to you but who does not live in the site town or city, he or she will, of course, have to make what contact he can in the media of the city where you are going to meet.

Get an energetic PR person. Ask him or her to show you a scrapbook of past accomplishments.

Be sure he can devote full time to your meeting during the days of the actual conference.

Ask for an outline of what he plans to do for you in advance of the meeting, during the meeting itself, and as follow-up after the meeting.

On your part:

Make your selection of a PR person early—six months ahead is not too long. (Remember that some magazines have to have material months ahead of the date of publication.)

Furnish all the information you can to your public relations person as early as you can possibly get it.

Be clear in your mind, and make clear to your public relations person, what you hope he will accomplish. At the same time, be realistic as to the results you expect him to achieve. Listen to his suggestions and ideas.

Do not expect him to call newspapers or other media to ask whether they will use material he sends or to ask why they did not use it. As we have indicated, he cannot do this and retain the good will of his contacts.

Cooperate with him during the meeting in every possible way. If possible, supply a properly equipped press room at the meeting. (For more on the press room, see later in this chapter.)

How to write a good press (news) release. The subject of writing news releases and news stories can fill a book. I hope, however, that after reading this section you will be able to prepare a respectable news release, if you have something significant to tell.

General principles:

1. A news release gives information; it does not "sell."
2. It is written in a certain way.
3. It should be easy to use, both from the standpoint of content and format.
4. No editor is under the slightest obligation to print it. (The term "release" is a misnomer in 95 percent of the cases.)

The first job is to marshal your facts. Be sure you know everything of importance before you start to write the release.

With respect to the form: You may use your organization's letterhead, a special letterhead that plays up the word NEWS, or plain white paper. Some associations like to use a light-colored stock if they are sending a lot of news releases to the press. An association which is prolific with releases may adopt a certain shade of tan, for example, as a mark of subtle identification. A large corporation that has a lot of appointments and financial announcements might do this. The fact remains, however, that most news releases go out on white paper.

In the upper left-hand corner of the first page of the news release go the association or firm name and address, if you are not using a letterhead. Below them you put the name of a person the editor can contact, in case he wishes more information. With this name, put his or her phone numbers—office and home. This identifying information is single spaced. The date of the release comes next, frequently on the right-hand side of the page. Next is a release line—"For Immediate Release," "For Release After 11 A.M. March 1," "For Release Afternoon Dailies of March 2," "For Release at Will," or whatever is appropriate to the event or the publications concerned.

The body of every release should be double spaced, on one side of the paper only, and have good margins—an inch or more. Always start the release half-way down the page. Editors get frustrated and irritated when they have no room to insert a headline over the story, and there is no psychological advantage in getting all of a release on one page.

If you wish to write a headline, do so. While the editor probably will not use it, it gives him an idea about the content of the story.

Use of a dateline (Washington, D.C., February 16—) at the start of the first paragraph is optional. If you use a dateline, you can dispense with the date of the release in the upper right-hand part of the first page, but not with the date the story may be run (the release line).

The so-called "lead" is the most important part of your news release. It must contain every essential part of your story, just as if it was all that would appear in the publication—and this is exactly what will happen if space is tight. Why the lead, and what is it?

One of the many "firsts" of the American Civil War, we have heard, is the now-established method of writing a news "story" for a newspaper. It seems that when Northern war correspondents put their dispatches on the telegraph wire to their metropolitan newspapers those pesky Confederates often cut the wire somewhere before all the story got through. There were, no doubt, other interruptions—priority military traffic and natural hazards like lines downed by storms.

As a result, it became the practice to give all the most important facts in the first sentence or two. It might have been more "literary" to hold the big "snapper" for the end of the story, but the reporter who did that might find that the last part of his message never got through.

Therefore, news stories and news releases now start with the most important information, go on to the next most important, then drop down to the even less important, and so on. Editors can rarely use all of a news release, if they can use any, and they cut from the end.

The importance of writing a news release in this fashion cannot be overemphasized. Read several long news stories in a good newspaper to see how the principle works in practice. Note that if a news story has two or more important matters to deal with, the writer of the story will mention both or all in the beginning, then switch back and forth throughout the story as he recounts the less important details.

When you begin your lead, you must say something of importance in the first seven words. Here are some sample leads:

■ Marshall Smith, president of the Notting Hill Chemical Corporation, will address the National Dye Association at its one-day seminar on March 7. About 400 chemical engineers are expected to attend the meeting, which will be held at the Moderne Hotel in Springfield, Ohio.

■ Solar power can fill 10 percent of America's electricity generating needs in the 1990s if proper steps are taken now. This is the opinion of Alex M. Gunderson, research director of Sunland Laboratories, who spoke before the Middletown Civic Club last night. (Note that a release must be written so that time references coincide with the time the reader sees the news story.)

■ Herbert Anderson, of 21 Pine St., was elected president of the American Society for Magnetometry at its annual convention last week in Hawaii. Professor Anderson, who heads the Physics Department at Upstate University, holds several magnetometer patents. (This is a lead for a local paper. If the release was for wider distribution, it would be necessary to give Professor Anderson's city of residence but his street address would be omitted.)

■ When the District 5 Paperhangers Union opens its annual conference on March 13, there will be something new. The Paperhangers will take over the cruise ship *Bali Ha'i* as their convention site, instead of the usual hotel. The ship will be moored in Port Everglades for the five-day conference.

Try not to start your lead with an article (a, an, the). Newspapers are no longer as conscientious in avoiding beginning leads with "The" as they once were, but often make an effort, at least on their front pages. A proper name is a handy first word—a person, organization, rarely a city. Also, prepositions, adjectives, and adverbs, if they do not make your writing contrived or stilted, are good.

In your lead put the traditional four w's—who, what, when, and where. Sometimes you need why. When picking facts for the lead, think of what will seem important to the reader, rather than what is important to your organization or company. The guest speaker may mean something to the readers of the publication you are aiming at, whereas attendance at the meeting is the most important thing for the organization.

Language. Through the release, use plain, simple words. Be precise. A number—five, ten, 350—means more to the reader than "many," "large," or "extremely successful." Gushy words like "beautiful" and "exciting" have no place in a news release. Use the active, not passive, voice when you can. Short sentences, short paragraphs, are best. Avoid overcapitalization—it's old fashioned. Look at current newspapers as your guide. If you have one important publication in mind as a target for your release, you may want to tailor one specially typed copy of your release to that publication's "style" in capitalization and punctuation.

What about explanation and background? Must you explain in your release what your organization or company does? Definitely yes, unless the average layman will know automatically. The magnetometry association in one of our examples needs to be explained within the first two or three paragraphs. If the R.J. Andrews Company sends out a release, it is necessary to tell all but the local media what R.J. Andrews manufactures or what services it performs.

Should you send supplementary materials? Yes, if you wish the editor receiving the release to have background material on your organization. Background material is particularly important if the release deals with complicated matters not of common knowledge. Additional biographical information about speakers and newly elected officers, and their photos, may be of use.

Broadcast media. News releases are prepared in the same way, whether they are to be submitted to print or broadcast media.

It helps to know editors and broadcast people personally. But remember that they are busy, that most releases they receive cannot be used. Do not ask an editor if he will use your release or has used it. If your release is about a subject important to readers, and is written in proper form and straightforward fashion, some part of it stands a good chance of being printed in some publication.

Before you send your release on its way, it is worthwhile to get the name of the editor of the publication to whom it should be addressed. If the publication is small you will send the release to the editor. If you are dealing with a large city daily it may be appropriate to send your release to the business editor or in some cases the scientific editor, but the usual addressee for the large daily for a release about meetings would be the city editor.

It is customary to end a press release with either of these notations:

–30–

#   #   #

How to have an effective press room. To the outsider, a press room at a conference appears to be an esoteric place, even arcane. The layman who walks in sees nothing particular happening. Perhaps one person is typing and two people are talking, or just one is at the typewriter. Yet out of this non-activity comes the news story that makes the front page of the local daily. It is here that the beginning of coverage on prime TV originates. How does this come about, and how does one meeting manager get successful press and television exposure for his conference and another does not?

The rules for a successful press room are simple:

1. Know what you are doing.
2. Equip and staff the press room well.
3. Work hard, before and during the meeting, to give the press what it needs.
4. Remember that you are the seller, the press and broadcast people the buyers.

Do not think that the full-fledged press room is only for the big convention. The small meeting can do a good job with a small room and limited facilities. Most of the ideas in this section will be applicable to all meetings, though some will be more appropriate to the larger one.

When you first plan your meeting, try to secure a good public relations person, one with press contacts and public relations experience, to put in charge of publicity and the press room. Failing that, look for public relations expertise among your membership or in your company. This can save much grief later. Because, in the end, you may have to be your own PR person, we are going to deal in basics.

Compile a list of all potential press/broadcast contacts. This includes daily, weekly, trade press papers, and television and radio stations.

Ascertain their deadlines. You may have to work months ahead with some of the monthlies or quarterlies. Three weeks is enough lead time for weeklies, dailies, and broadcast media.

In plenty of time, send advance material to your media list. News release or releases, pictures (identified on the back) of your principal speakers and officers. Background material is useful if the reporters you expect to attend may not be familiar with your industry or organization.

In fact, the major basis for a successful press relations job is advance work, lots of it. Try to get advance texts from all your speakers. Duplicate enough of these for all expected needs—advance copies to press and radio/TV, enough copies for all reporters at the press room, and for other people if it is your custom to give out copies on request.

While the advance work is important for any meeting, it is particularly necessary for the small meeting, as there is neither time nor staff to write many news releases or to set up procedures to see that all media receive copies of anything produced.

Record what is sent in advance, and to what media.

Set up a file of large envelopes for the press room itself. Each envelope is labeled with the name of the publication or letters of the station. In this you put all the material accumulated before the meeting starts, and take the envelopes to the press room when it opens. Add releases, pictures, or anything else that accumulates as the meeting goes on. Maintain a record of what you put in the envelopes, with the names of all the media listed in the left column, headings at the top of succeeding columns to indicate the releases you are distributing, and check marks below these column headings opposite each medium's name to show that the release has been put in the respective envelope.

It would be most convenient for *you* if each reporter left his envelope in the press room until the end of the meeting, but he won't do this. He will take the envelope when it is convenient for him. So, with each new release you bring out during your conference, save a copy for each publication, writing the paper's name at the top. Hand these to the individual reporters as they show up in the news room. Do not leave releases intended for the press out on a table where anyone can pick them up.

The public relations person, or an assistant, should be on hand at all times in the press room to answer questions, to arrange interviews with personalities, to assist the press—both print and broadcast—in any way possible. The person in charge of the press room should dispense tickets for lunch and other conference events to members of the press. It is also a good idea to give him possession of press badges, to encourage reporters to go early to the press room, where they will get their credentials.

Equipment for the "compleat press room" consists of the following:

■ Bulletin board, or blackboard and chalk.
■ One or more typewriters for the press (plus any needed for staff).
■ Telephones.
■ Duplicating facilities (at least nearby).
■ Paper, carbon paper, envelopes, pads, scotch tape, paper clips, stapler, pens.
■ In the morning, rolls and coffee, perhaps soda in the afternoon. (I don't think it is wise to start furnishing free liquor unless it has become a tradition with your meeting and you cannot break the precedent.)

At least one secretary should be in the room to substitute for the public relations person, who may have to cruise the meeting, to type releases, duplicate them, and perhaps do some typing and duplicating for reporters. Do not let your own people use the reporters' typewriters, unless the latter have no need of them.

How to promote via the membership. The best prospects for attendance at your next meeting are those who have attended in the past. (See the section on mailing lists earlier in this chapter.) Pay particular attention to those people who have been especially loyal in their attendance (see Chapter 3).

I like to send a special letter to people who have attended meetings in the past. They can be specially addressed (expensive, but perhaps worth the cost), or not. But in either case, the content of the letter should be directed right at the former registrant, reminding him of the benefit he has derived in the past and expressing the friendly expectation that you will see him at the coming convention. Be sure to enclose registration blank or coupon and "ask for the order." Remember to send the former registrant regular mailings, as well as the special letter.

It is important to stop solicitation as soon as any person registers, but it is particularly important with a former, faithful attender. He, more than others, has been led to believe that he is a special person. Don't disillusion him.

When you are close to cut-off time for registration for your meeting, a telephone campaign may bring good results. You might, for example, phone every person who attended two or more meetings in the past five years. More on telephone campaigns later in this chapter.

Various devices are used by some organizations to build attendance—for example asking each member to bring a guest to a one-day meeting.

Sometimes regional competition can help build attendance. The techniques involve frequent publicity, with ballyhooed progress reports, and numbers trumpeted to the skies. Select distinctive regional names for your competing groups.

Prizes can be anything you wish. They can be material—trips, articles of value, almost anything except actual cash. The prizes can be recognition alone, and any material prize should certainly be awarded in addition to adequate recognition before the entire group at your big meeting. The prize can be an object, yet be symbolic. One organization awards an old-fashioned top hat to the manager whose sales organization has the largest production for the year. The prize may, of course, be all-expenses paid to the annual meeting.

Regions of the country may vary in potential meeting attendance. In this case you have to set quotas of registrations and make your award on the basis of percentage of quota attained. Judging a contest designed to build attendance at a meeting must be on a simple basis. Each member of the organization who gets a given number of people to attend who have not done so for two years (or whatever) receives a designated prize.

Enthusiasm about coming meetings, if genuine, will spill over into letters to members. You should also miss no opportunity to promote your meetings orally. When you are speaking at one meeting, always mention the next one.

One organization has a number of small meetings during the year and one large convention in the fall or winter. To each of the small meetings the association sends a slide projector and sets it up in the registration/headquarters area. All day long, slides are projected on a screen showing attractions of the site city for the coming annual convention. A voice commentary accompanies the slide presentation.

Telephone campaigns. Telephone campaigns are not a good method of promoting meetings. A good telephone approach does bring in the stragglers. Unfortunately, however, it is self-perpetuating. The more often the device is used, the more it is expected, until it becomes a crutch. If it becomes necessary to use a telephone campaign for, say, an annual meeting one year, it should be avoided the next. The very fact that sufficient attendance required telephoning should be a red flag alerting the meeting manager to the need for more effective and early promotion for the next conference.

If you recognize that a telephone campaign is not the most desirable method, how can you make it most effective in those cases when you feel you have to resort to it?

First, unless you are resolved never to solicit attendance by phone, you must plan ahead for the possibility. Most telephone campaigns are mounted in the last two weeks before registrations must close, at the behest of someone who has become alarmed by the dismal advance registration figures. Humpty Dumpty is in pieces. He must somehow be put back together again, and quickly. No one has a telephone talk prepared, no one has proper lists with phone numbers, and no one is available to do the phoning. In other words, Humpty is scattered, and no one knows what he looked like when he was a whole egg, and all the king's men have other work to do anyway. This is why most telephone campaigns just lay another egg.

The first necessity is a good telephone talk. This should be prepared well in advance of the time it may be needed. It should open with identification of the caller:

"This is Mary Smith in (Atlanta, Chicago). I am calling for Mr. Martin Jones, who is chairman of the annual meeting of the Chemical Society this year."

At this point there will probably be some recognition on the part of the person called that he realizes the context of the call. Note that Miss Smith has suggested the importance of the call by indicating that it is a long distance call.

The next step:

"We see, Mr. Albert, that we have not received your registration for the annual meeting, and Mr. Jones asked me to call you to ask if you had sent it in."

At this point, the potential registrant, Mr. Albert, may make any of several responses. He has either decided to attend, decided not to attend and cannot be budged, or is persuadable. In the first two instances the remaining conversation will be short.

If Mr. Albert has put his registration in the mail, Miss Smith should thank him politely and end the call. If he has yet to mail his registration, she should try, in a nice way, to get him to take immediate action. The fact that he has decided to attend but has not evidenced that fact in writing marks him as a procrastinator or a busy man, and Miss Smith may have to follow up with another call in a few days.

Mr. Albert may say that he is not going to attend. Miss Smith should reply that that is too bad, because the program is very good this year; perhaps she will mention a specific speaker or event. Mr. Albert will probably then give his reason for not attending. It may be unanswerable—"I have to speak in Denver that day;" "That is the date of our stockholders' meeting and I must be there." Miss Smith then expresses regret, says she hopes that Mr. Albert can attend the next meeting, and signs off. She can also suggest that Mr. Albert send someone in his place.

But if Mr. Albert seems uncertain about attending the conference, or gives less than a hard-and-fast refusal, the telephone sales call really begins. The reasons for attending must be carefully organized and presented in summary form. I recommend three short sentences, followed by a "request for the order" ("May I list you as planning to attend?"). Miss Smith can then field objections, if necessary, but she should return to the request for an affirmative answer as promptly as possible.

What are the reasons for attending?

First, the program. Miss Smith should mention those topics that will most appeal to the person she is calling. Any topic that relates to a subject that is at present making headlines may well be stressed.

Second, she should mention the speakers, both those chosen as experts in their field and the headliner invited because of wide recognition by the public. If the program is worth attending, there must be good things to say about the speakers, as well. The trick is to devise what the telephone caller will say and see that it is said convincingly.

Third, there is a reason for attending a meeting that is often overlooked: Mr. Albert may change his mind and come if he hears that other companies in his category are sending representatives to the meeting. The fact that Amalgamated Dye and Tri-State Chemical Corporations are sending people may convince Mr. Albert to register. In competitive businesses people have to keep up.

A lesser motivator, but one that may work in conjunction with other incentives, is the faithful attender argument. If Mr. Albert has regularly attended for a number of years but is uncertain this time, the personal attention of a telephone call and mention of his regular attendance may persuade him to register.

Leisure-time activities or the spouses' program, however attractive, do not have a place in a telephone campaign. If the conference is to be held at Pebble Beach in California, however, there is no harm in saying "Pebble Beach" two or three times during the telephone talk. Any golfer will react to those words.

Any meeting worth promoting has something special about it. Perhaps you have shortened this year's meeting to two days without sacrificing important substance. Or, you are placing subjects on the program (such as . . .) that no other conference in the industry has dealt with. Or, the meeting place has been centrally located so that everyone possible can attend. Or, the entire meeting has been constructed in accordance with the wishes of the membership, as indicated in the answers to a questionnaire. The possibilities are numberless.

Any organization has to devise its own sales talk, but the ingredients are always present. In fact, if the meeting manager has been promoting in the right way, all the reasons for attending have been spelled out in mail promotion, publications if available, and advertising. These motivating ideas are just pulled out and reiterated in the telephone campaign.

Answers to objections must be devised from the beginning. Every possible objection must be anticipated and an answer formulated.

What lists should Miss Smith and the other callers use? The most obvious ones are lists of people who attended in previous years, companies that should without fail have a representative at this meeting, and all other members of the organization. Some good may be obtained from using membership lists of related organizations and sister disciplines (if you permit their members to attend).

First call the best lists. By "best" I mean those that are likely to return the best results from a percentage standpoint, though the people listed may not be the most prestigious.

A good telephone list must have phone numbers. Your file of past years' registrants probably shows them, and I hope that your membership roster does. Regular mailing lists do not always have phone numbers; but more and more do today.

Who does the calling? Women usually do better than men. They offend less because they keep their temper better. The people calling have to be thoroughly briefed and practiced in handling expected questions and objections. This training of the callers takes time. All the information is in the previously sent promotion, but it must be organized for telephone use.

The people who can be trained fastest to make the telephone calls are the meeting manager's own staff, as they are most familiar with the meeting details. But they may not have the time, or in all cases be well suited for telephone work. The number of people to be called, too, may be too large for a few people to handle. If it is necessary to hire outside people, or use volunteers, who are not familiar with the meeting they are trying to sell, briefing and practice before starting telephone work become very important. And someone thoroughly versed in details of the conference should be on hand during all telephoning to supervise and step in to answer inquiries the people phoning cannot cope with.

For large-scale telephoning a telephone committee is essential. Its members should be located all over the territory served by the organization, to keep toll charges within reason. Callers should be trained and supervised in the same manner as those who work out of the headquarters of the organization.

Once it has been decided to make a phone campaign, the meeting manager, or his public relations man, should write a telephone calling guide. This guide, on a very few sheets of paper, should give the sales talk and incorporate every possible answer to objections, sales closing, and helpful tip for the person who is doing the phoning.

Phone campaigns are not the best way to sell meetings, but if you feel you must resort to them, make them as effective as possible. They can be made to yield results.

5

The Meeting Itself, Part I

It will quickly become evident that many meeting details mentioned in this and the next chapter are not matters that can be left entirely till the meeting begins. Like most things connected with a meeting, advance preparation is required. However, most of the activity connected with the items in these chapters occurs at the meeting, and it is most appropriate to consider them here.

Signs

The big day has come. You are at the meeting hotel. You establish live contact with the hotel convention staff. It will be a few hours before the conventioners land, with spouses and baggage. The very first thing to do is to put up your signs telling members where to go. If you are handling rooms in a special way, apart from the hotel desk, direct your members there with a big sign as they come in the front door. Have a conspicuous sign to direct them to the meeting registration area, the premeeting cocktail party, if any, and to other places they may need to go. Then set up your meeting registration facility.

The Efficient Registration Desk

A smoothly run registration job at a big convention is no accident. It is evidence of good planning, advance work, and close supervision of the staff involved. This discussion of registration will focus on the big meeting. Managers of smaller conferences can use the ideas to their advantage.

The biggest favor you can do yourself is to have as many of your conventioners pre-registered as possible. (See Chapter 3.)

Separate sections. Have two main sections in the registration area, one for those people who pre-registered, one for those who are registering currently. Within each section set up separate lines to divide conventioners alphabetically.

Some meeting managers have a separate section in the registration area for VIPs. This is a good idea. Convention workers are often lent by local companies or hired from local firms, the convention bureau, or an agency. The past president who fumes in line is an important person to himself and to the organization, but to the registration worker behind the table he looks just like anyone else. To spare bruised egos, have a sign that says: VIPs—Officers and Former Officers, Speakers, Press, Guests. Include your Loyal Legion of regular, faithful attenders if you wish to, especially if you are giving them some special form of recognition to wear. One of the organization VIPs or a staff member should stand by at this location as greeter and trouble-shooter.

Pre-registered convention-goers. The people who registered in advance by mail give their names to the workers at their respective registration stations and receive their material. I favor having badge and tickets in a small envelope with the registrant's name on the envelope. This envelope is clipped to his record card. When the envelope is handed to him, he also receives his kit from a separate pile. (The kits are not marked with the conventioners' names.) The registration card remains in the box, the absence of the envelope indicating that the person has arrived at the convention.

Current registrations. The people who have not registered in advance are the ones that take the time and slow down your registration process.

You have to catch these people before they get in line—that is, before they get in the alphabetical lines—and have them fill out their own registration cards. This requires a large sign that says in effect, "If you have not registered in advance: (1) Take a registration card; (2) fill it out; and (3) take it to the proper alphabetical line for registration." You will have to provide writing space away from the registration lines for this filling out of cards, and pencils. Insist that the registrants print their names. Keep the card language simple.

To keep current registration moving, you need two workers on each of the lines. One takes the card and lays it down where he or she can see it but where it can also be read by the other worker, who is a typist. While the typist makes up the badge the worker who took the card is getting money or a check from the registrant and writing a receipt. (The receipt should be at least in duplicate so that the organization has one for its records.)

It is essential that the people processing the current registrants know precisely what they are doing. Use only experienced people if you can, and have a dry run before the meeting. You must be sure that they know what you want, and that they can do what they are supposed to.

Once the typist has made up the new registrant's badge (and we hope she used a machine with jumbo type in upper and lower case), she inserts the badge in a holder if she has time. If her fellow worker has more time, *she* puts the badge in the holder. Then the person who first received the registration card passes over badge, receipt, a kit from the pile, and anything else that the registrant should receive at that point.

Problems. As in any other endeavor, problems are better anticipated and avoided than solved on the spot. Make a list of the most common complaints: "I did register," "I paid and you have no record," "What can I do about a room?" and decide what you will do about each one.

Next, get the problems out of the registration lines. If someone gets to a registrar and there is a problem, move him out of the line at once. The way to do this is to have a staff member floating behind the tables of registrars to step in on call, or on his own initiative, when a problem pops up. He then takes the registrant to a problem table where one hopes his problem is solved. The conventioner is then escorted back to the head of the line for registration.

If this problem table is prominently labeled, the man or woman who needs help will very likely have gone there in the first place.

Some particular wrinkles. The registration area should be well lit. The tables should be supplied with adequate amounts of material—kits, badges, receipts, pens, typewriters, paper clips, staplers, and supplies should be replenished as necessary.

The signs are most important. They should be big, high on the walls, and never on the tables, where they can be hidden by lines of registrants. The signs should tell explicitly what people should do. They should sort people out so that their time, and that of your registrars, will not be wasted.

The pre-registrants should get the best possible treatment. The speed with which they complete the registering process will confirm the wisdom of registering for this meeting ahead of time and will serve as an example to others so that they will pre-register next time.

At your VIP desk, have a staff member ready to take speakers and other important guests under his wing. Speakers and guests, of course, do not pay meeting registration fees. It is a good idea to send members of the press to the press room to get their press credentials and tickets.

One problem area is the time-consuming process of qualifying delegates where there are conflicting claims as to who is the legitimate delegate. Such problems are often solved by a committee sitting in privacy in a hotel room. Refer the delegate to this committee, via the Problem Table. You should also have a conspicuous sign stating: Delegate Qualification—Room _____."

Tickets to special events should never be sold in a registration line. Sell them at a separate table, again with a conspicuous sign. If you wish to make sure that only registrants buy the tickets you can have the ticket seller insist on seeing a badge. You can also include a card without value in the envelope with the registrant's badge. He will then exchange this card for the tickets admitting him to the events he wishes to attend. (Unless you believe that the second method is absolutely necessary, I suggest that you dispense with this formality.)

Select the people who will handle money with care. Honesty is important, but the main problem is that there are many delightful people who are fine handling simple registrations, but cannot add two and two, to say nothing of substracting $7.50 from a $20.00 bill and giving the right change. Insist on a strict, careful handling of money. Tell your assistants that a ticket is considered money and that every one, or the equivalent in cash or check, must be accounted for. This is just good business.

For more complete control of tickets than some organizations impose, you can write down the number of tickets given to each person who will be selling or dispensing them, and get a receipt. Then you should get back money (cash and checks) and unsold tickets equaling the dollar value of the tickets you entrusted to the person in the first place. Some organizations number each ticket and charge the people handling them not just for a given quantity, but also for specific tickets.

Keep cash relatively low in your registration area. Packets of cash and checks, carefully labeled as to just what they are or derive from, should go constantly to the hotel safe, under adequate protection.

After the main rush of registrations—probably after the first day, usually not later than the second—your registration activities can shrink. Maintain all your services, and for the full time you should be open, but use fewer people. Keep the best and most experienced.

Frequently members will approach the registration desk to ask for the hotel and room number of another registrant. This subject was dealt with in Chapter 3 in considerable detail. One additional solution to this "where is he?" question I have seen was at a large meeting where a trade publisher maintained a large board that listed all persons attending and the names of their hotels. Wisely, the people maintaining the board omitted room numbers. This board provided a service and also, of course, a means of advertising the publication. (It looked like a great deal of work, too.)

Registrants who do not show. This problem will be treated in Chapter 7.

Two optional features the meeting manager for a large convention might consider are:

An information booth staffed to answer any question a conventioner could ask about the meeting or the host city, and:

A refreshment booth selling hot dogs, hamburgers, and simple sandwiches at low prices. At one meeting this booth was in an area through which the meeting-goer had to pass to reach the registration tables. Near the booth were good seating facilities, so that registrants could sit and socialize while they snacked.

I have kept until last the *sine qua non* of the successful registration process. You can call him the registration chairman, the registration director, or what you will. Without a good one you will have problems—

big ones. He is like the ringmaster of the circus. He must be tough, exacting, unperturbed, and confidence-inspiring. If you are he, good luck.

Meeting Room Details

It is now necessary to check the meeting rooms to be sure that they are as you want them, are arranged as you requested, and have the equipment you need.

Size. Is the room, after all, large enough? If it is the main ballroom, you can do little but squeeze in some chairs at the back. If you are crowded in a smaller room where you are running a simultaneous session, you can perhaps trade for another room running a session on your program where the room is too big. Happily, you know from advance registrations or will learn from a query at the opening session about how many people will attend each of your simultaneous sessions. Another solution is to take out some of the tables in the rear of a room set up classroom style and replace them with chairs, so that you have a room that is part schoolroom, part theater setup.

Is the room too large and you don't want to shift the audience to another room? Ask the hotel to put in a divider to make the room seem smaller. Dividers are often a sort of artificial hedge on casters, sometimes screens.

Smoking. Are smoking and nonsmoking sections of your meeting rooms properly marked? Are there ash trays in the smoking section? The smoking section should be at the rear of the room.

Schoolroom style equipment. If the room is set up schoolroom style, do the tables have pitchers of ice water and glasses? Are there three grease pencils on each table so that the people attending the session can write their names on the signs ("tents") included in their kits? If you wish to furnish pads and pencils, are they laid out at each place? Are all handouts in place, if they are to be put on the tables?

Speakers' props. How about speakers' equipment? Is there the right number of microphones, are they the right type, in the right places? You must have each microphone tested to be sure it is "live" just before a session starts and just before a session recommences after a break. Do this yourself or have a member of your staff do it.

Has the hotel provided the lectern you asked for—floor or table?

This is a good place to define some meeting-room terms. Giving their derivation may help you remember their meaning. *Podium* is not what a speaker stands behind when he reads or delivers his talk. A podium is what he stands *on*, a dais. Podium comes ultimately from the ancient Greek word *podos*, meaning foot. In fact, it is the word foot, just said a little differently.

Lectern comes, through French, from the Latin verb *legere*, to read. It is where the speaker reads his talk.

Rostrum is a sort of hybrid word in its meaning, though not in its derivation. It was originally the tip of a ship's prow, then the platform in the Roman forum from which orations were delivered. Today it can be used to mean either a podium or a lectern.

If a speaker wants a blackboard, is it there, with eraser and chalk? If he wants an easel, is it in place? Do you have all the speakers' name signs?

Is all the audiovisual equipment on hand, with a large enough screen? Is the screen placed high enough so that the audience, if sitting on one level, can all see? Do you have an operator for the AV equipment? (A special note for the small meeting: too often a small organization rents or borrows a film, rents a projector, and thinks it is ready to run the film. No one at the meeting knows how to thread the film and run it. Don't let this happen to you. Be sure someone with the know-how attends.)

Does one of your staff know where the light switches are? Does he know how to turn the lights down and up? And is he on hand to do the job at any time during the session?

Flag etiquette. A flag on a standard is placed to the right of the audience if it stands on the floor of the meeting room. If it is placed on a raised dais it stands on the audience's left (the speakers' or VIPs' right.) If the flag is displayed on a wall, its blue field is at the upper *left* corner as seen by the audience.

Meal room. If the room you are concerned with is being set for a lunch or banquet, be sure that appropriate equipment, mentioned above, is on hand.

If you have a big head table, say a double-banked one with a large number of VIPs on two levels, you can use an efficient method of getting them in the right order before they file into the ballroom. One way is to have chairs set up in rows in a nearby room where you are assembling the people who will sit at the head table. On each chair place a sign showing the last name of the VIP. Each person sits in his or her respective chair, in correct order. When all are assembled they are led into the ballroom.

It makes a good show to have the head table file in in order, with someone announcing the name of each person as he steps up onto the dais. (This is appropriate for a large gathering, but not, of course, for a small luncheon.) Sometimes, at Canadian banquets, the people at the head table are led in by a piper. This starts the banquet off in a truly memorable fashion. A more common way to introduce the people at the head table is for the chairman of the meeting to introduce them at some point after they are seated. He starts on his right (the audience's left) and usually passes by both the main speaker and the person who will introduce that speaker. These two people are introduced at the appropriate point in the program.

For a banquet, you will probably want one or more banners, and perhaps other decorations and lighting effects. One organization rented centerpieces locally for the tables, saving themselves considerable money.

These are the kinds of details that must be taken care of with regard to the meeting room or rooms during the conference. You will, of course, compile your own list.

Speakers

How much can you do for your speakers at the time of the meeting itself? The following courtesies are desirable, though you cannot always do all of them:

- Meet the speaker when he arrives at airport, railroad station, or hotel lobby. Reconfirm his return transportation.
- Make sure he is happy with his room.
- Attach a speaker's ribbon to his badge.
- Show him the room where he will speak, and see that he is satisfied with the equipment and setup.
- Introduce him to other speakers, especially those on his panel.
- Don't let him wander loose at the meeting. See if you can offer him entertainment of some kind during his free time.
- Introduce him to others at the head table if he will sit there during a meal.
- If he is paid an honorarium, give it to him after he speaks and before he leaves the meeting. (If his appearance was arranged by an agency, check with the agency to see how the check should be made out.) If you are giving him a small gift, present it to him immediately after his talk, before he leaves the dais. These gifts should be different for men and women, something nice and worth keeping.
- See that the speaker is invited to all social functions. If you can, entertain the speakers each afternoon at cocktails in your suite, where they can meet officers and other VIPs at the convention.
- Have a speakers' breakfast each morning where the speakers can meet and talk.
- Have a room near the ballroom where speakers can retire for coffee, to work on their talks, or to confer with other people.
- See that the speaker gets to his return transportation on time. Assistance in checking out so he does not have to stand in line at the cashier's desk, too, is appreciated.
- Thank your speaker by letter, whether you paid him or not. A letter to his boss or employer, expressing your appreciation for the appearance of the speaker and the value of his talk, is a good idea. Each letter should be different.
- If transcripts of the meeting are printed, be sure that the speakers receive complimentary copies.

While you will wish to do as much as possible for your speakers, you will find that it is easier to provide these courtesies if your meeting is a small one with a single speaker than if it is a large one with many speakers.

Entertainment by Others

Should we allow nonconvention entertainment, such as company hospitality suites? There is good news and bad news in permitting entertaining that you do not sponsor at your meeting. The situation is somewhat analogous to admitting outside exhibitors to your conference (see Chapter 9).

The good news is that it may solve a problem without cost to the sponsoring organization or those attending.

The bad news is that it may get out of hand and weaken the purpose of the meeting.

The meeting manager or committee may have to ask one of the following questions:

- If we're not allowing entertainment, *should* we permit it?
- If we are allowing it, how can we control it?
- If we are allowing it and want to stop it, how can we stop it?

Before trying to answer these questions, let's find out what is good about non-association-sponsored entertainment. (Let's call it outside entertainment, for convenience.)

Outside entertainment fills the holes in the program, an especially valuable service for the small meeting. In a small city or country setting, outside entertainment keeps a group together and makes it unnecessary for the meeting-goers to drive long distances to fill an evening. Not the least important service of entertainment like this is that a lot of business is accomplished and a lot of contact made at cocktail parties and in hospitality suites. Also, some hosts give parties just to be able to shake their friends' hands and express appreciation for a relationship they have enjoyed in the past.

What is bad about outside entertainment? First, in some cases it is conducted during program hours. It is annoying for a chairman to see a part of the audience drift off before the afternoon program is completed, to visit hospitality suites that have opened prematurely. One naive meeting manager we know arranged a cocktail party for his group only to have half of them attend another party. He had no advance warning of the competition, but every person attending the conference had received an invitation.

Entertaining can become competitive. One large convention with a serious purpose is plagued with an excessive number of hospitality suites. Each company feels that it has to outdo all the others in offering hospitality to potential customers. As a result, conventioners roll through the hotel halls at all hours, and many of them cannot make it to the 9 A.M. opener the next morning. Probably the companies would like to end the escalation of hospitality but don't know how to do it.

Some relaxation and fun at a meeting are desirable, but if outside entertainment competes with the meeting program, becomes competitive among the outside hosts, or too extensive, your meeting is sure to suffer. Time and energy of convention-goers are diverted. More important, the meeting can come to be identified as a fun convention rather than a serious business or educational conference. This label, once applied, will be difficult to remove, and future attendance will suffer.

If you do not allow outside entertainment now, should you decide to permit it? Ask yourself whether your meeting needs it and whether it will benefit from it. Consider the question very carefully. You will very likely decide against permitting entertainment in any organized fashion. (You cannot prevent Joe and Mary from inviting their friends Bill and Janice to their room for a drink.)

How can you control outside entertainment? The first rule is to know about it in advance. The second is, keep yourself in the driver's seat. The third, make the rules clear to everyone ahead of time, and enforce them rigidly.

To know about outside entertainment in advance, keep close rapport with the hotel. Have the people there tell you about anyone who reserves a suite or public meeting room during the time of your meeting. The hotel will do this; your business is more important than any side activity. If you find that a suite, for example, has been reserved where you suspect that some entertaining is planned, you should telephone the person in whose name the reservation is made. Say, "We understand that you have reserved a suite at the Super Majestic Hotel during the time our annual convention will be held there. We are interested in knowing whether you plan to do any entertaining." Inquire as to the nature of the entertaining, if any. "We wish to be sure that you understand our rules for any entertainment we do not sponsor, and I can outline them for you now. I will also sent you a typewritten (printed) copy." This puts the prospective host on notice that you *know* he plans entertainment and that you expect him to conform to the rules.

Suppose an outside firm or group defies you and runs a party anyway, at a time or under conditions you have forbidden. In this case tell the offender that if he persists in having his party or keeping his hospitality suite open during unauthorized hours you will advise the audience at a session not to attend (this has been done) and that he will not get into the hotel at the next meeting. If he persists, carry out your threat.

Here are some specific rules for control:

1. Allow no public notice, like signs, of entertainment.
2. Allow entertainment by individual invitation only.
3. Allow entertainment only during designated hours—when no conference activity is planned. For example, if you have a meeting

running all day Wednesday and Thursday, and through lunch Friday, with a no-host cocktail party Tuesday and a reception and dinner on Thursday, you might permit outside entertainment from 7–11 P.M. Tuesday and Wednesday, and 10–12 Thursday night. Restrictive? Yes, but worth insisting on.

4. If a host has a cocktail party, he may not have a hospitality room, and vice versa. One or the other, not both.

5. Have rules for outside hosts who wish to entertain at the same time. If there is a custom for one outside group to invite everyone attending the conference to a cocktail party on a given night it would be unfair to open that time slot to another party without warning the host who has had it in the past. If the customary host is a commercial supplier who has something to sell you may feel differently about this from the way you would if the local chapter of your organization hosted the party without hope of commercial recompense.

For example, one large organization is composed of salesmen for several hundred companies. Each year, about 25 companies host as many separate banquets at the annual convention for those of their salesmen who are present. Similarly, at the national convention of another organization, regional groups have their own respective dinners. In both these instances, all dinners for the association are held on the same evening.

It is not essential to follow all these rules to control entertaining, but if you incorporate some of them in your planning, your job will be easier. Don't be surprised if your outside hosts, too, come around on the QT and thank you. It takes a load off them.

If you now allow entertaining and want to stop it, what can you do? You can, of course, try to stop it short. Expect bad feeling and trouble, but if you have enough organization sentiment behind you, you may be able to do it.

In any case, bring it under control with firm rules as a first step in phasing out. Cut down the hours available for entertainment. Allow no more hosts to enter the list of firms on your permitted list, and replace none if anyone drops out. ("Sorry, the situation was getting out of hand. We had to cut down, and this is the way we decided to do it.")

If you have a large number of hospitality suites, you can reduce the number by allowing a firm to entertain guests only every other year.

You can offer your own competition by having the organization host programs in the evening to eliminate outside entertainment.

If you do intend to phase out entertainment by others, plan to accomplish this over a period of three to five years. Set your schedule at the beginning of the period. And be sure your people have something to do with themselves in the evening at your conference. If you don't, you will be known as the guy who shot Santa Claus.

6
The Meeting Itself, Part II

This chapter deals with running the actual sessions, audience reaction sheets, speakers at the meeting itself, honoring loyal attenders, security, transcripts, and other subjects.

The Sessions

Starting. Can a meeting be run on time? The answer to that question is a definite yes. You can run it on time if you want to. When you delay the start of a meeting to wait for late-comers you are unfair to those who arrived promptly and you are wasting the time—not of one person but of the aggregate of all who are there in the audience. You are, moreover, assuring from the outset that your program will run behind.

There is no magic technique to starting on time. Some things help, however.

1. Tell your speakers that your program will keep precisely to schedule.

2. Tell your conventioners in promotion and at the start of the meeting that every session will begin and end on time.

3. Start each session exactly on time. Don't wait for stragglers. Open the session if there are three people in the room, two, one person, or none (the last just doesn't happen). Your audience will come in fast enough if you start.

4. When you want your audience to come in, take seats, and quiet down, try this technique to get attention:

Start by saying, "Ladies and gentlemen, take your seats, please. We are about to start." You can usually point out that there are seats not yet occupied near the front.

As soon as the flurry of sitting is over, but certainly no longer than two minutes later, say, "Your attention, please!"

Then count three to yourself, slowly, and immediately start talking—giving your welcome, introductions, or whatever. Do not wait longer, or you will lose your audience.

5. Give the people in the hall a boost. One way is to buy a bell, a cocked hat, and a bandolier that says Town Crier. Put them on one of your assistants, who will walk around ringing the bell and crying, "Meeting is about to start. Please go in." If you don't want to go for the props, send your staff out a few minutes ahead of starting time to talk people in.

6. Want to get people to sit near the front in the meeting? Place handouts of papers or whatever you are distributing in the first few rows of seats only. If more people come in, have someone hand the late-comers material after they are seated.

Don't accept the idea that you can't start on time. Some people are running their programs on schedule. There is no reason why all cannot do so. It's only fair to the speakers and to the audiences, too.

Speakers

Introductions. The trouble with the way most speakers are introduced is that the introductions are too long. The truth is that often an oral introduction is too short to describe the speaker's accomplishments adequately but is long enough to bore the audience. The speaker then has to mollify the audience and try to earn the attention he should have as a matter of course.

Avoid this by putting full biographies, with pictures, in the program, or on other sheets supplied in the kit. Have them accompany the outlines of the speakers' talks if possible. When the first speaker is introduced to the audience the introducer says that full biographies are in the program (kits), and introduces the speaker by name and affiliation only. All other speakers are introduced by these two means of identification.

Problems. Some problems can arise when speakers are delivering their talks. One is the difficulty of keeping some speakers to their allotted time. I have mentioned before that you should tell the speakers in advance that you will keep strictly to schedule. Make up several 3 in. × 5 in. cards. On these type, "Five Minutes," "Two Minutes," "Time's Up!" and "Please stand closer to the microphone." Have several of each message.

The chairman passes the Five Minutes card to the speaker five minutes before he is supposed to finish, following in three minutes with the Two Minutes card, and then with the cut-off Time's Up! card. The fact that the speaker is getting warnings will be visible to the audience and puts them on the chairman's side. To allow a speaker to run over is unfair to succeeding speakers because it may force them to shorten their prepared talks. To allow any amount of run-over in speeches can put your program in a shambles.

A second problem with speakers is that sometimes they cannot be heard. The usual reason is that they are not standing close enough to the microphone. As you have guessed, the answer is to pass them the card that tells them to stand closer. Be direct. There is no other way.

It is harder to hear a speaker when he sits than when he stands. Therefore, if you have a seated panel, their faces will often have to be closer to the mike than they would be if standing at a lectern.

In some instances a speaker has such a strong voice that, in a small room, he can cut loose from a mike and be more effective using his voice alone. The speaker who has this capability is usually aware of it and does not have to be told.

Speakers should be heard, but they should also be seen—or rather, they *and the exhibits they present* should be seen. Sometimes a speaker uses a blackboard for diagrams or puts figures on slides to help illustrate his talk, but his exhibit can be seen only in the first few rows. The only solution is to have the same material reproduced as hand-outs to be given to the audience before the speaker begins talking. (Some techniques for making effective slides are described in Chapter 10.) Be sure there are enough hand-outs for the entire audience. Have more than you think you will need.

Speakers who do not show are a serious problem, which has been treated in Chapter 2.

I have previously discussed giving small gifts to the speaker and writing letters of thanks. The mechanics of making a presentation to a speaker on the dais—or to any other recipient of a gift or award—are as follows:

Turn your body so it faces the audience, but turn your face from time to time toward the recipient of the gift or award. Hold the gift, plaque, loving cup, or what have you, so it can be seen by the audience and pictured by the photographer. Present it with the left hand and extend your right hand. The recipient takes the award or gift in the left hand, leaving the right hand free for the handshake. Thus, left hands and right hands cross. If you want to get a really good photograph of the presentation, restage it after the session.

Questions. How do you handle questions addressed to your speakers? There are several ways.

1. At most meetings, when the floor is opened to questions, a member of the audience stands and puts his question aloud. This method puts a premium on aggressiveness. The shy person or one who desires anonymity does not ask a question. An advantage to this way of putting questions is that there are liveliness and the possibility of visual confrontation in the case of difference of views between the questioner and the program speaker.

Defects are several. Questioners may make speeches instead of asking questions. This uses up time and turns off both speaker and audience. Questions of most general interest may not get asked by this method, but people with individual problems may get satisfaction.

Another defect of this method is that usually the question cannot be heard by the audience. Where this conventional handling of questions is used, it is important that the chairman of the meeting repeat the question into the microphone at the rostrum before the speaker tries to answer it. This accomplishes three objects. The chairman can rephrase the question, if necessary, to make it more understandable. The speaker is given a chance to think before answering the question. And, most necessary of course, the audience has a chance to hear the question. Note that the *chairman* should repeat the question. If you rely on the speaker to repeat it, he will forget.

2. A variant of the first method is to have one or more microphones in the aisles, so that members of the audience can move to a mike to ask a question or to make a comment. This is useful where the speaker has delivered a learned paper and highly qualified people in the audience are expected to comment at considerable length, and where cross comment within the audience is expected. For the usual speech with short question period following the talk it is doubtful that the microphone placed in the audience is more than a gadget. It is time consuming.

3. Some meetings have a practice of allowing any member of the audience to interrupt the speaker at any time with a question. This can make a shambles of the speaker's organized talk and cause him to run out of time prematurely. The best way to stop this is to tell the audience before the speaker talks that there will be a question period at the end of the speech. If any member of the audience thinks he will forget his question, he can write it down.

If you are wedded to the idea of interruptions for questions, try this modification: have the speaker talk for a while, stop for questions to that point, and then talk again, with a question period following each section of his speech.

4. One very effective method of handling questions is to furnish the audience paper on which to write questions. You can get bandoliers that say, big and bold—very likely in red—"Questions?"—and have one or more young women walk slowly around the meeting hall during the talk and the question period picking up the questions. You use women because, believe it or not, they are less distracting to the audience than men.

The question people take the questions to the chairman, not to the speaker. At the conclusion of a talk, the chairman gives the speaker the questions he will answer. The speaker reads the question and then answers it. It is courteous, and you get better answers, if the speaker has a chance to look over the questions before answering them. You, as meeting manager, can help by scheduling two or three speakers one after another, then a question period for all three. In the case of a panel followed by questions and answers, the chairman should not call on the last speaker to answer his questions first, as he would not have had a chance to look at his questions before he started to answer them.

Written questions have these advantages: The writer will take care in phrasing them so that they make sense. They will be read through a microphone and therefore can be heard. They can be screened so that if time is short only those of most general interest will be answered. Two or more questions about the same subject can be combined, also saving time. More written questions can be answered, by a good deal, than is the case with the spoken ones. Try this. It works.

Liaison between dais and meeting manager. An important by-product of having people collect questions is that they can carry messages between the chairman on the dais and you, the meeting manager. This is essential, as you will have announcements you want him to make. Not all the speakers may be on hand when a session starts, and the chairman will be anxious to know if he may have to rearrange his program. You should keep him informed of developments, but you need an unobtrusive messenger. That messenger, for two-way communication, is the question girl.

The people collecting questions should be impressed with the importance of their job, which is not only to carry questions forward to the chair, but also to usher latecomers to seats, listen to speakers to see if they are audible in the back of the room (informing the chair of inaudible speakers) and provide liaison. If a question collector leaves the meeting room, she should have a replacement substitute until she returns. Be sure the question people understand that they *must* cover the room at all times. They should be allowed to sit, but not to have reading material. It is very frustrating to a chairman to have a note to transmit to the back-stage meeting manager and have no messenger in the room or one whose nose is buried in a magazine.

Messages for the audience. What should you do when you are conducting a meeting and a message comes to you that someone in the audience has a telephone call? Under no circumstances, or almost no circumstances, should you announce from the rostrum—or, of course, allow the chairman to do so if you are not on the dais—that Mr. Jones has a telephone call. To do so is unfair to your speakers, cheapens the meeting, and causes disruption when Mr. Jones leaves the audience. It also encourages others to have themselves called out of the conference.

How can you avoid this? After all, people can be expected to get messages.

Have all telephone calls come to your registration desk. Your personnel there will take down the essentials—person called of course, caller, phone number. This note will then go onto a bulletin board. To get your convention-goers to check the board, the chairman announces, perhaps twice a day, that no one will be paged, but that messages will be placed on the board. The chairman should tell the audience the telephone number of the registration desk so that those attending the meeting can pass it on to their offices. It is a good idea to print your method of handling messages in the program.

But how about the really important messages? Shouldn't you announce those? In answer to that we say that people's ideas of importance vary. What is important to one secretary may be unimportant in the scale of values of the meeting manager or chairman. Have your registration staff be firm with callers who insist that you must call someone out of the meeting. If they say it is important, make them tell why. The only exception you should make on paging members of the audience from the rostrum is in the case of illness, accident, or death in the convention-goer's immediate family. Make this plain to all attending. You will be surprised how well everyone will accept this.

The Sub-Conference

By *sub-conference* I do not mean a meeting concerned with submersible warships or understudies for players and actors who have to be replaced. I mean those annoying, discourteous conversations that go on in the back of the meeting room. They are rude to the speaker and distracting to the audience. If your group is a bunch of "talkers," the best cure is prevention, perhaps even going so far as to put a notice in the program.

The meeting chairman who finds side conversation going on during the session despite printed warnings has a responsibility to the speakers to step in and stop noise in the meeting room. You will do this, if you can, by a polite, firm word between talks, but if necessary be prepared to interrupt a speaker for the purpose. Naturally, we hope that this extreme step will not be necessary.

Sometimes the fault is not entirely with the people in the back of the room. They may have tuned the speaker out because they could not hear him. Far too many speakers do not stand close enough to the microphone to be heard. Far too often questions from the floor are asked orally (as noted above, the worst way to handle questions) and neither the chairman nor the speaker repeats them into the microphone so they can be heard. All the audience is the back hears is an answer to which they are supposed to dream up a question. True, the back-row people should nevertheless be quiet, but they do have some excuse for conversation.

We need both the carrot of good speakers, interesting and easy to listen to, and the stick of oral chastisement, where it is necessary. And why do some people read newspapers during a speech? This I will never understand.

If your noise problem is chronic, here is a suggested notice for the first page of your program:

> As a courtesy to the speaker and the other members of the audience, please do not conduct private conversations or read newspapers in the meeting room when a session is in progress.

Audience Reaction Sheets

How can you know whether your meeting is going over? During the meeting, keeping your eyes and ears open is very important. You should tell your staff members to take care of every complaint promptly, and when the complainer is out of sight to tell the meeting manager so that it can be recorded.

Also helpful are suggestions for the next meeting. Meeting managers have a harried job, but it is important to find the time to write these ideas down. Also, try to record the name of the person making the suggestion. He may later prove valuable in helping to carry it out.

Nothing is so helpful in planning future meetings, however, as an audience reaction sheet. You can give this any name you wish—reaction questionnaire, ideas and suggestions, tip sheet, the meeting-goer talks back.

Ask questions to get reactions to program, site, hotel or motel, meals, rooms, physical arrangements, conduct of meeting, and, if you wish, such matters as recreation, advance reservation procedure, and spouses' program.

Keep your questionnaire short—not longer than both sides of one sheet of paper. Make it easy to answer, with the responder mainly making check marks or circles. Leave room toward the end for the meeting attender to add comments of his own. A signature can be optional.

In soliciting information to determine the popularity of the program items, it is best to list all of them and allow the replier to do one of two things:

- Check the three, four, or five (you decide on number) he liked best.
- Mark his preferences in decreasing order—1, 2, 3.

We believe the second method will give you the more valuable information. Separate the topics and speakers in the ratings. This makes it possible for the person attending the meeting to give a good mark to a superior speech delivered by a poor speaker, and vice versa.

Always ask what people want on the next program. If your organization moves its meeting from city to city you may wish to ask where the responders wish to go next.

Have the completed questionnaires left in a box at the rear of the meeting room or mailed to you.

If you follow worthwhile suggestions from the audience reaction sheets, your meetings will increasingly reflect what your organization or company needs and wants.

But there are plus values for the audience reaction sheets beyond a contribution to the quality of the program and site location and similar matters. Here are some:

Audience Reaction Questionnaire

    To help us plan next year's conference, we would appreciate your taking a few moments to tell us what you thought about this one and what you would like covered at next year's meeting.

    Here are the topics and speakers at today's sessions. Please indicate your first three preferences, in decreasing order, by numbering them 1, 2, or 3.

	Most Interesting	*Most Useful to Me*
The World Today	_____	_____
Growth Stocks as Opportunity	_____	_____
Are Bonds in a Bind?	_____	_____
Mortgages in California Today	_____	_____
New Energy Sources—New Industries	_____	_____
The Future of Credit	_____	_____

	Most Effective Speakers
John Forecaster	_____
Adam Smuthe	_____
Frederick Wary	_____
Lisle St. Mento	_____
Oliver Ohm	_____
Henry Preteur	_____

Comments _____

_____

    How would you rate the following with regard to the conference? (Please check one.)

Hotel Facilities?   Excellent_____   Good_____   Could be better_____

Meals?   Excellent_____   Good_____   Could be better_____

Spouses' program?   Excellent_____   Good_____   Could be better_____

I would like next year's meeting held in (city):_____

I suggest the following topics and speakers for next year's conference:_____

_____

_____

Comments_____

_____

_____

(Signature)_____
(Optional)

■ The members of the organization have a sense of participation in the meeting. Just being asked for opinions is important, but the person who makes a suggestion and sees that suggestion followed will come to the next meeting if he can get there, if only to see his suggestion in action.

■ Audience reaction sheets result in sincere testimonials from attenders. These are useful in reporting the meeting that prompted them and in promoting the next conference. If you run an annual or semiannual meeting, continued promotion can make very good use of quotes from the questionnaires.

■ You may learn small things about your meeting hotel—mostly negative—that you would learn in no other way. This is a sort of negative "plus," but an important one. Hotel management will show its best side to *you,* but not necessarily to the rank and file convention-goer. He may tell you his troubles anonymously through a questionnaire where he would not do so in person. These matters, in total, might affect your decision for another meeting.

The audience reaction questionnaire shown is an example of one type of reaction sheet.

At the end of a session the audience should not just scatter. There should be a good ending. The chairman should express appreciation to the speaker(s) and ask the audience to join him in an expression of that appreciation (clapping). This makes the speaker or speakers feel glad that they made the effort to talk to the group.

Non-Session Events

By non-session events I mean meals, coffee breaks, cocktail parties and hospitality suites, and scheduled entertainment. For meal functions there is little to add to what was discussed in the last chapter.

Coffee breaks. Coffee breaks are not only a chance to pause and refresh, but also are an opportunity for plus values for your organization or company and for your meeting-goers.

You can get extra value by setting an interesting scene in the coffee area through the use of posters, exhibits, or demonstrations of association services and activities or company products in the refreshment room or corridor. Audiovisual may be worthwhile.

If your organization is large enough, have three or four of your major headquarters departments represented by their chiefs at various locations in the area. They are there to tell about their respective services and answer questions. Some likely services for this exposure are information/library, advertising, marketing department/membership, publications. Remember to use signs that can be seen a good distance away. Photographs and graphics help get the message across.

Selling booths to exhibitors helps pay the freight for the meeting.

Place these in the coffee area and you have another plus for your association. If you sell booths, don't forget to have one for your own organization. For more on booths, see Chapter 9.

The major benefits of a coffee break for those attending are a rest from listening to speeches and a chance to exchange views with other meeting-goers and meet new people. Conventioners, however, also benefit from knowing more about services that are available to them.

A couple of wrinkles: If you have simultaneous sessions, have them break at one time for a general coffee break where all can mix.

A variant of the ten- or fifteen-minute coffee break is the continual coffee break. With this, the people attending can step outside the meeting room any time for coffee or soda and drink it there or take it back inside. A two-minute stretch is allowed at the end of each speech, but otherwise there are no breaks.

What are the pros and cons of this continual coffee break, or more properly, *continuous coffee service?*

The one pro—and it is a big one—is that it saves half an hour to 40 minutes for the program by cutting out the morning and afternoon breaks. Or, alternatively, makes it possible to let the audience go earlier in the day.

The cons are several. One of the major benefits of a meeting, the opportunity for conversation among the registrants, is considerably reduced.

The continuous coffee service works for a one-day meeting. Even a dedicated group of information-seekers would, I believe, rebel at so much sitting if the meeting ran more than a day. Also, there is no time when people can make phone calls and the like that will not absent them from part of the sessions, except before and after the meeting starts.

Continuous coffee service requires an attendant all the time, or at least demands his frequent attention to see that the supply of coffee and other drinks is maintained. Of course, this must be paid for.

Cocktail parties. Most meetings that run two or three days have a cocktail party. You, as meeting manager, will probably be in charge of arranging this. In addition, your organization or company may wish to entertain speakers, officers, and other VIPs and their spouses separately from the convention-goers at large. This, too, may be your responsibility.

At conventions other than your own, you may be asked to set up and run a hospitality suite for your firm or association. Since the principles of running any of these types of cocktail parties or hospitality suites are similar, I will discuss them all here. I discussed the purchasing of liquor in Chapter 2.

When any organization or group runs a cocktail party or hospitality suite, someone should always be at the door to welcome guests. This person should greet the guests, introduce them to any important people in the firm or organization and to the host of the suite. Most of the time this is done. Sometimes this courtesy is omitted. It should not be.

Who tends bar in a hospitality suite? It is best to have a bartender from the hotel, especially during the busiest time your suite is open for visitors. If traffic is light, you can have the people who man the suite mix the drinks. Be careful, however. If one person is bartender consistently, he is low man on the social totem pole. Did you pay his expenses to the meeting so that he could be cast in that position?

Often a hospitality suite is opened for the purpose of entertaining customers and potential customers of a firm. If it is manned by salesmen, care should be exercised to make all the salesmen seem important. Perhaps each salesman should make drinks—at least the first one—for his own customers. In any case, the bartending should be spread around so that all who are on the same business level will seem to be equal in the view of the customers they serve.

Hosts for the hospitality suite should remember that they are representing the salesmen who were not able to come to this meeting as well as themselves, and should be cordial to any guest who comes through the door.

Whom do you invite to a hospitality suite? Your customers and potential customers, of course. Don't forget the officials and staff of the sponsoring organization. How about your competitors? Why not?

How do you get the word around? A note in advance to all potential guests is good, if you can get a mailing list. You may be able to get room numbers from the registration desk when the meeting starts. A pile of invitations on the registration desk may do the trick. If the sponsor will let you, large signs in the registration area and the hotel lobby will bring in the crowds.

I like a printed card, worded in polite, semiformal English. Such a card is most effective when mailed in advance.

Everyone recognizes that a hospitality suite is semisocial, semi-selling. Whether the hosts are a firm selling products and services or an organization trying to sell itself to new members, some sales objective is involved. How much should you have of each? My opinion is that the best selling is none at all. Keep the encounter entirely social. It is OK to have some literature on a table. It is OK to discuss a little business if a customer has a question. And it is OK to make an appointment to see someone later in his office. But the objective of a hospitality suite is to give an opportunity for people to meet, say hello to one another, and converse in a friendly atmosphere. And it would be a bad business/social fault to go to someone else's hospitality suite and start selling there.

A quick look at other aspects of a hospitality suite—limit the hours the suite is open, observing any rules laid down by the organization sponsoring the meeting. Be open any time you say you will. Limit staffing of the suite. Your people can make more contact elsewhere in the meeting, even though it is lighter contact. And when a lone guest walks into a hospitality room and five of your people rise to meet him, he won't think your hospitality is too attractive. Better to have only two people there.

Should you have hors d'oeuvres? It really is not too important. Peanuts, potato chips, perhaps pretzels, you should have these. Hors d'oeuvres are nice when you have heavy traffic. (They are also somewhat expensive.) Do not over-order on hot hors d'oeuvres. They are not much good when cold.

There is one last problem with a hospitality suite. It is the hanger-on who stays, and stays, and stays, after everyone is gone and you want to go to bed. Every drink anchors him more securely in his chair, and he isn't about to leave without suggestion. We have used a method that works invariably for us, and should for you. With a big, broad smile go over to him and take his hand as if to shake it. Draw him carefully to his feet. With great good humor, say, "It's time to go to bed. I'm going to bed. Everyone is going to bed!" Put an arm around his shoulder, walk him to the door, and still with a big smile on your face, put him out in the hall. No one ever objected to this. Perhaps by that hour of the night a guest is glad to be told that it is time to go to sleep.

Scheduled Entertainment

If you have planned a show, a dinner-dance type of program, or some other evening entertainment, your success in bringing it off will, as with other events, depend upon advance preparation. Observe particularly what has been said elsewhere about buying and serving liquor (see Chapter 2).

Honoring the Loyal

The faithful attenders—those who have come loyally to the association's conventions for several years—are best honored at a luncheon. Make it a part of the formal program at the meal. You have everyone there, with no one moving around. Choose a time when the meal-service schedule indicates relative quiet. Honor enough faithful attenders to fill about three minutes (five minutes at most). Start with those who are honored for the shortest period you are citing. Ask them to stand as their names are called and remain standing, with applause held until the end. Wind up with those who have the longest record of attendance. Say something nice about them and see that they get a good measure of applause.

Photographer

Is the wandering photographer at your meetings just that, wandering?—Or is he moving about and snapping pictures with a purpose?

Did you and he plan ahead?

Sending out pictures with your news releases can help improve your news coverage.

Furthermore, whether you have a simple bulletin or a glossy house magazine with four-color printing, photos of your meeting can liven up the publication, be informational for its readers, and stimulate interest in coming meetings. But the pictures must do what you and the editor of the publication want them to do.

What pictures should the photographer take? The editor of your publication is the best judge, but if the editor is not on hand, here are some tips:

You will want pictures of all your speakers. These are best taken of them sitting at the table where they are going to speak (especially with panels) or at the rostrum. You will also want audience shots, and these are most interesting from an angle—one side or another, or looking down from a balcony, rather than head on. If your meeting is a serious one, these pictures reinforce that fact with those who did not attend.

Officers and big wheels should be snapped. Get all who should appear, just as with the speakers. (Of course, avoid printing anyone's picture twice in the same issue of your publication.) Informal shots of people at cocktail parties are fine, but don't overdo it. Get identification for all pictures of people.

If there is a tour, be sure your photographer is on hand to record it.

The photographer should be alert to "news" opportunities. One meeting manager who takes his own pictures noticed a famous movie actress come into the hotel. He asked her if she would let her picture be taken with his president. She graciously consented, and the photo went in the association magazine. Another photographer was on hand when the hotel hosting the convention mismanaged dispatch of conventioners' baggage at the end of the meeting. His picture of a mountain of luggage moved the headquarters of the chain to change its system of handling baggage.

Finally, try to get excitement and variety. People seeing the pictures should recall the meeting with pleasure or wish they had attended.

Security

Few people like to talk about the subject of security, but nobody likes to suffer from a neglect of it. There are three main aspects involved. The first is making sure that only those you wish to enter have access to your meeting. Strict control of badges—making sure no unauthorized person gets a badge—will keep people out of a meeting room if you have the doors well guarded. You can also issue tickets to the sessions, though this would be unusual.

At the 1976 Democratic convention in New York, individual identification was excellent. No one was admitted to the floor without a large tag (color coded for function) and pocket credentials. Often it was necessary to go through a succession of check points. The advance planning on the part of the convention people and the police kept out those who should not be admitted and let those entitled to enter do so without having to prove ancestry and blood type.

Another aspect of security is the safety of valuable equipment and materials. Where everything is portable, carry it into the banquet department of the hotel and lock it up at night. If you have a good deal of machines and displays, guards can be a good investment. They are virtually a necessity at a trade show.

A third aspect of security is protection of the meeting-goers and their property. Here we are dealing with an unpleasant subject, out of tune with the atmosphere we want to prevail at our convention. But don't we have some kind of responsibility to our members attending a meeting, especially when some of them may not be accustomed to protecting themselves in large cities? Is it right just to let them fly by themselves? A person who is injured may bear the physical and emotional effects for a long time.

When we encourage someone to leave home and attend a meeting in a distant place, we are making him an expatriate even though he is still in his own country. If this person is injured or robbed he is away from his own doctor, his friends, bank and other sources of money, the area where he can exert any influence he may have. He is at the mercy of the medical, financial, and legal structure where he happens to be. The doctors in the convention city may be as skilled as they are at home and the banks as accommodating to their depositors, but he does not know them, and they and their people do not know him. The police may be as effectual, or as useless, as at home, and the courts may be no better than in his home town, but he can at least vote and raise his voice in protest to some effect at home, but it does him little good in a strange city.

In choosing a site for a convention you are assuming a major responsibility. If all goes well, you are a hero. If someone has problems, he becomes the victim of choices and circumstances over which he has no control. And a good experience can turn into a bitter one.

Travel literature will rarely say anything negative about a city or resort. The same is true of tourist bureaus and hotels. We wish they would be more frank. Even a desk clerk may not give you a warning to take a cab when it is safer than walking. I would like to see hotels and restaurants display discreet warnings to their guests about possible incidents. These warnings could prevent those actual cases of robbery and injury that ultimately do more harm to the hotel and restaurant business than any number of warnings could accomplish. We doubt that guests would be frightened off in any serious numbers. We do know of a young man who attended a hairdressers' convention in a Midwestern city and saw so many warning signs in his hotel that he didn't bother to unpack, but took the next available plane home. Few people are as timid as he was.

The major responsibility for people's safety rests with themselves. If they will not take care of themselves, no one else can. For this reason concrete suggestions on how to protect your person and property appear in Chapter 11 under the heading "Travel Tips."

Nevertheless, the meeting manager should give some warning to people who may not know the proper precautions to take. At least issue the old standbys—don't bring heirloom jewelry, put valuables (and money not needed immediately) in the hotel safe, put nothing of value in a suitcase (even a hard-cover locked one), put the chain on the door at night. Women's purses should be placed on the floor or in front of their feet at meals, not by their chairs, or even worse, suspended from the back of their chairs. The conventioner who buys something of value, puts it in his portfolio, and leaves the portfolio at his seat when he goes for a coffee break is asking for trouble.

Why not list these precautions, with perhaps other appropriate warnings on a slip to go with advance information to registrants before the meeting. For late registrants there can be a pile handy at the meeting registration desk. A less preferable alternative is to put a warning slip in each kit.

Transcripts

Transcripts—that is, proceedings of a conference—will be discussed at length in Chapter 7. Some action must be taken at the meeting itself, however, if you are to publish proceedings. Your options are to have a stenographer (your own or one you hire) record the talks, make a tape of everything said, or—and this is the most satisfactory—have the speakers furnish texts of their talks. With advance texts, you will still have to record questions and answers, in some fashion, if you want that material. If you have simultaneous sessions you will have to have a stenographer or tape recorder for each session if you want a verbatim record. Also, most panels—whether simultaneous or not—are usually unrehearsed.

Be sure to tell your stenotypist or the person making the recording what room of the hotel he or she is to go to and an exact time to appear, probably half an hour in advance of the time the program will start, in order to set up equipment and locate and plug into outlets. Give the stenotypist a program so he or she can get the exact spelling of speakers' names.

Some organizations furnish all those who attend a meeting with a complete transcript of the proceedings. Others try to sell cassette tapes. If you do this, price your cassettes high enough so that you do not discourage attendance at your convention, yet not so high that you cannot sell the cassettes. One large organization that encountered this problem tried offering cassette *players* at just over cost if the purchaser spent a certain amount for the association's tapes. This helped. Then it ran a drawing at its annual conference for a free cassette. But there was a catch. Before the conventioner could fill out an entry blank to try to win the free cassette he had to listen to a tape giving a sales talk on the tapes the organization offered its members. This was a good idea that worked.

Spouses

There is little to say about the spouses' and children's programs that was not covered ealier, except to see that the registration of spouses and the program designed for their and the children's entertainment stay on the track.

Liaison with the Hotel

Right now, at the meeting itself, is where all your advance planning and consultation with the hotel should pay off. From signs in the halls to microphones in the meeting rooms, meal service, coffee breaks, and cocktail parties, everything should go according to plan. But it won't. Some meeting rooms may be too cold or too hot. More people will show up at the round table on costs than you could have possibly imagined. It turns out that Senator Smith will consent to a news conference after all.

Nevertheless, if you have planned, made arrangements, and programmed, and the hotel people know what you want at each step, they will do everything possible to accommodate you. You will have fewer foreseeable problems and will be able to take the unexpected in stride.

I presume that you have communicated pertinent parts of your program down the line in the hotel to each person in charge of the various events for your conference. I assume that you have done this with the knowledge and consent of the hotel management. In addition, there must be some person in that top management whom you can deal with in an emergency. By the time of the meeting you will probably be on a first-name basis with this person. Since he or she cannot be available day and night, know who this person's alter ego will be, and meet the stand-in so that if any hotel problem arises, you can count on quick, top-level solution. If you cannot move an underling, you need to know whom to appeal to.

You yourself, or a member of your staff, must be in any room where one of your meetings is going on, to handle any problem that arises. You should be present when a meeting starts in the grand ballroom, but can leave an assistant to watch matters once the meeting is going well, if you feel you are needed elsewhere. If you have small, simultaneous sessions going, have a staff member sit out the meeting, and you should look in on each one at least once. Any problem should be immediately communicated to you. If you have an office that you use during the convention, let people know that that is where they should look for you first. If you leave that office—or any place where people can expect to find you—tell someone who will *not* be leaving that location where you can be found.

One matter on which hotels and conventions have never gotten together is that of check-out on the last day of a meeting. The hotels want their rooms emptied by noon or 1 P.M., but the meeting ends at 2:30, 4, or 5 P.M. Meeting-goers who want late check-out—often most of those attending the sessions—are frequently told to consult the assistant manager. Why does this have to be done on an individual basis? The meeting manager could consult the hotel to determine what it will permit for late check-out, then do as the meeting manager of one organization does— have someone from his staff sit in the rear of the meeting room and list the names of those people, with their room numbers, who wish late check-out. He then turns the list over to the assistant manager. Of course, an announcement about this service is made from the lectern.

Press Room

The organization, staffing, and equipping of a press room were discussed at length in Chapter 4. The object now is to keep it running well.

The meeting manager should check from time to time to see that the press room is operating as it should and to lend any assistance the PR person feels would be helpful.

Reporters attending your meeting will want to make telephone calls. Very likely the hotel operators will not let calls go out from a meeting room extension without a code word. Find out what that is and tell your staff in the press room so that they can pass it on reporters who wish to use the phone. Most reporters are responsible and most will want to make only local calls. A reporter for an out-of-town paper will very likely need to call his publication, and that, of course is a toll call. I have never had a member of the press who made a personal long-distance call from a press room who did not use his own credit card, reverse charges, or offer to pay for the call (offer accepted).

7
Post-Meeting Activity

When your meeting is over, do you fold your tents and silently steal away? Are you glad it's over and want to forget about it until next time? Think again. There are things to do immediately. There are many opportunities to get plus values from the meeting just past, to make the next meeting easier, and—in addition—there are responsibilities that ought to be discharged.

No-Shows

First, even before paying any bills you did not pay at the meeting itself, you must deal with people who registered in advance of the meeting, did not cancel within the required time, and did not show up for the meeting.

In earlier chapters we have made it clear that you should do your best to get all the money you can in advance. Offer inducements—a door prize available to advance-paid registrants only (for the small meeting), a lower fee (for a conference).

But now, you did all that and some people who registered did not show up. *Immediately*—that means the day right after the close of the meeting—send a kit to anyone who paid in advance and did not show. Bill anyone who did not pay, and, upon receipt of his check, send him a kit. My belief is that you should charge the full fee for the meeting to a no-show.

Publicity

If your conference has been important for the community in which it was held—if it was *news*—you have probably done your best to secure coverage in print and broadcast media. Now is the time to try for a wrap-up story in the local newspapers and on radio or television. Time is of the essence here, and your chances are really best if you have been working closely with the media people during the meeting.

Submit the same story you write for the newspaper in the city where the meeting was held to the newspaper in your headquarters city, but change the first paragraph or two.

Very likely some people qualify as personalities in your organization or company. Send short pieces about these men and women to their local papers, with glossy photos, if you can get them. (They need not be as large as 8 in. × 10 in. but passport size is the smallest a paper can work with.) One encouraging factor about getting stories about officers, prize-winners, and speakers in local newspapers is that many middle-income and upper-income people live in the suburbs, where weekly papers are important. The weeklies like to get news of personalities.

Here are some suggested ways you can start your story for a local paper—what journalists call "leads."

> John Johnson, president of Drinkwater Bearing Company, was elected 1981–1982 chairman of the Northwest Machinery Association at its annual meeting last week (June 22–24) in Minneapolis, MN. Mr. Johnson is one of the founders of the 30,000 member organization, which is ten years old. He resides at 21 West Garden St.

If the newspaper frequently runs several paragraphs of a story of this kind, you can add information about the meeting not given in the first paragraph, plus some more facts about Mr. Johnson's business life, perhaps something about his family and associations. In this case it is customary to keep his address till the end of the story. The date given in the parentheses in the lead is a guide to the editor of the paper—so he'll know when the event actually took place. He will probably omit it in publication.

Here is another lead:

> James K. Randolph, of Springfield, was recently (August 27) honored as one of the top salesmen for his company, Exactbilt Mobile Homes, at its sales conference at company headquarters in Indianapolis, IN. Mr. Randolph established a company record by selling 27 mobile homes in the final six months of 1980—more than one a week. Average sales price of the mobile homes was well above $15,000.

And another:

Doris Hammersmith was the recipient of the Award of Honor of the California Association for Youth Advancement at its annual convention in Monterey last week (July 13–15). Mrs. Hammersmith was honored for her work in founding and developing a shelter for runaway teenagers in Garden Bright, CA. The shelter has helped over 3,000 young people since its establishment in 1977. Mrs. Hammersmith lives with her husband and three children at 17 Ivy Way, North Centerville.

In your leads, be certain to tell who, what, when, where, sometimes why, and perhaps even how. Also, it is frequently of interest to the reader to know how many people attended the meeting.

If you are successful and do get some stories published, be certain to clip them and file them away in a spot you can easily remember. You will need those clippings later.

If your association or company has a magazine, a bulletin, or some other means of communication with the membership or employees, by all means write a story for the publication. Pictures are important here. This is a good place to use the candid shots your photographer took at the meeting. (See the section on the photographer and pictures in Chapter 6.)

Report for Yourself

I recommend that every meeting manager have a notebook—a three-ring loose-leaf binder is good—to contain plans and reports of meetings. Maintained cumulatively, this meeting notebook saves work and headaches in connection with the next meeting. The meeting manager should write a report to himself which is as complete and detailed as possible and contains everything he can think of that could have application in the future. He should write this while the meeting is fresh in his mind, from notes made during the conference.

The report should, of course, tell where the meeting was held, how many attended, how many meeting and guest rooms were used, and how much everything cost. It should be broken down by pre-registration, registration, meeting itself, and post-meeting follow-up (for non-hotel matters), and arrangements, cost per service, efficiency, cooperation, etc. (for hotel matters). This report will help whoever manages the next meeting—whether it is you or someone else.

Promotion

I said to hold onto clippings about the meeting. Those from newspapers in the city where the meeting was held are particularly valuable. Have photostats made of these and make a montage of the headlines and-first parts of the newspaper stories. If you can afford it, run this montage as part of a house organ story about the meeting or in a folder as a special report to the membership (or employees). In the months preceding the next conference, you can use the same (or a similar montage) in the same way. Do the same thing with photo montages if you run repeated stories. The clippings can bear repetition better than pictures.

Responsibilities

The meeting manager has a responsibility to write the report mentioned above.

He should also thank all speakers, people who have assisted him with committee work or in some other way, and, if appropriate, the hotel people who cooperated with him.

The meeting manager should pay all bills for which his company or organization is liable, after checking them for accuracy, and put his accounts in order.

Letter to Those Attending

Sometimes the meeting manager, or the head of the organization or company responsible for the meeting, should write everyone who attended. This is a particularly good idea for a small group, and where there is something to be "sold." We are using "sold" in a wide sense. A firm may hold a meeting to introduce its services and to build good will. Certainly a letter thanking people for coming and offering to supply more information if it is desired is a good move. The same would be true if prospective members of an organization had been invited as guests at a meeting. Good taste must be used in the letter and in subsequent follow-ups, but this is just one more plus-value that can be achieved.

Transcripts of Proceedings

Chapter 5 described action you must take during your meeting if you are to have transcripts made of the proceedings. This section discusses the subject of transcripts at greater length.

When you run meetings, you do so with the belief that they will add to the knowledge and expertise of your audience in its field of endeavor.

Few people take notes. You realize that unless you do more than have speakers give talks and answer questions, people not present will receive no benefit. Therefore, unless the content of the meetings is of only ephemeral interest, a desire will arise to get the meeting down in permanent form. You come to the question: to have a transcript or not to have a transcript.

Publishing a transcript can be expensive and very time consuming, and the published work may appear months after the peak of timely interest has passed.

Economical Methods. If you are willing, however, to cut some corners and if you can be firm with speakers on what you expect of them, you can save money and time and produce a timely transcript.

I suggest that you obtain advance manuscripts of prepared talks from all speakers. To get advance texts you cannot depend upon voluntary cooperation from speakers alone. You must insist upon advance texts as part of the agreement to speak. See that the texts arrive some weeks before the meeting, to allow for the inevitable extensions of time some speakers will request.

The most common objection you will encounter from speakers is that they never have a prepared speech and talk only from notes (or even without notes). In this case you should ask the speaker to deliver his talk in his office, either to his secretary or to a dictating machine, and then have it typed—good, clean copy.

When you have the typed texts of the talks, you have the great majority of the material you need for the transcript.

If you stop at this point, you will save time, effort, and money. You can reproduce the texts just as you have them, merely adding some biographical material where necessary about each speaker.

If the variation in typing of the different manuscripts troubles you, you can have all the material retyped so as to appear uniform. It must then, however, be carefully proofread for accuracy. If you are going to the trouble of retyping, you might as well edit the manuscripts for uniform "style" in punctuation, capitalization, and similar matters before they are typed again.

Adding other material. Although stopping at this point will give your membership the great bulk of what was said and you will have contributed considerably to the literature of the subject, some meeting managers and chairmen, and possibly some other people, will not be satisfied. You will not have introductions—about which more shortly—or questions and answers and panel discussions. You may want to include these. If you do, you will have to have this material tape recorded, stenotyped, or taken down in shorthand. It is best, in a formal transcript, to omit speaker introductions and replace them with biographical sketches. Most introductions sound better when spoken than they read in cold print.

You cannot, however, cut corners with questions and answers (Q and A) and panel give and take. Either you omit them or you pay the price in time and money for taking down all the words as they are said.

With Q and A, you make things easier for yourself, and the transcript more accurate, if you have all questions posed by the audience presented in written form, addressed to the speaker who is to answer. (These are collected, carried to the chairman, and passed by him to the speaker.)

As each speaker reads the question into the microphone and answers it, someone must be recording his words, in shorthand or on tape. The chairman should collect the written questions from the speakers at the end of the session and turn them over to the typist to serve as a check against her notes or the recording tape.

The typist then prepares a typed copy of the questions and answers, indicating by name the speaker reading each question and answering it.

Panels are more difficult, inasmuch as several people may comment on the same matter. Stenographic notes must indicate who is talking. If the discussion is being recorded someone should backstop the tape by very brief notes identifying a speaker by name and the first few words of his comment. Notes for this part of the transcript, of course, now are typed.

Should you get professional help in recording the Q and A and panel questions of your program? By all means yes, if you can afford it.

You can try the do-it-yourself route. If your organization is too small to afford commercial help, you may want to try to handle the Q and A and panels yourself.

Obviously, there are two ways:

1. Some member who has a secretary with good shorthand skills persuades her to attend the meeting, or
2. Some member with a recording machine volunteers to tape the material and have it typed.

In either case, have a back-up—another person good at shorthand and a second knowledgeable operator of the machine. People do get ill or fail to show up for one reason or another.

Remember, too, that if you run simultaneous panels you will need a stenographer or tape recorder for each panel.

If you have pursued the process this far, you have a transcript in two parts—the prepared talks, with short biographies and the typed Q and A and panel discussions. You need not send the speeches to your speakers for review—after all, they wrote them. You must, however, send copies of the Q and A and panel discussions to the speakers so that they can edit them for correctness of grammar and fact. (This should *not* be an opportunity for a speaker to revise his remarks from what he did say to what he wishes he had said.)

At this point your real time problem can begin. Give the speakers a deadline, saying that if you do not receive their copy back by the given date you will assume that there are no changes. The next step is to have the Q and A and panels typed.

Before you have final typing done, of any of the material, consult your printer to determine the best form so that he can do a good job for you. If you use only the manuscripts sent you by speakers you will, of course, have nothing to retype, provided they are all clear enough and dark enough to reproduce well. The material *you* have typed, however, should benefit from the advice of your printer.

When you have copy that is perfect for reproduction, take it to a good offset printer or offset duplicating shop and have it run off. How about collating? If the print shop has the facilities to collate, take advantage of them. If you try to do it yourself for a considerable number of members you can find yourself up to your elbows, with paper confusion all over the place.

What about a cover? Early on, consult the printer for his suggestions. The possibilities vary a good deal, depending on the degree of formality you wish, the number of pages to be included in your transcript, and how much you wish to spend. You may want to see what a stationer can offer in the way of paper folders. Some of these folders have a "window" cut in the front cover. Careful spacing of the title page can result in the title and other identification appearing framed in the cut-out in an attractive fashion.

Formal transcript. We have discussed above procedures whereby you can put before your members in printed form an inexpensive transcript that will embody most or all of your meeting. The formal, elaborate, book-type transcript, set in type by a composing house and printed by a regular book printing company, is quite different from the less formal transcript we have described. Some of the procedures are the same.

It is still important to get advance manuscripts, compile bios, and secure a transcript of questions and answers and panels. It is customary to have the respective speakers look over pertinent parts of the manuscript before it goes to the printer. The printer's copy should be prepared by a competent editor, not only for the sake of uniform style, but so that he or she can question places where meaning is unclear or language should be improved. Avoid sending proof of the typesetting to the speakers. If they have reviewed the appropriate portions of the manuscript, they should be content.

Typesetting can be the usual kind, with "justified" lines (that come out exactly even on the right) or with an electric typewriter (ragged right margin, but much cheaper).

If you are having the book typeset by a printer, he will want the copy to come to him double-spaced. Since most manuscripts prepared for speakers are single-spaced, you must first edit the speakers' texts and then have the material retyped. To minimize variation between the text approved by the speakers and the finished product, have the proofreaders read from the speakers' manuscripts you edited, and not from the later copy sent to the printer.

Binding can be paper or plastic, or hard cover. If you are producing a record that you wish to be considered permanent, hard cover is well worth the difference in cost.

8

Small and Special Meetings

This chapter first discusses small meetings in general, and then discusses specific types of small meetings. For the sake of completeness, some aspects of a meeting that were covered earlier in this book are repeated here. (For more detail on these matters, the reader is referred to the sections of the book dealing with larger conferences.)

Meetings of all sizes have certain things in common. A site must be selected, arrangements must be made with the hotel or restaurant, theme and program must be decided upon, the meeting must be publicized and conducted, and so on. The small meeting cannot opt out of any of the major obligations and opportunities that affect the large convention. But the way the job is accomplished may be quite different for the small meeting from what it is for the large one.

The Small Meeting in General

Small meetings are of many types, but these remarks pertain to a one-day meeting of, say, 50 to 500 people, with lunch but no breakfast, cocktail party, or dinner, and with none of the people attending needing hotel rooms. Enough information is provided about luncheon arrangements so that readers interested only in that aspect can profit from this chapter.

One characteristic of the small meeting of the organization type is that the meeting manager is frequently someone who has the position for a single year, and is therefore a novice at the job. His title is likely to be "program chairman" or "annual meeting chairman," and he is often backstopped by the president of the organization. Sometimes little is done until too near the date of the meeting, and then the president has to step in to save the situation. This should not happen. When it does, it simply means that the wrong person was chosen for the job.

Therefore, the first rule in assuring good meetings is to choose the right person to arrange and run them. When the person functioning as meeting manager is a neophyte, it behooves the association to select a meeting manager who is energetic, has sufficient time to do the job, has a good business head, can deal easily with people like banquet managers, is good at detail, and, most important of all, has a track record of getting jobs in the organization accomplished on time. These qualities will go far to compensate for lack of experience.

The inexperienced meeting manager can get valuable information and counsel from his predecessors in the position. He should not be bound by their advice, however, and should try to make his meeting outstanding and superior to any in the past.

The job. Once chosen, the meeting manager—and I will assume it is you—will have to address himself to several tasks:

1. Selection of site and facility, and, perhaps date.
2. Advance promotion.
3. Advance registration.
4. Decisions on theme, development of program, selection of speakers.
5. Consultation and planning with manager of meeting facility.
6. The meeting itself:
   Registration
   Conducting the meeting
   Dealing with personnel of the hotel or restaurant
   Meeting, introducing, and entertaining speakers
   Lunch
   Paying bills
   Post-meeting wrap-up

Site, facility, date. Your officers or executive board will almost certainly make the final decision on the site city and the date for your meeting. If the organization has a regular meeting date which is monthly or more frequent, it will probably use the same hotel, restaurant, or club each time. In this case there is no decision required unless you plan to make a change.

In the event that the selection is not cut and dried, several elements are involved in choosing a site location. Consider the nature of the organization and its meetings. A scholarly group might not care for a resort area, but a less serious organization might like to go there. For a one-day meeting there is usually not much choice in location, but there is some. What can the site location offer of particular interest to the members (field trips, for example)? Where can the members afford to go? The most important consideration is the desires of the membership. The officers and meeting chairman may feel that they know their members' preferences. A minority of organizations actually poll the membership. The time to do this is at a meeting some months or a year or more (depending on the frequency of the meetings) in advance of the meeting for which you are preparing. Offer several places and ask for a show of hands on each site. Do not feel bound by the vote, but it can be a valuable guide. Ask for a vote two ways:

"We would like your opinion, in an advisory way, on the site for our next annual meeting. We are considering holding the meeting in Greenvale, Springfield, Centerville, or Smithtown. By a show of hands, how many prefer Greenvale?" "How many for Springfield?"

But there are some people who might like the idea of meeting in a particular town who could not afford the time or perhaps the money to go there, so also ask, "If the meeting today had been held in Greenvale instead of here, how many, by a show of hands, would have attended?" Repeat for the other cities.

Remember that this expression of preference for site city is advisory only. Selection of facility and date should *not* be voted on by the membership, even in a nonbinding way. The selection of the facility is the meeting manager's job, with approval of the president or executive committee, and will be discussed a little later.

Considerations in selecting a date are custom (not binding), weather, competition from other meetings for the same audience, availability of the site and desired facility, holidays (patriotic, secular, religious), and school calendars. If members will be pulled away from their business or work to travel, a one-day meeting is best held on Monday or Friday so as to minimize time lost from work. The usual local one-day meeting, however, does not ordinarily involve travel and hence can be held any day of the week.

It is important to mention the date of a coming meeting to the membership as early as possible and to continue to repeat it, so that they will mark it on their calendars and keep the date clear of other engagements. If the facility—hotel, motel, restaurant—has been decided upon, you have a good opportunity to do a real selling job at meetings and in promotional material, because you can describe the attractions the members can look forward to.

When choosing a facility, the first rule is, shop around. Prices vary, and atmosphere, efficiency, and the quality of food vary even more. Choose a place where your membership will be comfortable and happy, that has rooms large enough for your meeting, can be reached easily by most of those who will attend, and has good food and service. We are dealing here with the small meeting. Usually the small hotel does a better job with this sized group than does the big hotel. There are exceptions.

Advance promotion. The meeting manager or program chairman should start to promote the coming meeting at the earliest possible moment following the selection of the date. He asks for a few minutes at meetings to talk about the big up coming event. He sees to it that all mailings to the membership mention the coming meeting and try to build enthusiasm for it. If the organization is local, the publicity chairman should see that regular reports of the association's meeting go to the local newspaper and include information on coming events. The smaller the locality the better press cooperation the organization will receive.

In your communications to the membership promoting the meeting, mention the essentials each time—name of the meeting, theme, place and facility, date. Try in addition to say something new and exciting in each mention. Assume that the members will not want to miss the event, and give them every possible reason for attending.

Advance registration. Try to encourage advance registration, even if your meeting is only a luncheon. When you send your meeting notice, have a coupon at the bottom, and ask for a check. People who have paid are more likely to come than those who just picked up the phone and said they would be present but sent no money. It saves time at the meeting itself if most of the people have already paid, and it helps keep finances straight.

One small organization I know meets once a month for lunch. Every member who phones in his meeting reservation or returns a coupon in advance of a deadline stands a chance of winning a door prize.

Names of advance registrants go into a hat, and someone picks the lucky name. The winner gets a bottle of whiskey. If a liquor prize bothers you, something else useful to a man or woman will do.

This is a good way to help you, as meeting manager, fulfill your lunch gurantee.

Theme and program. It is customary for the meeting manager to choose a theme. This is not only an aid to unifying the program and transmitting the idea of the meeting to the membership, but it also helps the meeting manager to organize his own thoughts and create a meeting that will define a whole concept, with all parts of the program contributing and reinforcing one idea.

Try to choose a theme which ties into some important new trend in the world or the country at the time. For example, a group of exporters might be interested in a meeting with the theme, "Trade Opportunities in Japan in the Eighties."

The theme may be much more limited. Suppose a group of booksellers is having its annual meeting next year, and you are the meeting manager. It occurs to you that there is considerable interest in a new trend for initial publication of authors' works in paperback (as opposed to publication first in hard covers). You sound out a few people in the organization and find a positive reaction to this idea. The theme of your meeting becomes, "Paperbacks challenge hard covers in original publication field." A paperback publisher who is pioneering in the original publication field is a natural for your loud speaker. You will want to have others talk on the attitude of authors, marketing, sales possibilities, and other aspects.

In almost every case, each speaker should talk within the subject to which the meeting is devoted, and address himself to the interests of his audience. There is sometimes a temptation to ask a big name because he is willing to come and will help swell attendance, but unless he is willing to talk on the topic of your meeting, and can do so, he is weakening the program as a whole. Such a speaker is excellent at a luncheon with no other program during the day. If he speaks at a program with other subjects scheduled, ask him to speak at lunch.

Planning with manager of meeting facility. When you chose the site town and the hotel, motel, or restaurant for your meeting, you talked to a number of managers of facilities, and selected the place that best fitted the needs of your group. You will now go back to that hotel or banquet manager and discuss the details of your meeting.

There is wide variation in practice. Some hotels make specific charges for meeting rooms; others let them free if a function, such as a luncheon, is held in the room used for the session. The most frequent charges are for the following:

Use of rooms
Meal(s)
Liquor (bartender, bottles, or corkage)
Coatroom (if members do not tip as they check)
Audiovisual equipment and microphones
Service fee
Sales taxes.

Be sure that you have an understanding *in writing* as to what charges will be. An exchange of letters is a good way to accomplish those agreement.

It is a good idea to set your gurantee at meals a little below what you are pretty sure the number will be.

The meeting itself. Since this is a small meeting, there is a good chance that when your meeting opens, other groups will be holding functions in the same hotel or motel, or that you will have only part of the restaurant to yourself. Your registration booth, therefore, will be a table just outside the meeting room or be one of the tables in the dining room.

Be sure the secretary or other person registering the guests has a complete list of all those who are expected to attend. Those who have paid, we hope, are duly noted on the list as being paid. Anyone who pays at the door should be noted on the list as paying by cash or check. Unless the check bears the legible name of the person attending, the secretary should mark the check in the lower left corner with the name of the person for whom it pays. (And why not make your organization the first in town to provide the secretary with enough small bills at the start of the meeting so that he can make change without digging into his own pocket and messing up the bookkeeping?)

The secretary should personally hand out all the badges. They should not be spread out on the table. This guarantees payment for those who might be forgetful, and, more important, guards against gate crashers.

The chairman of the meeting has the biggest job. He is responsible for introducing guests and, personally, or through another, for running the meeting on time, seeing that all microphones work, the food is hot and served to everyone, that no foul-ups of any kind occur. He has to see that speakers are met—though someone else should actually perform this job—and must pay the bills after the meeting is over.

Since Chapters 5 and 6 dealt with actual conduct of a meeting, this chapter will not cover many aspects of handling the meeting itself.

Just a few tips, however. If you are in charge of the head table, remember three rules: Don't seat too many at it (not more than 10 or 12), have a list of *everyone* you will introduce, with written comments about him in case your mind goes blank, and introduce the head table from *your* right. . . . Some paid guest speakers who are registered with a speaker bureau expect to be paid after they talk and before they leave the meeting. The usual practice in this case is to hand the speaker an envelope containing a check made out to the speaker bureau. When you contract for the speaker you should determine when and how you should pay. If you have to conduct business during the serving of a meal, and sometimes this is unavoidable, it will help to tell the head waiter in advance that you would like the waiters to be quiet at predetermined times. Once the members receive their dessert, you can talk freely with little chance that the waiters will make enough clatter to drown you out.

After the ball. The post-meeting wrap-up involves thank-you letters to your guest speakers and anyone else responsible for making the event a success, perhaps letters to those attending, and any publicity you can achieve. This publicity may take the form of a report for the organization and the local newspaper and coverage of the meeting in the organization's publication if there is one.

If your responsibility for the meeting is an on-going one, or if you wish to help the chairman of the next meeting, you may well write your own report, for your and his eyes alone, on what went well and not so well with arrangements.

The small meeting has a great deal of flexibility not available to the large one. No one writing on running a small meeting could possibly suggest the wealth of devices and ideas that are available to the innovative meeting manager. Much of the satisfaction you can have from running the smaller, informal group meeting derives from the ideas *you* generate as you go along.

Here are some specific types of small and special meetings.

Sales Meeting

Sales meetings are much like other small or in-house meetings, but it is appropriate to consider a few special aspects and suggest some ideas.

Keep firm control of the physical set-up of the meeting. The composition of the program will be a joint effort between you and the sales or marketing department. The top brass will speak, and the program will be heavy on information and motivation.

Location. One of the important aspects of your planning is where the meeting will be held—in the office or elsewhere.

If you have no classroom or board room, don't hold the meeting in your office. Sitting salesmen and women at desks in an office area destroys the meeting atmosphere and makes the salespeople uncomfortable.

Even the use of a board room leaves much to be desired. Inevitably, people will be called out of the room to answer phone calls or deal with problems that subordinates feel cannot wait. Each time this happens, damage is done to the image of the sales meeting. It becomes obvious to the salespeople that some outside problem of the moment is more important to the company than its sales conference.

If you have a classroom, use it, but exclude outside distraction.

In most cases, it is best to hold the sales meeting away from the office. Unless your meeting is entirely local, you will have to house the out-of-town salesmen somewhere. Hold your meeting at the hotel or motel. It will not cost that much more. The status of the meeting is enhanced, you can keep interruptions and distractions to a minimum, and the meeting facilities will be better than any office could probably provide.

Here are a few ideas used in connection with successful sales meetings.

Promotion. Let's say that you are trying to promote your company sales convention. And let's suppose that the salespeople have to meet a quota to qualify for the meeting—and a higher quota to qualify their wives or husbands. Spouses' encouragement can assist greatly in boosting production.

Get spouses on your side by developing their interest. Letters from the sales vice-president or the company president addressed to Mr. and Mrs. Salesperson and recognizing the spouse's importance to the husband/wife team can help.

Keep Mr. and Mrs. Salesman informed about progress toward the goal of qualifying them both for the conference. Keep telling them who else has already qualified.

Run a contest for spouses: "Tell in 150 words or less why (Michael or Michelle) and I are both going to Paradise Mountain" (or wherever the convention site will be). The prize could be so many dollars toward the convention wardrobe, with the prize essay printed in the company house organ.

Above all, keep the spouses informed of elements of the program that will interest them—details about sightseeing, shopping, tours, clothes they will need—to make them want to go and therefore encourage the salespeople to meet their qualifying quotas.

Content. In Chapter 1 I mentioned the idea of a program based on the theme of spring baseball training. If you are holding a spring sales meeting, here is a way to carry that theme through the conference. The meeting was actually sponsored by an association of salesmen, and was its annual sales congress. The idea could easily be adapted to the needs of a company sales meeting.

For its sales congress, the group used the baseball theme and promoted the event with bright, colorful mailing pieces. To convey the spirit of the promotion campaign, here is an excerpt from one piece:

SPRING TRAINING FOR INCREASED SALES

An exciting program following a baseball game format is planned:

- Warm-up with 50 members at tables of 15, starting at 8:30 A.M., with coffee.
- Two innings starting at 9:30 and 10:30 A.M. will feature 9 leading players, coaches, and specialists. Each will conduct a session in separate rooms—giving each fan an opportunity to visit two programs.
- At 11:30 A.M. a panel discussion on Confusion in the Marketplace will be led by three experts, one from each of the morning groups.
- At 12:30 P.M. a Ball Park Lunch of hot dogs and hamburgers will be the seventh inning stretch.
- All will be topped off by the ninth inning "Big Hitter" (main speaker).
- The program will be exciting and educational—and a chance to talk with many top salesmen and specialists in our industry.
- A souvenir program will be distributed to all fans.

A successful piece, it maintains the theme throughout. The theme suggests the message and gets it across. Another approach to a part of a sales meeting and one that is usable for other small meetings as well is a "Hot-Ideas Session."

Do many of your group have common problems? Sales problems, dealing with irate or otherwise difficult customers, explaining technical matters or delays in delivery? Have some of your salespeople found good solutions to these common problems? An adult "Show and Tell" is an excellent way to share ideas, and is good for audiences of up to 400 people. That's a "Hot-Ideas Session."

Pick eight or ten men and women whose solutions to problems have worked for them. Have each prepare a two-minute talk (no more) on what he or she did, how it was done, and the results.

Have a good-humored way to get the speaker to sit down at the end of two minutes sharp. Cut him off with a bell, a popped paper bag, or a raucous horn. Have the next speaker go on quickly. No introductions except name and briefest identification (like branch or territory).

Your "Hot-Ideas Session" will be over in about half an hour, and your audience will love it. Remember two essentials—your salespeople must have common problems and you must run the program fast and snappy!

In-House Business Conferences

More often than not, internal business meetings are a waste of time. If this is the case, why do we have more and more of them? Why waste many hours of high-priced managerial time in dragged-out, inconclusive conferences?

Everything bad ever said about such business conferences is true. Some of them are nothing but ego trips for the executive who calls them. He feels large, but often communication should be achieved some other way. Committee meetings are a means of spreading responsibility when it should be personalized. And the cost of a meeting should be estimated in terms of salary time, before the conference. Unfortunately, this is seldom done.

Objectives. Nevertheless, in-house meetings (whether of a company or association) are sometimes the best way to—

1. Communicate information.
2. Train.
3. Motivate.
4. Secure information, evaluate it, and come to a decision on action to be taken.

Most in-company meetings and conferences have as their primary purpose one of the above four aims. The meeting will have one or more subsidiary purposes, but one objective will dominate.

The major purposes of meetings are expressed graphically as shown in Figure 3. Note that in-house business meetings can be divided into two main groups:

One is where the flow of talk is toward the audience from one general source, representing meeting types numbered 1, 2, and 3 above.

The other is where there is a free flow of talk among the participants, identifying with the type of meetings in group number 4.

Seminars and workshops are types of training meetings, sales meetings are primarily motivational, and committee and staff meetings derive from the desire to secure and elevate information and come to a decision. Nevertheless, with the first three types particularly, we find interrelationship. A training session, for example, is at least partly designed to communicate information and to motivate those who attend. Motivation *must* communicate some information, and sometimes it also involves training.

Despite the linking of types of meetings, however, it is important to assign only one major purpose to any meeting or conference. To do this you must organize your thinking sufficiently to clarify your meeting aims. Just as any meeting should be responsive to a need (otherwise, why hold it?), you should be able to determine the type of meeting necessary to accomplish the purpose.

Planning for the meeting differs according to the type. So does the

FLOW TO AUDIENCE

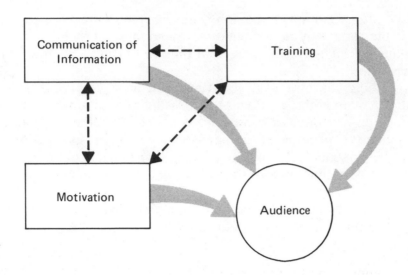

FREE FLOW AMONG PARTICIPANTS

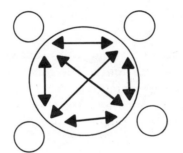

Figure 3. Purposes of business meetings.

conduct of the conference, the selection of those who are to attend, and other factors.

Communication. Where the main purpose is communication of information, the flow of talk is mostly from the dais to the audience. This puts heavy responsibility on the planner of the meeting, who is often its chairman as well. If you are that person, sit down and ask yourself:

1. What do I want to communicate?
2. How can I best pass on this information to the audience and at the same time be sure that I do not lose their interest?

What you wish to tell must be carefully thought out. First you will have to tell the audience what you are going to talk about, talk about it, and then review it.

You, as moderator, must keep a firm hand on the meeting. If others participate as specialists, you must delineate for each his exact field and the amount of time he can have to talk about it. You must know just what each subsidiary speaker is going to say, so that you can prevent overlap. You must sum up after each is through speaking.

Visual aids and audiovisuals are particularly appropriate for the communication type of meeting. They can convey information faster and in more memorable form than a good deal of talk. They should, however, not overpower the listener.

Whether the subject of the meeting is a new product line, reports of officials or salespeople, or a complete change in company policy, advance planning, allotment of time, and firm control are essential.

How about questions? One sure way to ruin a meeting called for the purpose of disseminating information is to allow members of the audience to interrupt with questions. All speakers should have their say, and then have a question period for the audience. If the meeting has been conducted right, the questions will be few.

As with any other meeting, plan intensively, start and end on time, keep your speakers within their time slots, and your meeting should be a success.

Training. Like meetings designed to communicate information, those devoted to training involve a flow mainly from the dais to the audience, without free flow of talk among the participants.

This is important, because the training sessions, to be successful, must be even more authoritarian than the meeting designed to communicate information.

As with any other meeting, advance planning, strict timekeeping, and a firm hand on the material and speakers are required.

The training meeting is more difficult than the type of session that is designed primarily to impart information. In the training session, the leader of the meeting not only has to *tell* his audience, but he also has to get them to perform. He must teach them how to do things, to accept ideas or methods, and to act in accordance with these ideas and methods. Since training by definition involves new concepts, methods, and products, and since people have ideas of their own that are usually resistant to change, the trainer must be much more than the usual communicator. He must be able to arouse in the people listening to him enthusiasm for doing something they would not normally want to do. He must then be assured that they have learned what he has tried to teach them.

Needless to say, the meeting leader's assistants should have a clear idea of the areas they are to cover at the training session. There should be no overlapping, and it is the responsibility of the conference chairman to see that he has reviewed the material of each assistant or expert to be certain that there will be no conflict in their presentations. A pre-meeting run-through is recommended.

How much participation should you expect from the audience? There should be a good deal, but it should be controlled. The training meeting is not designed to discuss methods—they have been decided upon—nor to reach a conclusion; it's not that kind of meeting. Questions from the floor should be invited. Run-through demonstrations by members of the audience are particularly valuable. Questions from the learners directed to members of the audience who are somewhat experienced in the subject of the training are an asset to the meeting.

The training session needs plenty of props. Samples of the product, audiovisuals, films, flip cards, demonstrations with actual materials—all these are grist to the mill.

Training sessions are essentially meetings that try to help people do things or say things in a certain way. Whether they are being trained to operate a new machine or to conduct a membership or fund drive for an organization or to sell a new product, they deserve the best you can give them to develop their skills.

Motivation. Motivation meetings are the third type of conference where the flow of talk is from the dais to the audience. (In the next section we will examine the meeting where there is a free flow of talk among the participants.)

Any intelligent person who can talk on his feet can prepare himself adequately to handle meetings that communicate or train. Special qualities are required for the motivator. Whether the purpose of the meeting is to inspire salespeople, fund-raisers, employees, or coreligionists, the speaker has to have something of that magnetic quality that, for want of any more suitable word, we call charisma. He has to be able to arouse enthusiasm, even emotion, in his listeners and, having done so, persuade them to *act* in the direction in which he is motivating them. The number of speakers who can do this well are few.

Most motivation meetings have only one main speaker. To allow others to address themselves to the subject would result in diluting the desired effect. Frequently, however, the main speaker is preceded by two or three "warm-up" people, who help to prepare the way for the principal talk. These speakers usually are on the podium only briefly.

A special form of the motivational meeting is the sales meeting. It is a true art to conduct a good sales meeting where the main object is motivation rather than information or training. The principal motivator is usually a successful salesperson, but he should be more than that. His speech and manner should be, if possible, above that of the salespeople he is addressing. He should be someone they can look up to and emulate, as a salesman and as a person. And, in addition, he must be able to motivate.

The meeting to secure information, evaluate it, and come to a decision on action to be taken. We can call this the decision meeting for short.

In meetings for communication, training, and motivation, the main flow of talk is toward the audience. The meeting leader is perforce something of an autocrat. In the decision meeting, there is a free flow of talk among the participants, and the leader's function is one of subtle guidance with a minimum of pressure.

Like any good conference, the decision meeting starts with an agenda and advance work on the part of the meeting leader and any other participants whose cooperation he can gain. At all costs, however, advance decisions or hardening of positions should be avoided. No one knows all the answers, and the job of the coming meeting is to solve a problem.

Other types of in-house meetings can be large or small and, according to size, can be held in someone's office or in a large room, theater style or schoolroom style. The decision meeting, to be effective, must be essentially a small meeting, held in a room with a wide, preferably rectangular table. (The table can be circular.) These conditions rule out an individual's private office, a large room, or a hotel room. Avoid these if you can. A board room or conference room with a wide, rectangular table, with plenty of room around the table and a lot of light overhead is ideal.

Get the air conditioning going, rule out all interruptions, except at scheduled breaks, and seat your people. Seating is important. Seat people individually, not by sections or departments. Do not let potentially hostile points of view line up on opposite sides of the table. If Joe and Bill don't like each other, seat them at opposite ends of the table.

The meeting leader can sit at the head of the table or, if he feels that confident, half-way down one side.

What have these physical arrangements accomplished? They have emphasized to the participants in the conference that they are meeting on a basis of near equality. A meeting in the boss's office underscores what the law considers to be the master-servant common-law relationship. A meeting in a large room, schoolroom style, reminds those present of listening to teachers in grade and high school. Here, however, around a table, the meeting leader is down on a level with the other participants, emphasizing the search for information and the making of decisions.

Having a table to sit at gives the participants a surface on which to rest their materials and also gives them the confidence they may lack when sitting in the open with a pad on their knees. Suppose the meeting had been held in the boss's office. He sits behind his desk, as in a fort, while his subordinates are outside the wall, undefended, trying to storm the citadel of *his* mind with *their* ideas. Is it any wonder that decision meetings held in private offices often become adversary, special pleading, and competitive shouting matches?

In passing I mentioned the possibility of using a circular table. I don't recommend buying one, if your board table is rectangular. A circular table, however, proclaims that everyone present is equal. (You may remember that King Arthur's table was round so that no knight would feel superior to any other.)

So, your decision meeting starts in a favorable physical environment, with everyone able to talk with everyone else and no one able to fight too easily with an opponent.

The leader should explain the purpose of the meeting, say that those present are there to learn the facts (secure information), weigh the problems and possible solutions (evaluate), and come to a decision as to what to do. He should say that everyone will be encouraged to talk, that no decisions have been made in advance, and no solutions prejudged.

Then, from the agenda previously distributed, the meeting leader should pose the first problem, start calling for information about it, then discussion, and so on. His role is the get people to talk, lead them into fuller explanations of their ideas when they tend to express themselves incompletely, encourage comment and counter ideas, and gently pull the discussion back onto the track when it tends to get too far afield. He should try for a decision—even a small one—when discussion on a topic seems exhausted. Each decision is a sign of progress to those participating; it tells them that the meeting is worthwhile, and, incidentally, that the leader is effective.

If at all possible, no matters should be put over for decision at a future meeting. Each deferral is a sign of weakness. It may not be possible to complete the agenda during the scheduled time, but scheduling another meeting for the uncompleted portion is preferable to failing to decide on matters that should be wound up at this meeting.

The meeting leader should break firmly for rest periods and see that the meeting ends on time.

Good notes should be made, and a report typed. Normally every participant will receive a copy of the typed report of the meeting. If secrecy is essential, the meeting leader alone will have a copy, but will be prepared to answer orally questions posed to him by participants.

If further meetings are necessary, new agendas will, of course, be prepared, advance work done, and the new meeting will commence with a brief review of earlier work accomplished and an explanation of what remains to be done.

Committee meetings. These are a special form of decision meeting that will be discussed at some length later in this chapter.

Staff meetings. Years ago there appeared a cartoon showing a movie mogul sitting at the head of a long table filled with his subordinates, in various stages of nodding their heads. Mr. Big was saying, "Dammit, don't say Yes until I ask a question." If the staff meeting—another form of the decision meeting—is held merely to broadcast the executive's decision or to feed his ego, it is a waste of time. But if it is held to feed information among the participants, evaluate data and knowledge, and come to intelligent decision, it is of great value to any enterprise.

Staff meetings should truly accomplish something. If a weekly staff meeting fails to do this, then schedule staff conferences less frequently. If you do not hold them on a regular basis, try to save up several interesting, solvable matters for a special meeting.

Much has been said in these discussions of various types of meetings about the preparation the meeting leader should make. He is, indeed, the most important factor. He should plan, make an agenda, do advance work, and adhere to his time schedule. He has a right to expect all other persons attending the meeting to do their part, too. It is usually appropriate to distribute advance materials and information, so that the other participants can prepare as fully as possible.

No sudden, spur-of-the-moment meetings should be announced, except in emergency situations. Perhaps Joe has the greatest sales idea ever to come down the road, but it is not fair to call everyone together without notice to discuss a change in accepted procedure when only Joe is prepared to talk. Have Joe put the outline of the idea into a memorandum, circulate the memo, and only then schedule a meeting to discuss it.

It should not be necessary to say it, but use tact, not only in the meeting room itself, but also in planning and announcing a meeting. The decision meeting frequently involves interdepartment representation. Notify all participants at the same time and in the same way of the meeting. If you tell Bill of R&D to tell Jim of Sales that there is a meeting this afternoon at 3:00, Jim may not be in the best frame of mind when he walks into the meeting room. Also, if Jim had a previous important appointment elsewhere at 3 P.M. he is not going to like having to choose between meetings. Better to clear the time with all participants before setting it definitely, then announce it to all simultaneously.

Another way to queer a meeting is to allow interruptions. A sales manager I knew accepted telephone calls while he ran staff meetings. His meetings were a waste of time for everyone but himself and a useless expenditure of company salaries.

There is, however, no way to compile a complete list of dos and don'ts. Properly planned and run, in-house business meetings can be productive. You *can* confound the critics and prove that your meetings are not a waste of time.

Press Conference Pointers

Schedule press conferences for Tuesday, Wednesday, or Thursday. Monday and Friday are bad.

Know the deadlines of those publications you most want to "make." Don't schedule a press conference too close before the deadline for most of the publications. And of course if your press conference is held after that deadline, your coverage is definitely hurt.

Invite the press ten days to two weeks ahead. A postcard or telephone reminder will help.

Indicate in your invitation what food or drink, if any, is involved. If your press conferences is scheduled for 10 A.M. or 2 P.M. no one expects any refreshments. But a starting time like 11 A.M. (or 4 P.M.) should be followed by:

The press conference will end by noon (5 P.M.)
or
We hope you will be able to join us for lunch (or cocktails, or coffee) after the press conference.

The news to be given out at the press conference should be important enough to be worth the time of the reporters sent to cover the meeting. Kits are best given to reporters before the talks start. (See Chapter 4 for guidance on writing news releases.)

The speaker or speakers should give information beyond what appears in the press kit. They should avoid reading word for word from any of the press releases being handed out. Otherwise reporters will feel that they could have gotten everything from a kit sent them through the mail without coming to the press conference.

Questions by reporters should be answered in straightforward fashion, without fudging. If a question cannot be answered, the speaker should politely refuse to answer. Such refusals should, of course, be rare. The speakers should do their homework before the meeting to be prepared for all likely questions.

While the timing of a press conference may depend upon deadlines of major publications, any favoritism should be avoided at the conference itself. The smaller publications may be the ones that actually give you coverage.

Here are some comments about a press conference I attended where everything was done just right.

The press conference seemed to run effortlessly, but this was because of careful advance planning. Cocktails, the press conference, then lunch constituted the meeting.

The reporters were met as they arrived by members of the public relations firm, who greeted them and placed a pressure badge with the reporter's name and affiliation on the reporter's chest—on the right-hand side. Then came drinks and introductions to the officers of the firm. After about 20 minutes the press conference began. There were plenty of press kits, with releases and pictures of the client firm's officers and the new product it was introducing. Three short talks were followed by a long question period. The speakers had done their homework and were forthright with their answers, despite a few questions that verged on the abrasive.

The president of the company cut off questions from the floor at a point that I thought was slightly earlier than the reporters expected, saying that all the officers would be available to answer questions throughout the lunch.

The bar was still open, and a few reporters availed themselves of the opportunity for another drink.

Lunch was buffet, but of excellent quality. The public relations people saw to it that each reporter sat with at least one person from the firm who could talk knowledgeably about the new product. Their enthusiasm was strengthened with facts and reasons.

Certainly not all the reporters wrote a story about this new product, but all went away with more information about it, and this is all the PR people and the manufacturer could expect.

There are many types of news conferences, depending upon the purpose. Some, of course, have no food or liquor whatever. But for this type—cocktails and lunch—the job could not have been done any better.

Class Reunions

A successful school or college reunion depends 90 percent on the energy and imagination of the chairman.

The chairman can skip no bases on promotion, arrangements—including menu and perhaps lodging—and costing. However, he has a number of things "going for him," as they say, that the association or business conference director does not.

The reunion is social, not business. Out goes planning a program of topics, speakers, controversy, varied opinions, weighty papers. This is a fun time! Bring in the funny hats, costumes if you wish, the master of ceremonies who was the class humorist, the songs, the reminiscences (inevitably improved with time).

Another thing going for you if you are promoting a reunion is loyalty. This is as strong a mover to get people to travel miles to a reunion as is self-interest in drawing conventioners to a business meeting, perhaps stronger. Don't forget, too, the common experience of classmates who have known one another in the same physical setting for some years.

All right, let's be concrete about practical ideas.

Promotion. The very first thing you need, naturally, is an up-to-date list of the living graduates. Sometimes it can take an entire year to compile such a list; you should have your committee working early to whip that list into shape.

Start with the school or college. If that fails, ask graduates you know where their class friends are now, and pursue these people for more information, in widening circles, until you have located everybody possible.

Notice #1 should go to class members nine or ten months in advance of the reunion date, telling them when the reunion is scheduled, so that they will keep the date open. College and university alumni magazines frequently do this for you by printing the schedule of reunion dates at the beginning of the college year.

About January, start getting tentative commitments (Notice #2). From this list, extract the names of those expecting to come to use as "bait" in your next mailing. This mailing (Notice #3) will go out in March or April. In it you will ask for reservations and banquet deposits. More than with any other kind of meeting, people who are on the fence about attending a reunion will want to know who plans to be there. Your "expect to attend" list is a big motivator.

If your class is really well organized, you can have a telephone committee call class members in their respective areas following your spring mailing.

Notice #2 should be the big sell. It should tell all about the reunion, sell the banquet—site and meal—arouse enthusiasm (without giving away the show), and capitalize on the anticipation of entertainment and anything else that is going to happen.

This same mailing should include an information sheet, to be returned whether the graduate will attend or not. The sheet will ask for marital status, name and occupation, names of spouse and children, graduate's hobbies, and similar information.

Notice #3 will go to all class members, give final information on the reunion, including hints to the women on what clothes to bring.

Meeting costs. How about budget for reunions and their promotion? Colleges will often send mailings for classes planning reunions. (High schools rarely can.) If you use the alumni office to mail for you, you save money, but allow a lot of time. Such offices are often understaffed and overworked. If they do get your mailing to the post office promptly, the postal service frequently is very slow at handling mail paid for at the low, nonprofit rate. It is embarrassing to have a mailing reach addressees a month later than you planned. And it can be disastrous to your promotion.

If your class has dues, you have a source to tap for printing and postage. Some classes have annual dues, while others collect a small amount from each person attending one reunion to make up a kitty for the next.

One way to help build a fund for reunion promotion is to ask in Notice #3 that people *not* planning to attend the reunion send a check for a dollar or two to reimburse for postage, etc.

You can save money on Notice #1—and make extra mailings—by using postcards.

Housing and meals. College reunion classes frequently can be housed in dormitories, and the college will probably offer some meals at moderate prices. The same is true of residence prep schools. Notice #2 or #3 should give information on alternate housing (motels, hotels) with addresses and telephone numbers.

The reunion program. Tradition rules reunion programs. Who would want to break the famous tradition at one college of competitive step-singing among reunion classes, with each class in uniform costume? If the 25-year reunion class customarily makes a gift to the college, that presentation will be an inevitable feature of the program.

But the smaller, less structured reunion can do entertaining things, too. For a recent high-school reunion the master of ceremonies awarded humorous prizes for:

- The graduate who came the farthest (a kite to fly back home).
- The graduate with the most children (headache pills).
- The man and woman who had changed least (hair dye and facial makeup).
- Male graduate with the least hair (a wig).

- Sexiest woman (*Xaviera*, by Xaviera Hollander).
- Most unusual occupation (a corkscrew for a circus contortionist).

The information needed to award these prizes came from the sheet returned as a result of Notice #2. They could have been voted on at each table, with finalists determined by applause.

Make up your own list of what you will award prizes for and what the prizes will be. This can be a really fun thing. Don't miss the possibilities.

One 40th reunion class had every returning alumnus or alumna dress in period costume, not in the style of the year of graduation, but in the style of every year since. Each graduate had a year assigned, and had to live up to a style he or she could document for that year. It was a lot of work, but the results, say the people who were there, were fantastic.

On the more serious program side, a class reunion is a good time to honor someone in the class who has made a real contribution to the community through volunteer work or who for some other reason deserves recognition.

A number of reunion committees are using a helpful device to make it easier for returning alumni to recognize one another. On each name badge they place a Xeroxed picture from the class yearbook. Besides helping to tell who's who, this makes for easy comparison between the before and after. You would wait at least ten years before doing this for a reunion class, however, as there should not be much change in the first decade out of school or college.

Each member of a class attending a reunion should be furnished with a list of the entire class, first names of spouses where available, and a footnoting system that tells which class members are attending the reunion and who are deceased. If you wish, have three sections to the list—those attending the reunion, those living but not present, and those not living.

Further program ideas include optional tours of new buildings on campus or a new high school, presentation of a few popular faculty members who have been invited to the banquet as guests, dancing, of course, and entertainment in which members of the class are somehow involved.

Any reunion should allow a lot of time for people to talk with one another and renew old acquaintanceships. This is the best part of a reunion.

Irregular reunions. One drawback to holding reunions on a strict five-year schedule is that the class members don't have an opportunity to gather with members of the other classes who were in school or college at the same time they were.

One answer is to hold reunions in irregular years. Perhaps the term "cluster reunion" is more useful. For example, the class of 1975 might meet in 1980, but so would the classes of '74 and '76. In 1985 the reunion classes would be those of '75, '74, and '73. A schedule can be worked out for a longer time.

Most colleges using cluster reunions have been very satisfied with them. If you wish to promote the idea, you may be able to work through your alumni office. If you find that your alumni secretary is too conservative on this subject, it may be better to work in a grass-roots fashion, trying to interest officers of classes just ahead of yours and behind yours in grouped reunions. Then get support from membership, and then express your wishes to the college.

The Committee Meeting

Most of us serve now and then on a committee. We may not always be formally named as a member, but whether we are working with members of a committee to set up a huge conference or are just called in by the boss as one of two or three people he wants to have listen to a report he has written, we are on a committee. Where we can exercise some influence or control it behooves us to make things run as efficiently as possible. Whether the committee is formal or informal, the chairman should apply some realistic rules.

Committees exist to carry on accustomed functions (standing committees) or accomplish special projects (*ad hoc* committees). In a committee meeting we want ideas from all the members—otherwise, why get them together? The position of the chairman is stronger than that of the others, especially in the case of the standing committee, but an effective chairman will encourage as much self-expression among the other committee members as possible. Results will be better if produced around a board-room table than in the chairman's private office.

Time. It is most important to start on time. Why? For several reasons. Because starting a meeting on time shows that the chairman is in control. It indicates that the subject is important. It is a courtesy to those who arrived on time. It saves money—delay costs a total of the salaries of everyone present, including the chairman. But, someone will say, you can't start until everyone is there. Oh yes, you can, unless the chairman is missing. And when late-comers enter the chairman can express some displeasure, perhaps in a light way, and quickly bring the tardy ones up to date on what has happened.

The chairman, and all members of the committee, should stop all phone calls, and not permit other interruptions. The reason is not only courtesy. Every interruption wastes the time of every other member of the committee and drags out the length of the meeting interminably. It is safe to say that nothing lengthens meetings so much as interruptions, except getting off the subject during discussion of the topic itself.

Agenda. The chairman should see that the agenda is followed. If this is a formal committee meeting, the agenda should have been circulated to all members several days in advance of the meeting date. If the conference is informal, and you are called in just to give a critique on the boss's report, then *that* is the agenda. The capable executive will not introduce another subject, unless the report ploy was just an excuse to talk about something else.

In most meetings, someone should be delegated to take notes. Whether this is a formal secretary or one named on the spur of the moment, he or she can keep an eye on the agenda and nudge the chairman to get discussion back on the track when people seem to wander.

The chairman must keep a firm hand on the meeting. He should see that the agenda is followed, point by point, and that people stick to the topic. It is his prerogative—and duty—to interrupt when necessary and say, "What you are saying, Joseph, is that . . ." and, "Marie, let's save discussion about that until later, when . . ." Far from resenting a firm chairman, most people like to see a meeting proceed efficiently.

It goes without saying that only topics on the agenda are discussed, even if the agenda is informal, as noted above. The secretary will note any subject that has to be carried over for another meeting.

Participation. The chairman should see that all people present engage in the discussion. There are various ways of doing this. One is to have each person speak as he sits, going around the table. Another, which is less obviously formal, is to ask the most junior person to state his views and proceed upward from there. Either of these methods will get you good, fresh ideas. There may be political problems if your company or organization likes to see original thought filtered through the minds of executives. It seems to me that this risk is worth taking. If we wait until everyone else has spoken to ask the new, young people what they think, we may get only an echo of what someone higher up has said.

Another way in which the chairman must be something of an autocrat is to guarantee the floor to each speaker as long as he keeps to the subject and does not repeat himself. Let him have his way without interruption from other committee members. The person speaking may raise several points that other members may wish to answer. The chairman should jot these sub-points down and then, when the speaker has finished talking, take up the points one by one for discussion. The person who originally makes a proposal that is then subjected to criticism is entitled to time to rebut the objectors and defend his idea.

A skillful chairman saves his own views till last. Presumably the chairman is the most knowledgeable in the field under discussion or has the most authority in the firm or organization. For him to express his views too early can direct the thought of the committee into a predetermined channel or discourage the expression of unorthodox and perhaps valuable ideas. He should, however, keep the discussion moving.

Gathering the ends. As the end of the meeting approaches, the chairmen should sum up and tell what decisions have been made. If there has been a difference of opinions, he should tell what the result of the discussion has been—what action will be taken and how it may have been modified by the minority view. If the differences expressed were sharp, he will make clear the action decided on, but will then pass quickly on to the next decision of the committee, not dwelling on controversy.

If there are still decisions to be made or areas of discussions for the next meeting, the chairman will list the major items for future discussion. If any of the members are to do research or specific jobs he will give them their assignments, and after the meeting deal with them individually to tell them what he expects.

The chairman then sets the date and time of the next meeting, perhaps after consulting the members, and he is ready to entertain a motion for adjournment. The meeting should adjourn no later than the time stated in the agenda. Any work not accomplished should go over to the next meeting. Note that if the meeting has started on time there has been a maximum opportunity to accomplish what was laid out in the agenda in the time alloted to the meeting.

The notes. The secretary should get the meeting notes typed and send them to every committee member present at the meeting, to members who could not attend, and to other interested parties designated by the chairman. If the meeting was confidential, only one copy of the notes or minutes should be prepared, and should be put in the chairman's care.

Whether you are the chairman or not, it will be useful to keep a log of the committee meetings, in which you enter *your* estimate of their value. "This meeting was beneficial to the association (or company), because. . . ." If you are hard put to find value in the meeting, the committee may be unnecessary, may be meeting too often, may not be doing its homework in preparing for committee sessions, or may be poorly conducted.

Summing up. Committee meetings deserve much more attention than they usually receive. They greatly outnumber all other kinds of conferences. Good meetings accomplish a lot, but bad meetings waste monumental amounts of time. Good chairmen make good meetings. They circulate good agendas, start meetings on time, keep discussion on the track, make sure everyone is heard, end the meetings when they say they will, and make sure that good notes record and reinforce what the committee has accomplished.

Miscellaneous Meeting Ideas

Break it up! Is your meeting pretty large? Are there just so many people that it is a major effort to get them all together? Do you have just one event where everybody can eat together and you turn the members loose the rest of the time?

Why not encourage smaller groups to hold luncheons and dinners— even breakfasts? Some meeting managers look askance at any development of this nature. They should not. We are not dealing with separatism, but with the natural wish to eat, some of the time, in a group small enough to enjoy a sense of community. Catering to this desire will only enhance the over-all meeting.

These single-interest luncheons are most successful when the wish arises spontaneously, but there is no law against planting the seed of the idea.

What common interest is the basis for one of these gatherings? The bases are many—a section of the country, people associated with a company, with a particular discipline within the larger group, people who are outstanding within the organization (e.g. salesmen), large contributors of money.

A few precautions: The luncheon or dinner should be approved by the board of directors of the organization. If there are several of these events, they should be run simultaneously. If there are speakers they should not deal with subjects that could better be presented on your regular program. Often these special-interest groups are most successful when they are mainly social.

An interesting variation—even a reversal—of the single-interest meal was recently proposed at a meeting of a large organization. The large group is an estate-planning council, which meets several times a year, bringing together trust officers of banks, attorneys, accountants, and life insurance men. This organization is itself an interdisciplinary group. It was proposed that smaller interdisciplinary meal meetings be held, presumably to concentrate on some topic of current interest. If these mini-meetings are instituted they will not violate the principle of noncompetition with the major program of the organization. The large association has no annual conference, and the limited number of meetings held each year cannot deal with all the subjects of interest to the membership.

Informal educational meetings. A person running small, educational and sales training meetings wanted the meetings to be informal, but found that the people attending would not talk to a speaker they did not know. I recommended that the manager of the meeting arrange the tables in a U shape, avoiding the schoolroom style which places them in rows. I further suggested that after the meeting manager had introduced the speaker and he had started to talk, the meeting manager print the people's names (first and last names) on a piece of paper for the speaker. These should be written down showing each person's position at the table as seen from where the guest speaker is standing. He can then address them by their first names—"Jim, would you agree with that?" or "Mary, how would you handle that objection?" Soon the members will be speaking up on their own.

Another way to enhance audience participation is to have perhaps two meetings during the year with the program entirely table discussion. Each table has an agenda, circulated among members ahead of time. Certainly the first time the same agenda would be supplied to all the members. Later, if you wish, you could try the more complicated approach of different subjects for different tables. Each table will have a discussion leader. It helps if he is an expert, but it is not essential.

This type of program has proved successful many times. It is important, however, to have strong support from your membership. Bring up the suggestion at an earlier meeting and let the members discuss it thoroughly, making sure that they will truly participate when the opportunity comes.

Buzz sessions. The term "buzz session" has been used to describe a session where speakers do nothing but answer questions put to them by an audience. Usually this is after the main, formal program.

I have seen the buzz session used in two ways:

■ One has several speakers in scattered areas of one large room (perhaps the ballroom), each with a number of convention-goers around him. Each speaker is dealing with a specialty, and the questions put to him, of course, are within a rather narrow range.

■ The other way is with all the speakers on the stage at one time. The audience is in one body in front, and any member of the audience can address any question he wishes to any speaker. Sometimes, after a speaker has answered a question, another speaker will comment on his answer.

Sometimes the buzz session works well, and other times, in my view, it does not. A good buzz session requires speakers who are willing to stay after the end of a formal, and perhaps long, program. It calls for more dedication than I think most speakers have. They must be willing to field questions for which they are perhaps unprepared and which are often of interest only to the person who puts the inquiry. The last, of course, could be said of any question, but in this case since the queries are put orally, the speaker cannot pass the question by, as he could if it were put to him in writing.

On the positive side, the small group type of buzz session (the first kind described above) has considerable merit. An intimacy is achieved between a speaker and a small group of people who are within a few feet of him, that helps establish good rapport and communication. I would opt for the small group as the preferred way.

Last meeting of the year. Here are two ideas from organizations that hold a monthly luncheon meeting. They are each local organizations with a membership of under 100 people. One of the ideas is good for the end of a fiscal year, no matter when it might occur. The other is usable only in December.

One organization closes its business year with a free lunch for members only. There is no free lunch, you say? Of course, strictly speaking, you're right. This free lunch is provided by charging sufficient dues and making luncheon tickets cost a bit more than the actual outgo during the year. This puts some extra money in the kitty, for the year the association might run in the red. In the meantime, the practice does something special for the faithful regulars, in providing one free luncheon.

Another association plans its December meeting as a Christmas party. Companies are solicited to provide merchandise as gifts. The individual gifts are not of great value, but collectively they include many useful and acceptable things. To be eligible to receive gifts, the member must have sent in his reservation in advance of the meeting—a practice this organization consistently encourages. Gifts are drawn by lot, and they are so numerous that every pre-registered member gets at least two or three. Incidentally, the organization promotes this party as a regular, formal meeting in its notice to members. The reason is that the members' employers often pay the dues and luncheon fees of employees who attend the meetings, and one or more firms will not pay for a party that is not part of a formal meeting. At the last Christmas "meeting" the business session was not onerous, consisting of one of the witty members giving a short, humorous talk on inflation and its effect on the members.

9

Of Cabbages
and Kings

This chapter deals mainly with subjects that do not fit easily into the organization of earlier chapters or that affect a minority of meeting planners.

Jointly Sponsored Meetings

Suppose that another association wishes to cooperate with yours in putting on meetings. Suppose, further, that the following situation obtains:

The membership of the other organization has a common interest with yours in certain areas of legislation. There could be some advantages. The committee for the other organization will take your membership list and handle direct-mail promotion for both organizations. They propose joint planning and fulfillment of a series of several meetings, to be followed, probably, by a permanent joint meeting cmmittee to handle all future conferences.

Although some joint meetings have been conducted successfully by cooperating organizations, I believe that a very clear understanding, in writing, is necessary before the venture is undertaken. It is difficult to separate functions and assign to each meeting manager or meeting committee what he or they can do best. It is also a problem to foresee all the stumbling blocks that may arise.

For example, suppose that one meeting manager is given the exclusive right to select speakers, while the other has the say on hotel and meeting arrangements. What if the first selects a speaker that is absolutely unacceptable to the organization represented by the second meeting manager?

If the meeting generates just enough income to meet expenses there is rarely a problem, but if it makes a good deal or loses a lot, there can be disputes over money.

Who gets top billing in promotion and conduct of the meeting?

Almost inevitably one organization throughout is the junior partner, and the other has the final say.

In other words, there are few cases where two associations or two companies jointly sponsor a meeting, and with good reason. Usually, each organization would be better off running its own meeting, though they may trade information as to program content, dates, and sites so as to avoid unnecessary duplication.

Before you consider joint sponsorship, be sure you cannot go it alone.

Presenting an Effective Slide Show

Years ago, children used to be enchanted by the magic lantern, which could project on a sheet or the wall pictures of marvelous far-away places, exotic animals, and things the young boy or girl had never seen in a somewhat restricted life.

Today speakers use the equivalent of the magic lantern to illustrate their talks. Do they always receive uncritical attention like the rapt interest of young people watching an old-fashioned lantern show?

Well, uncritical attention, of course, is too much to hope for. But does the modern speaker get as much attention from his audience as he has a right to? This depends on his subject, what he has to say about it, how he says it, and his visual presentation. We are concerned here only with the last aspect of a slide show—visual presentation.

Why use slides at all? Some people seem to feel that *any* talk is better with slides. I cannot subscribe to this idea. Slides should be more than a gimmick. There should be a positive reason for illustrating the talk, and the slides should proceed naturally from the content of the talk.

Where there is reason to use them, slides can be an effective supplement. Slides capitalize on the fact that people get 90 percent of their information through their eyes. If the subject is one that is clearly made more understandable by pictures and graphs, then the adage "One picture is worth a thousand words" clearly applies, and the speaker should consider using slides.

Slides hold the viewer's attention on a single idea while the speaker talks about it. Pictures that truly illustrate the speaker's words are good. Words on the slides reinforcing the pictures are acceptable. Do not use slides for a lot of words or words and figures. If you have "heavy" material, it is better to furnish a handout to every member of the audience so you are sure he can read the material. Words and figures on a projected slide should be read aloud by the speaker.

Consider the viewer. Sometimes a speaker puts slides together without a thought as to the size of his audience. Part of the success of the old-fashioned magic-lantern show was the fact that the audience was small, intimate, close enough to the projected pictures to see them without difficulty. Too often today a speech is illustrated with slides that are only a blur beyond the first third or half of the audience. The speaker babbles blithely on, waving his pointer—*he* can see fine—while people in the back row catch 40 winks if the lights have been dimmed and chat with one another if the lights are still on. The slide show works best with a small audience. If there are more than a couple of hundred people, get a very large screen and very good slides.

Quality slides. For the best slides, turn the job over to an artist familiar with this kind of work. It will pay off in audience results. I have said that the best kind of slide material is pictures and graphs. An artist making these needs to use bold line, both in drawing and in any labeling.

Many speakers, however, want words on slides, and the rest of this section will deal with putting words on slides in such a way that they can be read.

The worst slides are typewritten. If your speaker insists on typed slides, get them typed double-spaced on a jumbo-type machine, upper and lower case (not all caps), with the typist using a very dark ribbon. You can reinforce the darkness of the type by having the typist place a piece of carbon paper behind the sheet, with the carbon side toward the sheet.

Much better slides are made when the material is typeset. Let's go through the process that should be followed, from raw material through finished slides.

Your slide talk starts with a speech or script. If you can skip the speech, fine, but you must have a stripped-down script written by someone knowledgeable about the subject of the slide talk. For simplicity, let's suppose this is you. You should work with someone who is good at organizing material and who knows how to make slides. The two of you should work together as a team.

The first objective is to write the script for perhaps 25 master slides, which will be sufficient for a talk of 25–30 minutes. These master slides will be divided later to make slides with less reading material on them. Each master slide can comfortably hold ten lines of copy, with spaces between lines. Since typesetters like to have typed copy from which to work, have your secretary type the script four or five words (say, three in.) wide and not over 2½ in. deep.

This material goes to the typesetter. If you like plain, undecorated (sans serif) type, specify a type face like Spartan, Kabel, Helvetica, or 20th Century. Good sizes are 18 point and 24 point (¼ in. and ⅓ in. high, respectively). These sizes may seem small, but they really are not. Discuss with your typesetter the sizes and faces he has, and listen to his recommendations.

Tell the typesetter you want a film negative with a reader proof for reading. He will know what you want and you will have a proof on which you can make corrections.

Making slides. When you have reached the film negative stage, you can have your slides made. Break up each master slide into small segments, using the master slide in some cases as the first you will show of the group, in others as the summary slide. Use color to emphasize the thoughts you wish to reinforce. Use more than one color on a single slide if you wish. The color effect is achieved by using strips of colored gel. A good slide maker will show you how.

One further note—if your crowd is sizable, you will need a large screen so that people in the back rows can see. A large screen leads inevitably to the need for a high-ceilinged room. Bear this in mind when you are looking over facilities for your meeting. Room sizes are usually given in square feet or audience capacity, with ceiling height often not indicated.

If you have a small screen, for a small group, be sure the screen is elevated, so all can see.

Slide talks are not appropriate for all topics, or all speakers, but they can be effective. A good slide talk is the product of good writing, good design, and good presentation.

Booths and Other Exhibits

Should you allow guest exhibits? Should you have a booth of your own at your convention? These two questions are the subject of this section.

Whenever someone exhibits at someone else's convention, the one exhibiting gets a ride. Whether the ride is free or paid for makes a big difference.

Certainly, the first time a meeting manager gets a request to open his conference to an exhibit, his reaction will probably be to say yes. Everyone wants to be a nice guy. But it is wise to slow down and think before saying, "Go ahead."

Why have exhibits. The primary objective of a convention is to benefit those attending. All other considerations are secondary. If exhibits will be of great benefit to the conference attenders—enlighten or educate them or offer them opportunities they could not otherwise enjoy—then the exhibitors are not getting a free ride, even if they pay nothing for permission to exhibit. There is a *quid pro quo.* Usually, however, exhibits are not simon pure. They are not entirely designed to enlighten and to offer opportunity to the convention-goer. Most exhibits are selling something. Even an exhibit for a nonprofit agency is selling the idea and inviting support for the agency's activities.

There is nothing wrong with an exhibit's selling a product or service, but we should recognize that benefit from the exhibit will accrue more to the seller than to the individual attending the conferences. Since this is generally recognized, the exhibitor is frequently required to make some form of payment for the right to have a booth.

Payment. The payment need not be cash, but it is frequently money or a cash substitute. For example, an exhibitor may pay for the printing of the convention program.

One large organization gives convention booths free to advertisers that have purchased a certain amount of advertising space in the association's magazine during the preceding 12 months. As with other "free" space, there is usually a small hotel service fee which the exhibitor is expected to pay.

Less frequently, the exhibitor will provide some other service of value to the company or organization sponsoring the meeting, such as furnishing equipment on loan or at a reduced rate for a period, giving free advertising space (if the exhibitor is a publisher), or making a mailing list available.

Nevertheless, most exhibitors pay cash rather than cash substitutes for space, and the fee is based on rent for a certain number of square feet.

Because exhibitors are paying to have their booths at the meeting, they are entitled to a good location, with a reasonable amount of traffic, good lighting, and appropriate cooperation from the sponsoring organization. The meeting manager should tell all exhibitors the hotel rules and the local practices on moving materials.

Rules for exhibiting. It is up to you to set the ground rules for who can and who cannot exhibit. If you decide that one type of firm can exhibit you are at least morally obligated to allow any responsible exhibitor in that category to have a booth. You are perfectly justified, however, in deciding that only certain types of products or services may be presented. You should stand firm on this, once your decision is made. You will also want to set ground rules on exhibits that are overly distracting because of noise, lighting, or bad taste.

One side issue that will arise if you have a number of exhibitors is that some of them will want to run hospitality rooms to entertain the conventioners. You may decide to permit only exhibitors to have hospitality rooms. I think it wiser to divorce the subject from the exhibit question. In either case, make sure the hospitality rooms are closed during your scheduled events.

It is customary to make at least one meeting registration available gratis to each exhibitor. This usually permits someone to attend the sessions of the convention but does not always include meals or cocktail parties.

Having exhibits at your conference that do not promote your own company or association adds some commercialism to your meeting. If this is a concern to you, restrict the exhibits in number and size.

Now that we have had the caveats, let us suppose that you actually want exhibits, and that you plan to solicit them, but you still wish to keep them under control.

Promotion. The first principle in promotion of exhibits is to reach every firm that might wish to have a booth. The second is to furnish all necessary information in the first mailing. Repeat mailings should include all the material that was in the first, or say that it is available, with updating.

Your promotion should:

1. Tell price and size of booths.
2. Include a diagram of the space available for booths, with each booth area marked off and identified by a letter or number. The diagram should show the exhibit room, identified by name, and its relation to other areas on the floor of the hotel.
3. Give the days and hours when the exhibit area will be open.
4. Tell what arrangements, if any, must be made with the hotel with regard to exhibits, name a hotel contact, and give the address.
5. Tell when exhibit materials may be moved in.
6. If decorating or drayage must be done by only one firm, a common practice in large cities, list the firm, its address, and phone number.
7. Inform your exhibitors of how to make hotel reservations.
8. Let exhibitors know what courtesy you will extend in the way of meeting registration and other charges.
9. Give a deadline for removal of exhibit material.
10. Include:
    A cordial message, inviting participation.
    A form applying for exhibit space.
    A list of restrictions on exhibitors (two copies).

It is useful to go into more detail on the application form and the restrictions.

Application form. Your application form should identify the exhibitor by name, address, phone number, and the person in charge of exhibits. It should ask what service or product will be on view and require a brief explanation of how it will be displayed or demonstrated.

A place should be provided so that the exhibitor can indicate what size space he wants—single booth, double, or the dimensions if more than single or double booth spaces are available. He should also be able to specify corner or island or other special positions he would like, and competitors whose locations he wishes to avoid.

Include blanks so the exhibitor can indicate his preference for booth location—from first to sixth choice.

State that booths will be assigned in order of receipt of applications.

A deposit should be required with the application form, and the exhibitor should be told whether it is refundable and the date when the balance must be paid.

Restrictions. The dangers of exhibits are possible excesses. These lie in the direction of too much commercialism, bad taste, and, for meetings not primarily shows, too many exhibitors, a situation that can result in overshadowing the formal conference.

Here is a list of conditions and restrictions that a meeting manager may wish to impose on exhibitors. The list is inclusive, representing what a really up-tight organization might feel was necessary. The list is informally worded. It can be shortened or reworded as desired.

- The sponsoring organization (SO) reserves to itself complete control of the entire exhibit area and the assignment of booth locations. The SO has final decision on the acceptance or rejection of an application to exhibit, and can cancel permission to exhibit at any time. (Spell out the financial obligation of the SO in case of cancellation.)
- Exhibits will be restricted to the exhibit area and cannot be advertised or promoted elsewhere.
- Printed matter can be distributed only within the booth.
- Selling or order-taking at the convention, within or outside the exhibit area, is prohibited.
- No exhibitor may allow another firm to use his booth nor can he promote products or services of another firm.
- The SO will furnish without charge tables, drapes, and chairs for each booth. Hotel property shall not be damaged or defaced in any way. (No nails or staples in walls or columns.)
- The SO assumes no liability for exhibitors' property or equipment. Insurance, if any, must be provided by the exhibitor.
- Displays shall be in good taste and shall not excessively distract from neighboring exhibits. (Flashing or strong lights and recorded presentations may be prohibited.)
- Exhibitors are responsible for their employees and hired booth attendants. They are expected to be of high caliber and suitably dressed. (No bikini-clad models.)
- Alcoholic beverages are prohibited in the exhibit area.
- All displays and presentations must bear on the general subject of the convention or show. (Irrelevant displays to catch attention or promotion of products not usable in the SO's trade or profession are prohibited.)

I recommend that a place be provided on the list above for the exhibitor's signature, showing that he agrees to these restrictions, and that the SO retain the signed copy.

Your Own Booth

A meeting or show manager thinks of booths as something that other meeting managers set up at his conference. Actually, he himself may have the job of setting up a booth at other shows. Furthermore, if he is now running shows where his company or organization does not exhibit, he should consider it. Why not toot your own horn?

Form of the booth. You can exhibit with only a table (which is common at meetings where exhibits are not the main object of the meeting), with a standard booth, or with one specially constructed for your own needs. You will, of course, make your choice based on the nature of meetings at which you wish to exhibit, frequency of exhibit, the cost of construction of a booth and of shipment, and a consideration of what will appeal to the audiences you wish to reach.

A primary principle of booth design is flexibility. You cannot possibly foresee all the features you will need in a booth. Movable shelves, pegboards, panels that can be used flexibly—all make sense. (A specially constructed booth you will use over and over should include everything when folded and closed and must be rugged.)

Banner. Even though a booth is manned, the booth itself is a silent salesman, especially from a distance. Therefore you need a large sign or banner above the booth to attract attention. The name you use will probably be that of your company or organization, but not necessarily. If the name of your company is little known to those attending the meeting, but the name of a product is well known, use the product name.

The sign or banner should be lightweight and durable. If you have a traveling booth, see that the sign can be hung on the booth itself or supported by rods extending up from the booth. If you do not have a booth and will use a table provided by the conference at which you exhibit, buy extendable poles for the sign or banner, or be prepared to affix it to a wall with tape. (It is important to know whether your booth will be against a wall or in the middle of a room.) Incidentally, it is surprising how few exhibitors bring the normal, minimum essentials for setting up a booth. I have been asked at most shows at which I exhibited for the loan of a screwdriver, shears, tape, stapler, and string.

The "attraction." Your large sign or banner provides identification at a distance. You also need an attraction at the booth to hold the convention-goer who gets close. Some companies put a salesman out in the aisle to collar as many people as possible and start a sales talk. Sales are made this way to some prospects, but others are put off and don't come back.

Your booth "attraction" can be a slide film, a working model of one of your products, a stock reporting machine (at a financial meeting), or even a pretty girl (hired from a local temporary agency) to hand out literature. Some booths have a "sweepstakes" box. On the box is a sign that says, "Win a Free Tape Recorder"—or free color TV, trip to Honolulu, or whatever you are offering. You have printed slips that the meeting-goer fills in, giving his name, title, company, address. You try to get every person going by to fill in a slip so that he or she will have a chance at the prize.

The sweepstakes stops people at your booth, builds your mailing list, and gives people a chance at something for which they have paid no money. While the list of prohibitions I listed in the section dealing with other firms' exhibits at one's own meeting would seem to rule out a sweepstakes box, the list of prohibitions in that case was intentionally strict. I would not go that far at my own meeting, and see no harm in a sweepstakes box for any booth.

The encounter. You now have attracted your convention-goer from across the room, by the banner above the booth, have made him stop with your attraction and spend some brief time there, and now you have a chance to talk with him.

A booth is both a means of advertising and an opportunity to make sales (if the sponsoring organization allows sales). I use "sales" in the broad sense. If you have a booth to promote an organization you are as much in the selling business as if you were promoting the interests of the company. An organization needs to sell memberships, interest in the association, its services, its publications.

But which is more important to you—whether in business or organizational work—advertising or selling? Only *you* can decide this, but it will determine where you put the emphasis in the material you display in your booth and in your conversation with the meeting-goers who stop and talk with you.

So, as you talk with the prospect, you will be dispensing information alone if you are advertising, but will go on to try to sell if on-the-spot sales are important to you.

When the conventioner leaves your booth, be sure he takes something with him. Your association or company literature is good for *you*. Why not give him something that will be good for *him*? You do want him to feel that he enjoyed his stop at the booth and was not just held there. Give him something usable—pen, note pad, diary, travel sewing kit, or rain hat. You can take his picture to send to him. (This also builds the mailing list.) A good idea, of temporary benefit to him and you, is a shopping bag, printed with your company or organization name on both sides, to carry the literature he will collect from booths as he visits them.

What goes in? A frequent question of people setting up a booth involves what to put in it. I have already mentioned the attraction and giveaways. If you are responsible for the booth you must, of course, make the specific decisions, but here are some guidelines:

- Have several giveaways, of small value but of real use to the people who get them, and of considerable variety to appeal to different needs. Have neat signs saying "Take One" to identify the giveaways.
- Offer some products or services at a reduced price—a price available only at this meeting. Be honest about this and don't offer the

same product in any other way at this price. Signs should make your offer very clear.

■ Don't give away, completely free, anything of value except your sweepstakes prize.
■ Have order/membership blanks on hand.
■ Make your booth look orderly and efficient, but also, somehow, comfortable and attractive.

Location. Try to get your booth in the best possible location. A successful booth requires traffic—lots of it—going by. Good places are in corridors, from the middle to about two-thirds of the way out in large exhibit rooms, and at entrances to registration areas. Worst places are at the end of dead-end corridors, far corners of exhibit halls, and in a separate room from all other functions (unless there are so many exhibits that their sheer number compels attendance).

A corridor with a lot of traffic may still be a poor location. There is no percentage in being located just outside the dining room.

It is wise to avoid being next to a direct competitor.

Bring in the artist and PR man. When designing your booth and planning what you will put in it, get your artist and public relations person involved. They will help with ideas and execution.

Meeting and Program Embellishments

Advertising in the program. Selling advertising space in your meeting program is one way to help defray expenses. Your prospects are your suppliers, companies associated with your membership, and local firms in the site city. Have only a few standard sizes: one full page (or of course two full facing pages), one-half page, one-quarter page. This simplifies layout. Charge for a quarter page more than 50 percent of what you charge for a half page, for the half page more than 50 percent of the full-page rate.

Special recognition. You are planning a sales convention to which you are bringing 300 salespeople. Most will be accompanied by their wives or husbands. About 40 of these people have been top producers and you wish to make them noticeable. What can you do?

You can try special color badges for your top group, or distinctive hats, neckties, extra-large badges with ribbons carrying the words "Top Club" or other appropriate legend. The women would be pleased if they were each given an orchid to wear.

You can also fit each man in the top group with a distinctive jacket. A variant of using a jacket in this way is to supply uniform jackets to all your headquarters staff (men and women) if you are running a large convention.

Invite a representative. Here is an idea for any organization. Invite a representative of an independent organization in your field, or a representative of a related group (education with psychology, auto dealers with sales executives, for example). Ask such a person to speak. Your organization may be invited to send a representative in return, and both groups will gain information and ideas.

Building Membership

If an organization wishes to build membership it is customary for members to invite guests to meetings. How can this exposure to the association's program and members be made more effective as a recruiting device?

First, the meeting to which a prospective member is invited should be a regular meeting. To ask someone to a Christmas party may be a nice gesture, but it gives the person no idea of what he will usually experience if he joins, and may, indeed, leave him with the suspicion that the group is less than serious. On the other hand, asking him to the annual business meeting will make him sit through proceedings that he feels he has no business listening to, and, worse, that bore him.

Regular meetings should be of distinct benefit and well run if you are to interest guests. Indeed, they must be all of this simply to hold present membership. If you don't have good meetings you have nothing.

If you have a good "product," then get the people who might "buy" (join) to take a look at it. How? The best way remains for a member to bring a friend or acquaintance as a guest. The old motto, "Every member get a member," is still good. Members must be encouraged to do this, but it is easier to get them to want to invite a friend if they believe in the organization and are enthusiastic about their own membership. Even then, however, they must be urged to recruit.

At the meeting itself, it helps if the chairman sells, but by indirection. The aims and activities of the organization and the benefits to members can be mentioned in such a way that they do not constitute a sales talk. When it comes to reporting on membership efforts, one or two members can tell how they have been successful. If there is a polite competition in securing new members, all the better.

A guest at a meeting should be made to feel welcome in every possible way. The chairman should ask the member who brought the guest to introduce him. The chairman should ask each new member to stand and should give some pertinent information about the new member. Thus someone considering joining sees how he or she would be received into membership.

It is especially important that any organization be friendly. This should apply not only to old-time members who know one another, but to any stranger who comes to a meeting. Every person present who possibly can should come forward to meet the guest, be introduced, and chat with him. Any organization that wants to grow should get to know a prospective member and let the individual know its members. If the current members talk only with themselves, only the most determined visitor will turn into a member.

If our prospective member attends a good meeting and finds himself in friendly company, he will be favorably impressed. There is no need to back him into a corner and try to sell him on joining. If he seems interested someone should see that he has an application blank in his pocket when he leaves and should tell him where to mail it. A follow-up call the next day or a few days later to see how he enjoyed the meeting will do no harm.

Meetings are not the only basis for recruiting membership, but they can be very effective.

Canceling a Meeting

Dropping a conference after it has been planned and after work has been done to bring it into being strikes a blow at the pride of the meeting manager and of the organization that scheduled the conference. It is instructive to look at *why* the meeting was dropped. Out of this negative approach it may be possible to come to some positive principles that will make cancellation less likely in the future. Here are three case histories.

A promoter of a one-day meeting planned to have a conference on founding new businesses. He had some experience in this field and believed that members of the audience would want to trade experiences that they had had. He did not, however, secure speakers who would represent points of view and fields other than his own. He depended too much on his own ability to carry the conference, and relied too heavily on the audience—always a weak policy. When his registration was small a few days before the conference he recognized its failure, cut his losses, and canceled it.

Another meeting ran into a conflict of dates. The sponsors of one of the meetings relied on a news release to intimidate other organizations into keeping the date clear. Either the competitors did not get the word (most likely), or they ignored the message. Registrations flopped and the weaker meeting was washed out.

A third conference, customarily two and a half days, had acquired great prestige during the decade it had been held. It was an annual event, the strongest spring conference in its field. At a time when other organizations in the industry were expanding the meetings they held, it canceled its annual conference. Why? A look at the personnel handling the meeting indicated that they were incapable of planning and executing a conference of that importance. That man who had run the successful conferences was no longer with them.

As one considers the three actual cases of canceled meetings, one thing becomes evident. All three were instances of poor management, whether planning, promoting, or executing. The first conference should never have been projected and the other two needed better management than they were allowed.

Suggestions to Speakers

This book is for meeting managers, not for people who are going to make speeches. I do, however, have a few suggestions for speakers that I have not seen elsewhere.

Cafeteria talk. I once gave a talk where I faced a fairly common problem. The audience had a good many common interests, but they came from firms of all sizes, ranging from quite small to very large. I thought it would be difficult to keep everyone interested throughout the talk.

The conventional way of handling this problem is to give a general speech and then field questions. I was afraid that only a few questions could be handled in the time we had, and that too often the answer to a question might be of interest only to the person who asked it.

I decided to try something different. After a talk filled with hard facts and information, but geared to appeal to as many of the audience as possible, I announced a "cafeteria period." I pulled a list from my pocket and said, "I am going to take questions in a little while. First, however, I have a 'laundry list' of subjects that may be of interest, individually, to some of you. I will give the name of a subject. If you want me to talk on it, put your hand up. If you are not interested, keep your hands down and I will pass on to the next topic."

My list consisted of 20 topics, all aspects of the main subject, for which I had prepared comments of 30 seconds or so each. I had time to mention only about ten and actually discussed only six. The procedure seemed to work well, however. Following this, there was time for a few questions, handled in a conventional way.

You could try this "cafeteria talk" procedure if you have a very varied audience consisting of not more than 100 people.

If the entree is late. I was once the guest speaker at a luncheon where table service was very slow. It became obvious that if I waited till dessert was on the table to begin my talk I would have only a few minutes before people would start to leave for other engagements.

After waiting perhaps 15 or 20 minutes for the entree to arrive, I suggested to the chairman that I start my talk, interrupt the speech when lunch arrived, and resume it later. He agreed, and I had made my first main point before we were all served and I sat down.

I started speaking again when the dessert first came in (the waiters were quiet with their work). Everybody stayed till the talk was finished (I omitted a question period), and the meeting broke up not much later than it normally would have. The chairman said that the talk may have gained interest because of some suspense caused by the interruption.

Obviously, I tried to make the best of a bad situation. This solution should not be used in every similar case. I offer it as an idea you may wish to bear in mind in case of need. It goes without saying that if there are other matters that can be taken up during a lull in the meal, such as the organization's business meeting, it would be preferable to splitting the speaker's talk. Nothing else was available in this instance.

A big-type guy. You are going to make a speech and you are going to read your talk, but you don't want to look as if you are reading it. Have the speech typed double spaced on a jumbo typewriter. Of course, have it typed in upper and lower case, the way this is. (Upper and lower case is much easier to read than all capitals.)

Can we be heard? When you deliver a speech, you should stand if possible, talk into the microphone, and have confirmation from someone in the back of the room that you can be heard there. If there is no microphone, and you know your voice does not carry well, try to stand where everyone can hear you. An example: ten people at a long, rectangular table, no mike, and a speaker with a soft voice. He is wiser to stand in the middle of the table than at one end. This requires him to turn frequently from one side to the other to maintain eye contact with his audience, but he can be heard more effectively.

Speaker's trick. I am continually surprised at the little tricks speakers use to get audience rapport and participation. At one conference a speaker who based his talk on facts plus opinion several times hesitated over a fact. He knew that many in his audience were familiar with the facts, and someone was sure to supply them. No doubt this helped draw his listeners into the subject and made them more receptive to what he had to say.

Unusual Problems with Speakers

This short section is addressed to the meeting manager or meeting chairman. These are two unusual problems you may have with speakers.

Sales talk. What can you do about a speaker invited to talk at an educational meeting who gives a sales talk for the services his company sells? You cannot do much while it is actually happening. This is one of those things best headed off at the pass—prevented. Tell all speakers in writing, before your meeting, that no commercialism is allowed. If one of them steps out of line with a sales talk at the meeting, give no sign that you approve; don't even thank him for his talk. Don't ask him to speak again, and tell your friends. The word will get around. Most speakers, however, will cooperate if they know the ground rules in advance.

The executive who shouldn't speak. There are executives in some of our organizations and companies who just shouldn't speak at a meeting. What can we do about it? The solution has to be individual, because this is a political problem, but here are some ideas.

Incompetence on the podium can be of several kinds.

What the speaker says can be bad—embarrassing, condescending, or faulty in some other way. In this case you can talk with the person or write his speech for him. He *may* stick to the script.

His English is bad. There is nothing you can do about this. He dresses wrong for the occasion. You may be able to change this, but really not by much. Language and dress may not be all that important, though. If your vice-president wears a narrow tie when most men wear a wide one (or vice versa) he may be aware of the difference and just wishes stubbornly to express his individuality. Idiosyncrasy in a speaker will be accepted more readily by an audience if the speaker is financially successful than if he is not.

The speaker just cannot deliver a talk without irritating or boring his audience. In other words, he just can't speak. Fortunately, a lot can be done about this. Good instruction can raise the level of speaking ability in an extraordinary degree. The good can be made better, and the poor can be made good. Dale Carnegie courses are available at moderate cost, but any sizable city has excellent individual teachers for people who wish private instruction. The trick is getting the person who needs help in speaking to accept it. Very likely he has no idea that he performs poorly on the dais. He will not relish learning about his deficiencies, at least from subordinates or equals. And he will not get much benefit from a speech teacher unless he *believes* he can do better and wants to improve. Moving the poor performer to act is a personal and political problem.

If nothing else works with your poor speaker, try to keep him from talking at all. Give him other important work. If his ego is not too strong he may be accommodating. One job that is ideal is asking him to meet and greet an important speaker and take that person under his wing.

Related to the problem of the poor speaker is the association officer or executive who is adequate for normal occasions, but who cannot handle hostile people in the audience. There may be a dissident group within an association, a labor union, company stockholders, or the audience at a political gathering. Proper advance preparation is an essential before going into a meeting where trouble can be expected. Many executives, however, are aware that the manner of meeting opposition in a meeting may be as important as the content of answers to belligerent questions. There are speech advisers who concentrate on preparing speakers to handle difficult people in an audience, and their help can be well worth the fees they charge. (Floor microphones that suddenly lose their power can be helpful, too.)

Coming to Terms about Conventions

Years ago I came across an article about a "teacher's convention." I was bemused by this phrase, because I could not see how one teacher could have a "coming together"—that's what "convention" means. But of more concern than misplaced apostrophes is the misuse of entire words. Certainly experienced meeting managers have no need for a glossary of convention terms. For the benefit of the meeting manager who is just starting out, Chapter 3 gave some definitions of guest rooms and in Chapter 5 podium, lectern, and rostrum were defined.

Curiously, there is no completely satisfactory word to describe someone who attends a convention or other meeting. I have used, in this book, conventioner, meeting-goer, registrant, and similar terms. Conventioner seems somewhat far out. Why not attendee? Well, the ending "ee" actually indicates someone to whom something is done, not the person doing it. Thus, a donor is someone who gives, and the donee is the person to whom it is given. The payer is the one who pays, and the payee the one who is paid. A person who attends a convention should, therefore, be an attender, but we don't say it often. Attendant has a special meaning and cannot be adopted for use here. Conferee attracts the same objection as attendee, and for the same reason, but it has gained some respectability with much use. Yet conferer would have an utterly different meaning. Perhaps some reader who is concerned about language has solved this problem of what to call a person attending a convention.

It is useful to take a look at some other convention-associated terms to facilitate dealing with hotels and restaurants.

- *European plan* means room only with no meals included in the price.
- *American plan* includes three meals.
- *Modified American plan* includes two meals in the hotel rate. They are usually breakfast and an evening meal.
- *Continental plan,* not common in North America, means hotel with breakfast only.
- *Bermuda plan* gives you continental plan with a hearty American breakfast.
- *Full pension,* which you may get when traveling abroad, is three meals a day, with a hearty breakfast.
- *Demi-pension* lets you have continental breakfast and your lunch or evening meal.
- *A la carte* is, as I'm sure everyone knows, a restaurant term indicating that each item selected for the meal bears its own price.
- *Table d'hote* means that you pay for the whole meal, not for individual items. There is a choice of entree (main dish).
- *Continental breakfast* is tea or coffee, rolls of some kind, and a spread like marmalade or jam.
- *American breakfast* is a meal with juice, eggs and bacon or ham, sometimes cereal, and a beverage.

10
The Effective Participant

Most of the time we view meetings from the side of managing them, but it is worthwhile to cross over and try to help those who attend get more out of conferences. Here are some ideas you can either use yourself at meetings you attend but do not manage, or pass on to your members if the meeting is in your charge.

Preparation

A person who wants to get the most possible from a conference should sit down with the program in front of him. For each subject to be discussed write down what you hope the speaker will cover, what problems you have to which you hope some solutions will be offered, and the questions you would like to ask if answers are not provided in the prepared talk.

If the meeting is small, with perhaps only one subject to be discussed, it is still important to make what preparation you can. Think about the subject and jot down questions you would like to ask—areas where your information is weak. If members of the audience will be able to make comments, is there anything *you* know which would increase the knowledge of other people who attend?

You should list the people you want to see at the meeting and make some notes on what you wish to talk about with them. Make sure that these people will actually attend, tell them that you wish to see them, and find out what hotel they will be staying at. Some convention-goers make luncheon and dinner appointments ahead of time with their business contacts.

Another area of advance preparation is to list the new contacts that you wish to make. These may be with firms where you now know no one, or new areas of interest in your specialty where you feel you will benefit from exposure to new ideas.

What do you want to see in the city where the convention will he held? Are there field trips you wish to make? Sights to see, plays or games to attend? You should prepare for these, making advance reservations where they may be necessary and planning sightseeing routes.

Shortly I will have suggestions about organizing your meeting material.

At the Conference

At the meeting itself it is best to get your main objectives taken care of early. Arrange meetings right away with the people you want to see. You also need to program your time. Some people do just that—have their meeting program serve as their record for all engagements during the conference. They simply enter business and social appointments right in among the formal program entries in the proper place. I consider this method far superior to making such entries in the regular appointment book we carry with us at other times.

Notes

Many people make no notes while they listen to speakers at meetings. Some of these people, no doubt, have very good memories and can recall any information they wish when they need it. Others of us are not so lucky, and need to take notes. Good notes also make easier the writing of any reports you may have to provide after the conference.

The making of notes and their subsequent use are easier if you use a few mechanical tricks. One is to draw vertical lines or fold the paper so you have three narrow columns to work with. In this way, when your hand reaches the right-hand end of a line it has only a short distance to move back to the beginning of the next line. You also tend to write smaller with short lines. Both these factors save energy. It is important to date the notes at the beginning, jot down the name of the organization or meeting, and identify the speaker. A rectangular box around the speaker's name helps make it stand out when you go back over the notes.

"S1013(c)(1)," "periosteum," "threaten legal action." These are phrases with precise meaning themselves. Some people go home from a meeting with their notes consisting entirely of a few such phrases scrawled across a piece of paper. This kind of shorthand can jog memory for a few days, but after that these bare words are stripped of any further meaning. Who can remember what the speakers said about these things? Notes need to be sufficiently complete so that the main ideas are carried out far enough to convey meaning if you look at your notes a few months later.

Depending upon your needs, your notes may be very full or consist only of carefully described main ideas. There is no need to get down a speaker's words exactly as he says them—unless you intend to quote him, and then be very careful—it may even aid your understanding to make notes in your own words, rather than his. If the speaker is well organized and numbers the points he makes in his talk, you should do so, too, as your notes will be more usable.

Speakers at many meetings, large and small, give away handouts of material to those attending. Whenever you get a handout, immediately write on it the name of the speaker and the date you received it.

You may also leave the meeting with a good deal of other material, besides the notes you made of the talks, handouts, and supplements. Very likely you have names and addresses and phone numbers of people you talked with or who have special knowledge or expertise in subjects you may want to explore later. Date all these notes. Keep them in a handy place. Make continuing use of them over the months ahead.

One person with a lot of meeting experience writes the year on each business card he receives. He keeps the cards alphabetically by firm as a sort of informal address file. The date on the card warns him that an old card may be out of date because the person who gave him the card may have changed affiliation or address.

Organizing Your Meeting Material

Large organizations with large meetings prepare large amounts of material, some of which they send out in advance of the convention, and some of which is distributed at the meeting.

Some people are naturally organized, while others are not. Some don't want to be. My own inclination is a desire to be organized, balanced by a difficulty in achieving that state. Here is my system, which works reasonably well:

Before leaving home for the meeting I take all advance material I have received and separate in into piles by the days to which it applies and place a labeled top sheet on each pile.

Some material is always left over. This is anything that applies to the whole conference, or at least to more than one day. I label this "general" and place it before the material for the first day. If I am lucky I have that prime aid to organization—an advance program.

I often receive releases and advance texts of speeches. If there is a printed program, I start at the beginning of the program and number every talk or event—1, 2, 3, and so on. The next step is to turn to the piles I have laid out and number every news release, complete text, or other piece of paper dealing with a talk or event with the appropriate number appearing in the program. As I thus tie in all the loose material possible with the program, I also mark, beside the number in the program, "Have text," or "Have release." This information will come in useful later. Then I gather each pile separately—with paper clips or rubber bands, and put the piles aside for packing.

When I arrive at my room in the hotel where I am staying for the meeting, I lay out the material, by days, side by side on the desk. On any day I need to carry only the papers for that one day, plus the program. Each night I put my badge and program on the pile pertaining to the next day.

Even with this much organization, however, I find that some meetings produce so much material that it tends to drown my system. There are three things, however, that I must be able to put my hands on immediately at any time during the meeting. These are the meeting program, my appointment book (to make business appointments for dates after the meeting), and my business cards.

I like to keep all these in my jacket pockets, so that I have them handy whether at a business or social function. The only problem is the program that is too large to fit in a pocket. (Not a problem for the woman whose handbag is large enough.) An oversize program goes in front in a briefcase or on top in an attaché case but I wish meeting managers would design programs that would always fit in an inside jacket pocket or an ordinary-size purse.

As noted above, mark all engagements that are to be fulfilled during the conference in the meeting program. Do *not* mark any of them in your appointment book. If you cannot bring yourself to use your program in this way, mark appointments in one book only, not in both.

Keep all your notes in one place. Handouts, numbered to correspond with the programmed events, go in the pile of the applicable day. Each day, if possible, or near the end of the meeting, try to throw out any papers you do not need to bring home. Then, when you leave the meeting just pick up everything, as is, and take it home with you.

The imaginative meeting-goer will set up his own organizational system, perhaps arranged by subject matter instead of by program for the day. The important thing is to have a system where you expect a lot of paper so that you can concentrate your efforts at the meeting, miss no important events or engagements, and not be hunting through a mountain of paper for something you need in a hurry.

After You Get Home

Some people have their notes typed up when they return from a meeting and place them in the appropriate subject files. If you don't do this it is generally best to keep a file for each organization and put all material from the conference in that folder. Some highly organized people using the second procedure maintain a card file by subject with cross references to the location of the material they have collected.

Even if your company or organization does not require that you render a report on the meeting, why not write one? Writing the report not only benefits those who were not able to attend but also forces you to identify the most timely and relevant information provided at the meeting. Writing a report helps to reinforce your memory of what you have heard and therefore extends the lasting benefit the conference can provide.

Often at a meeting people from the same company sit together in the meeting rooms, all sit at the same table for lunch, and socialize with one another in the evening. Why not split up—spread out at the meeting, have no more than one person from a particular company at one table at noon, and go out in the evening with new acquaintances? You can talk with the people from your company any time. Isn't it more personally rewarding to make new friends? And isn't it good for business, too?

Finally, a person planning to attend a meeting should remember that information and contacts are two-way streets. He should go to the meeting in a rested, relaxed state of mind, anxious to meet new people of any company or specialty, glad to give of his own knowledge and expertise. In this way only will he get the most benefit to be derived from the convention experience.

The Meeting as Job Mart

It is a sad truth that most of the time some people are looking for jobs. Inevitably, some of them are using an old ploy—attending a meeting in an attempt to make a connection. If you have a job and are not looking for one, you need read no further. If you are looking for a job, however, some of the following ideas may be of help to you. If you are that much-sought-after type, the person who is trying to hire someone to fill a spot, you might read on and derive some benefit by indirection.

Generally speaking, you will get best results in looking for a job at a meeting if you do a good deal of pre-conference writing and phoning. Unless you want to blow your present job I do not suggest that you state in a letter what your real interest is in seeing so-and-so at a meeting. It is better just to say that you would like to have a few minutes with your friend at the upcoming conference. The more people you write to along these lines—provided they are chosen with care and an eye to your job safety—the more chances you will have to market your abilities at the meeting.

When it comes to the conference itself, be sure your badge can be read several feet away. If your association has furnished convention-goers with a typewritten badge, take a piece of white cardboard or paper and print your name with a broad pen or a brush in upper and lower case and attach this as a patch to your badge. The association people may not like it, but presumably they do not have your problem.

Be as much in evidence as you can at the meeting. This may mean attending fewer sessions, but you will find corridor patrolling and standing of more immediate benefit.

If you can do so safely, be sure that the people in your association who are the most widely known and therefore likely to talk to the most people know that you are job-hunting. Encourage them to spread the word.

Carry a portfolio with evidence of the things you have accomplished. A supply of data sheets (don't call them résumés) will come in handy.

Attend every cocktail party you can. A glass of ginger ale, however, instead of a highball will be a good idea.

Finally, remember those people you wrote to? Make a point of looking every one of them up. It will probably be one of them that comes through with the job.

11
Travel Tips

This chapter is concerned with ways to make travel easier. It is addressed to anyone who travels, whether you are a convention-goer or a meeting manager. In the latter case, the travel tips are for your own use and, where you think appropriate, for passing on to the people for whom you arrange meetings. These suggestions arise from experience of many years of travel. Most of them involve only common sense. But do you *do* them? If you don't, I hope that putting them in black and white will move you to act on them.

Air Travel

Overbooking. If you are bumped without your consent from a flight, the airline must pay the fare to your next destination, with compensation—$37.50 minimum, $200 maximum. If it cannot arrange another flight that is scheduled to reach your destination within two hours of the original flight (four hours on an international flight) the amount of your compensation doubles. There are a few exceptions.

Lost tickets. A lost ticket is one of the most difficult problems to deal with. From the airlines' standpoint, airline tickets are almost as negotiable as money. They make as certain as possible that they will not carry anyone free or pay an unjustified refund on a turned-in ticket. This makes it hard for you if your ticket is left behind at home or the office, or is lost or stolen.

First, never pay cash for a ticket if you can help it; use a credit card, a check, or buy it through a travel agent. Second, record the number of your ticket, and keep that record separate from the ticket so that if your wallet or purse is stolen you can tell the airline the number. Third, carry enough travelers' checks separate from your wallet or purse to pay for the balance of your trip, if you should have to.

For authoritative information on overbooking, lost tickets, lost baggage, and many useful things, get a copy of "Fly-Rights," issued by the Civil Aeronautics Board. Write the CAB Consumer Information Center, Pueblo, CO 81009. Some of the information is aimed at the less sophisticated traveler, but much of it is helpful for the business person and professional.

Saving money. You can save money on travel by planning well ahead, dealing with a good travel agent, and using family rate, excursion rate, or "tours." But check *all* costs in your planning. If you depart a day earlier in order to get a special fare rate, you will have to pay extra for room, meals, tips, and incidentals. And those expenses may completely wipe out the "savings" that a special rate would get you.

Timing. (This is a note for meeting managers only.) A large convention, with several thousand people, was held on the West Coast. About two weeks before the meeting the convention committee announced that charter flights, at rates well under standard scheduled airline fares, would be available from Chicago and East Coast points. This announcement came too late for many people, who either had to forgo the charter rates or scramble through cancellations and rebooking. Something as important as transportation should not be left till the eleventh hour.

Carry-on luggage. When you are boarding a plane and have carry-on luggage, don't get a seat right behind a partition. You may not have enough room for your bags. The carry-on luggage that you wanted with you may then go to the baggage bin in the hold of the plane.

Cosmetics. If you are a woman who travels with cosmetics, particularly liquids and hair sprays, try to travel light. Carry odds and ends—the half tube of tooth paste, the half can of hair spray, part bottle of vitamins. As part of preparation for your trip put aside containers that are part empty. A word of caution—you may want to carry liquids in a tote bag with you in the cabin to minimize spilling.

Clock problem. My wife and I had a delicate but very accurate travel clock. Twice we packed it in my luggage and on unpacking found it would not work. Our jeweler repaired it, but the second time said, "You must have been very rough with this clock. The works are in very bad shape. Did you throw it across the room?" We had not dropped the clock or otherwise mistreated it. Either it received rough treatment from baggage handlers or the lack of pressurization on flights was bad for it. We suspect the latter, as we had it packed in clothes in the middle of a suitcase. You may wish to carry delicate clocks in your carry-on baggage.

Tedium in the air. Take a good map of the area you fly over, to relieve boredom. Watch for geographic features—the seacoast outline, bays, points of land—and rivers, mountains, cities. Sometimes you'll fly above clouds, but, more often than you'd think you *can* see ground and water. Spotting points of interest below and matching them with the map makes the trip more enjoyable. *National Geographic* maps are excellent for this aerial sightseeing travel game.

Food, drinks, movies, and reading help pass the hours, but do nothing for cramped legs and inactive muscles. SAS (Scandinavian Airlines) has an exercise program for its passengers that you can practice in your seat as you fly. In a small, illustrated, folder SAS tells you how to jog, roll your shoulders, rise on your toes, exercise neck muscles, do bends, liven up ankle and wrist movements, and exercise knees—all without leaving your seat. That is just one program. Another involves movement, with one exercise pulling you up out of your seat briefly. The booklet is not for general distribution, unfortunately, and is handed to passengers en route. Perhaps you can devise your own exercises.

Some people take off their shoes in a plane. Fine for most travelers, but there are some whose feet swell, making it difficult to put the shoes back on. If you have this trouble, why not just loosen your laces or slip your feet only half-way out.

Meal flight. Plane seats are not designed for eating. Put your necktie in the pocket of your jacket, or tuck most of it under your shirt. Hook a corner of the napkin in your collar instead of putting the napkin in your lap. This will provide the best protection for your clothes if the plane runs into turbulence while you are eating.

Arrival at the airport. When you get to your destination, check to see if there is a courtesy car to your hotel. Resort hotels and airport motels, particularly, offer this service.

Better yet, inform the hotel ahead of time so that it can send the courtesy car to meet you. Of course, if you are the meeting manager for a group, you will inform your members of the availability of the courtesy car.

This advice about using a courtesy car may sound elementary, but sometimes no one tells us that the car exists and there is none at the airport at the moment. So we do not know there is any.

Lost luggage. One of the most annoying things that can happen to the traveler is to have his bag lost by the airline. Some people regard it as nothing less than catastrophic.

Here is what you can do (1) to prevent a bag's being misrouted, and (2) to recover it if it has been lost or to receive compensation for your loss.

■ Lock your bag.

■ Always have a permanent tag on the handle of your bag that gives your name and city of residence. It is a good idea, as well, to have the complete address on a piece of paper inside the bag.

■ Mark your luggage in some distinctive way, such as with a design in bright masking tape. Put some on each end of the bag as well as on the sides. This makes it easy for you to recognize and minimizes mistakes by others. It also discourages thieves.

■ When you present your luggage for check-in, be sure there are no old destination tags on the bags. These old tags can confuse handlers and send your bag in one direction while you go in another.

■ Watch the airline agent while he puts the tags on the luggage. You can usually read the destination on the tags. Be sure the right destination goes on.

■ Occasionally, if you have to change planes, you can watch baggage being transferred. This is particularly true at smaller airports. If your bag is plainly marked so that you can spot it at a distance, you can be sure if it is on the right truck to be loaded on the plane you are going to take.

Bags tend to fall out of step with their owners when passengers change planes. Missed connections, particularly, play hob with the smooth flow of luggage. If you know you are going to change planes it is best to put your most essential needs in a bag you carry onto the plane with you.

■ Take special care when going through customs upon entering another country. It is your responsibility to see your bag through, and a little extra care here will pay off.

■ When you arrive at your destination, claim your bag promptly. Bags unattended for a considerable time are likely to be stolen or have their contents pilfered. (For this reason you should not check luggage more than an hour in advance of plane departure time, either.)

Suppose, despite these precautions, that your bag does not appear on the carousel at your destination. What should you do? Immediately tell the airline people that you do not have your bag and fill out a loss form. Be sure to get the name of an airline contact and a phone number you can call during the coming 24 hours so that you can check on the progress of the search for your luggage. If it is night, the airline may lend you some toilet goods and perhaps even provide a little clothing to tide you over until your bag is located. Ask. The airline probably will not volunteer.

When the airline finds your bag it will usually deliver it without charge to your hotel or home. Airline people are anxious to cooperate and restore lost luggage as promptly as possible. The bag will be delivered by the final airline on your trip, even though this carrier may not have been the one that lost your luggage.

The present limit of liability for lost luggage is $750. The contents of a lost bag are depreciated, and you may be asked to show receipts to justify your claim to the original cost of items. The difficulty you may encounter is obvious, and it frequently takes considerable time—months—to settle a claim. Inflating the value of the contents of a lost bag does not endear a person to the airline and can delay claim settlement. If your luggage is really worth more than $750 after depreciation, it will help your peace of mind to buy insurance for the amount over that limit.

If you are dissatisfied with the way the airline handles your lost-luggage problem you can write to the Office of the Consumer Advocate, Civil Aeronautics Board, Washington, DC 20248.

Automobile Travel

Traffic. Will you be driving in another state for the first time, perhaps in a distant part of the country? Check traffic laws. They may be different.

In Los Angeles a car can speed from a ramp into freeway traffic without slowing. In New York, doing the same thing can get a car—and a driver—clobbered, as traffic coming onto an expressway in New York, or most other Eastern states, is supposed to yield right of way. Some states allow a right turn on a red traffic signal after a full stop. Others do not.

Some of the most frequent differences in traffic laws concern speed limits in town and country, access to highways, passing, and school buses. Your road map will sometimes tell about these laws. Otherwise choose the more conservative of alternatives when driving and observe other drivers carefully to determine local practices.

Hot weather driving. If you drive in hot weather and the back of your shirt gets wet from perspiration you can buy an air-conditioned car. You can also put a shirt or jacket you don't care too much about on the seat behind you to absorb the sweat and make you more comfortable. (I am skeptical of wire mesh back rests. I had one once that eventually cut into the upholstery of the car.)

Another tip about hot-weather driving. If you have to park your car in the sun, spread road maps or something else over the seat. The seat will not be so hot to sit on when you return to the car. Also, if the car will stand in the sun for any length of time, open a vent and the top of a window slightly (opening a wing window will do). The resulting circulation will keep the temperature inside your car lower and may save you a cracked window. (Expanding hot air has been known to crack windows when the heat could not escape.)

Don't leave a pet in a car on a hot day, even with the windows somewhat open. It's cruel.

Sightseeing. If you are about to drive a circular route, you have the option at the outset of the direction in which you drive. To have a better look at the scenery, drive on the side of the road nearer the attraction. This is particularly important when the attraction is water (for example, Lake Tahoe), as water lies below road level, or where you will wish to look down into valleys.

Laundry. When you travel by car, take a laundry bag to put your soiled laundry in. This makes room in your suitcases for souvenirs and gifts.

Safety. Don't drive more hours in a day than you normally work! And of course you should fasten your seat belt. Seat belts save lives.

Exchanging Homes

There are some good programs for exchanging homes during vacation. Occupancy of a house is exchanged for a stay in another house or an apartment, an apartment for an apartment, or perhaps a house for a yacht. Two families move themselves, with clothing, but find everything else they need in the home they go to. These exchanges are almost always for a week or longer, and therefore not very appropriate for the convention-goer and family unless some vacation at the convention location is added to the meeting period. Sponsorship of exchange programs has changed from time to time, so there is little use giving you addresses. Ask for information at your local public library.

Food and Drink

Water. Does change in water upset you when you are away from your home city? Bottled water may be your answer. But read the label carefully. Not all bottled water is straight from a sparkling mountain spring. If you're stuck on where to buy bottled water, try room service, especially outside the United States, grocery and variety stores, and (in California) liquor stores! Best of all, do what athletes and entertainers do—take your water from your home. Two quarts, stretched with more appetizing beverages, may last you through a two-week trip.

Left-handed tip. To minimize contact with germs while on the road, hold the handle of your coffee cup with your left hand.

Foreign Travel

Credit cards. Don't count on being able to use credit cards as freely outside the United States and Canada as you can at home. American Express is pretty universal, but some others are not always accepted off the mainland. Personal checks are particularly hard to cash in Bermuda and the West Indies, as well as in more distant countries. It is better to rely heavily on travelers' checks when leaving the North American mainland.

Language. Are you in a country where you don't know the language? When you leave the hotel take a book of matches carrying the name of the hotel. When you wish to return, show it to the cab driver.

If you are in a country that does not use our Roman alphabet, such as Japan or Russia, and you are going to a specific address, ask an English-speaking employee of the hotel to write the address for you in the language of the country.

Passports. If you are going out of the country and no passport is required for return to the United States or Canada there is no need to get a passport, but if you already have one, carry it. You will save time getting into and out of foreign countries, and it is nice to accumulate the stamped evidence that you have been in those places.

A passport is an important document. It may be more important to you than money. Guard it well. Don't give it to anyone unless local law requires that you surrender temporary possession. Take it with you whenever you leave your hotel room, both for safety reasons and because showing it can sometimes facilitate duty-free purchases. Because entry into America is still a goal of many people abroad, stolen passports command a good price. If yours is lost or stolen you can experience considerable trouble and delay before you replace it.

Shaver. If you are going to a meeting away from the continent of North America you may not be able to use your electric shaver or hair dryer. They will work in Bermuda and in the Caribbean islands but not in Europe. For other places, check the current. (Your travel agent may know.) Converters sometimes help, and can be purchased in some hardware stores.

Medicines. If you carry medicines abroad, it is a good idea to put a label on the outside of each vial telling what is inside, if your druggist has not done so. Some customs people are so concerned about illicit drugs that you might be delayed at borders if you had no indication on the medicines as to what they were. Labeling your medicines is worthwhile in any case, as it can be a help to you.

Have prescription, will travel. If your doctor has you on medication and you are going to Europe, have your doctor write a prescription in Latin. Then if you run out of your medicine over there, you can have the prescription filled in any country.

Carry extra copies of your eyeglass or contact lens prescriptions, in case you need replacements.

People who may be subject to a sudden attack of a medical nature should carry a Medic Alert bracelet.

Shopping. A problem in buying clothes abroad is that sizes are expressed in different systems. For men's suits and overcoats, shirts, and socks and women's stockings, the sizes are the same in England and America, but different on the Continent. For men's hats and women's shoes, sizes are expressed differently in all three areas. I suggest that you go abroad with a tape measure (cloth) that has inches and feet on one side and centimeters on the other. When abroad buy only what the country is famous for (there are few true bargains in clothes for North Americans abroad these days).

Here are a few equivalent sizes for people shopping in England and on the Continent.*

Men's Suits and Overcoats

American and English	36	38	40	42	44	46
Continental	46	48	50	52	54	56

Shirts

American and English	14	14½	15	15½	15¾	16	16½	17
Continental	36	37	38	39	40	41	42	43

*From "Shopping Abroad," TWA booklet #4-5745. Used with permission.

Women's Shoes

American	4	5	6	7	8	9	10
English	2	3	4	5	6	7	8
French	36	37	38	39	40	41	42
Italian	32	34	36	38	40	42	44

Out of the country long enough to make purchases you wish to bring home duty free? Put all purchases in one bag, alone or on top of any other packed articles. Have all receipts in one place. This makes passage through customs easier for you—and for the customs people. Do customs men of your own country seem much tougher on you than those of the places you visit? They have to be. Unfortunately, home-going travelers are more likely to smuggle.

If you are going out of the country with a valuable item, such as a camera, you can show it at the customs desk and get a document certifying that you had it when you left the United States. This saves possible trouble at customs when you come home. You cannot do this with jewelry.

Health and Comfort

Do not take brand-new shoes on a trip. Break them in first. You will be on your feet a good deal at the meeting, and your shoes, if new, can be tight and painful.

(Also, see *Medicines* under the "Foreign Travel" head above.)

Home Security Checklist

This is a checklist to make your home as secure as possible any time you leave for a trip and your house or apartment will be unoccupied.

With no intention of exhausting the subject, here are a few quick hints to help you protect your home.

Although your locks should of course be as secure as possible, your best protection is to convince strangers that the house or apartment is occupied. To accomplish this:

- Use light. Use timers that turn on at least one light, preferably two, as though someone had moved from one room to another, and turned off the first light before going to the second room. The first light should go on at dusk, the second somewhat later.
- Use sound—or sound and light. A timer can turn on a radio or television set and turn it off later.
- Stop all deliveries—mail, milk, newspapers—and have a helpful

neighbor pick up anything you can't stop, like pennysavers and other flyers.

- Leave shades and curtains in a normal or near-normal position. But they should be arranged so that no one standing at a window can get a clear view through the house.
- Leave no notes telling anyone when you will return, where the key is, and so forth.
- Don't disconnect your telephone, unless you will be away for several months, so that the saving may justify the risk that a potential burglar will check occupancy of the home by telephone.
- If you want the newspaper to report on your meeting or trip, wait till you get back to send the item to the paper.
- Close your garage door, and lock it.

Suppose you have done your best to convince strangers that you are at home, but some burglar just doesn't believe you. How can you guard against an actual attempt on your home? The following tips may help you:

- Tell the police you will be away. Ask them to watch the building. Tell them when you will be home. You may wish to give them a phone number where you can be reached, or the name of a neighbor who will have it.
- Arrange for a neighbor to check regularly on the house or apartment. Tell him or her the names of anyone you have authorized to enter the house, and tell anyone who will enter the house to make himself known and identify himself to the neighbor. If the neighbor sees any other activity of any kind, he or she should call the police and give the license number of any suspicious vehicle.

  In two cases a few years ago, self-assured burglars backed a truck up to the door of a house whose owners were away and moved out all the furniture. In the first case a neighbor watched without being suspicious. In the other instance the activity aroused suspicion and the neighbor called the police. They were a long time coming, and the truck was gone when they arrived. The neighbor did not have the license number of the truck, and the thieves—and the furniture—got away.
- Leave your neighbor your itinerary, with phone numbers.

Hotel and Motel

Reservations. I like to travel with all hotel reservations made in advance and with assurance that we will have a bed no matter how late at night we arrive. In order to do this we have to guarantee our reservation, which means that if we do not use the room we still have to pay for it.

Discounts are available to members of some groups—the American Association of Retired Persons, members of some travel clubs, employees of certain corporations, and members of some professional organizations. Too often, unfortunately, the hotel, or more often motel, is more anxious to get the patronage than it is to give the discount. Frankly, you may have to fight. Sometimes you will be given a better room at a lower room rate, but this does not seem to me to meet the idea of a discount. If you are trying to save money you want an inexpensive room at the discounted rate. Mention the discount when you make your reservation. This is almost always a condition of the deal. If you have trouble, report your experience to the organization through which you learned about the discount.

If you are going to a convention but planning to stay at an inexpensive hotel away from the main meeting hotel, reconsider. The money you save is rarely worth what you lose in benefits the convention can give.

Twin beds. You wanted a double or queen-bedded room and you are stuck with a twin. What can you do? The two beds, just as they are, can be pushed together. The beds can be put side by side, the mattresses placed cross-wise, and the combination made up as one bed. The sheets and blankets are then placed the long way across both beds. This is called bridging, and is better than the simple side-by-side expedient.

(You may wish to refresh your memory of hotel room terminology by referring to Chapter 3.)

For the ladies. You are unpacking and find that you did not bring enough plastic hangers for your dresses and blouses. You feel that the wooden hangers the hotel furnishes are too rough. Cover the wood with paper—either by making a small hole in a large piece of relatively heavy paper and passing the hanger hook through the hole from underneath, or wrapping the upper shoulders of the wooden hanger in tissue paper (facial tissue or toilet paper will do). If you need a cross piece for slacks, wrap the cross piece of the wooden hanger in the same way. Your clothes then will not come in contact with the wood and you will have no snags.

When you leave your wet shower cap in the bathroom overnight is it sometimes wet in the morning? Put it somewhere else to dry. Things dry slowly in bathrooms. After stockings are through dripping you can move them out of the bathroom, too.

Late at night. When you are in a hotel or motel and expect to get up at night, leave the light on in the bathroom and close the bathroom door. It's easy then to find your way through the unfamiliar territory while still half asleep.

Pants presser. Wrinkles in men's pants tend to shake out overnight if you hang them full length from a dresser by shutting the cuffs in a top drawer and letting the pants hang. You need a tall dresser, but this works better than putting the pants on a hanger.

When leaving. To be sure nothing is left behind, make a last-minute check of the entire bedroom, bathroom (including the back of the door), closets, drawers, under the bed (for shoes). This sounds like simple advice, but it is needed. Every year thousands of travelers leave things in hotel rooms.

Forget to leave your hotel key when you checked out? Don't drop the key in a trash can. Thieves at airports and train and bus stations watch for this, extract the key after you are out of sight, and use it to gain admission to what was your hotel room. Give some thought to the next guest in the room. Someone else may have the same consideration for you. Send the key back through the mail.

Lost or Strayed

Keep a business card in your raincoat, topcoat, hat, attaché case. If you lose any of these it may come back.

Luggage

Kind. What kind of luggage do you like? Color is a matter of widely varying taste, but how about weight and durability? My wife and I have tried the light, fabric type. This is certainly easy to carry, and some of our friends have had good success with it. After many years of extensive travel, however, we have in recent years bought only the most rugged suitcases we can find at a reasonable price. We make sure that the catches and locks are strong. Luggage that rides many planes is certain to be dropped, bumped, and scratched. For this reason, too, we think it a mistake to buy expensive leather luggage.

The tag. Have only your name, city, and state or province on your luggage tag. No street address or phone number. If your bag is lost, your name, city, and state will identify it. Unfortunately, additional information is sometimes communicated to burglars in the traveler's home town. There is no need to make things easy for crooks.

The key. What do you do with the key to a suitcase when you are not traveling? Do you leave it on your key ring, where you may already have too many keys? Do you put it in a desk or bureau drawer and hope to find it when you need it? It's better to tie it with a piece of string to the handle of your suitcase. When you need the bag, untie the key and put it on your key ring. Of course, when you return from your trip, you should take the key off the ring and tie it back onto the suitcase.

(See also, *Lost Luggage* under "Air Travel" in this chapter.)

Mail and Telephone

Important papers. As is well known, if you have mail sent to a hotel, to get there before you do, it should be marked HOLD FOR ARRIVAL. We like to expand this to HOLD FOR ARRIVAL ON, and add the date.

You may wish to send a letter or envelope by certified mail. You can do this, but do not require a return receipt if the envelope is to arrive before you do. This can cause problems.

Telephone. I went to a meeting of several hundred people that was held during the summer on a college campus. Meeting-goers lived in the dormitories, ate at the cafeteria, and met in the college theater. This was a meeting of professionals who use the telephone a great deal. There were very few pay phones, with only two in the building where we met. Long lines developed at every break, with frustration and irritation evident. When the meeting was over, one of those attending confided that he had found a pay phone in the gymnasium 200 feet away and had used it throughout the meeting. He never had to wait. The gym was not used during the summer, but the door was open. He had slyly kept this information to himself. I was no more observant than the others attending the meeting. So, it pays to look around, not follow the herd. Element'ry, Watson!

Packing

Checklist. Want to get your packing time down to as little as 15 minutes? Use a checklist. Put on the checklist everything you could possibly want to pack, at any time of the year, for any type of meeting. Run off a number of copies and put a few in each of your suitcases.

When you come to pack, take a copy and, as you put the item in the bag, put a dot in front of the listing. Cross off items that don't apply (like an overcoat in July) and put a dot in front of the listing you crossed off. Connect adjacent dots. A solid line beside the column then means that you have packed or eliminated everything listed in the column.

Your checklist makes it possible for a willing helpmate to pack for you, reducing your packing time to zero. The list is also invaluable if your bag should be lost.

Shoes. Shoes are the single heaviest article of a man's wearing apparel. When you take short trips, build your wardrobe around one pair of shoes—the pair you are wearing. I find black shoes best for short trips.

Living from the suitcase. When can you unpack fully? When do you live out of a suitcase? The rule of thumb, for my wife and me, is that if the stop is for one night, live out of the suitcase. Put nothing in drawers or on closet shelves (though it is OK to hang up a very few things). If the stop is for two or more nights, unpack everything and put it away. We find that clothes get too confused if we have to dig into a suitcase two nights running.

On a trip of several days, with a series of one-night stops at motels, we take two small bags, in addition to the larger ones. In one bag we put everything we will need the first night and the following morning. In the second bag we put everything for the second night and the following morning (except toothbrushes and toothpaste and a couple of other things that can be transferred). By the third night we have to reorganize. We then use a laundry bag (if we are traveling by car) or one of the small bags for dirty laundry and try to use the other to set up the fourth night's needs. If you suspect that this system is not perfect, you are right—but it helps. We can leave most large bags in the trunk of the car the first two nights.

Restaurants

Two meals a day. When traveling we usually eat only two meals a day—a large breakfast and good dinner. It saves a lot of time. You cannot do this if your meeting schedule calls for something different, of course. (For meal terminology, see Chapter 9.)

Sightseeing

Going to do some sightseeing on the next convention trip you take? Several weeks before you leave, sit down with guide books and folders and list everything you want to see, marking those places and sights with the highest priority with an asterisk. Then get out maps of the city and area and plan your routes—driving and walking—so that you will waste as little time and effort in your sightseeing as possible. Plan each day's activities if you can. This preplanning will make your trip much more rewarding and enjoyable and will save you valuable time.

Taxis

See Chapter 3.

Thieves

It is distressing to have to warn travelers about thieves, but big cities are not what they used to be, and even resorts offer opportunities to sneak thieves. You can never be 100 percent safe, but here are some suggestions.

Preparing for the trip. Travel light. I don't mean just clothes. I mean as regards cash, jewelry, credit cards, and other documents. Virtually all your money should be in travelers' checks. Unless your bank has a branch in the city you are going to, leave all your blank bank checks at home in a safe place. If you have family heirloom jewelry, whose loss would cause you particular pain, leave it behind, preferably in a safe deposit box in your bank. Credit cards for local department stores and other businesses belong in the same deposit box. The same advice goes for passports and other important documents you will not use.

When you get your travelers' checks, put your list of the check numbers in a separate place from the checks. Consider this list of checks a valuable document.

A current technique of thieves is to steal travelers' checks from the center of the packet. This way the owner is not likely to notice the theft immediately. So keep your travelers' checks safe, maintain a good record of which ones you use, and count the remaining checks every so often to be sure they are all there. Also, do not carry travelers' checks in your wallet.

If you and your spouse are traveling together and have duplicate major credit cards—American Express, Diners, Visa, MasterCard—that are usable most places you are likely to go, take only one of each. Leave the duplicates in the safe deposit box. Split the cards you take between you. (If husband carries Visa in his wallet, wife carries MasterCard in her purse. If her purse is snatched or his pocket picked, credit on only one card need be frozen.) Having some credit available to you can be very important. There is also something to be said for splitting the cards as described above, but putting the duplicate cards in the hotel safe.

Carry your key to the hotel safe deposit box in a pocket, not in a wallet or purse.

Husband and wife should each try to have with them some identification with a picture. If you live in a state where your photograph appears on your driver's license, you are fortunate. But do not carry your passport for this purpose alone.

En route. Remember that whenever you are in transit your property is at risk. Driving, in a cab to an airport, your luggage when checked, on the way to the hotel at the other end—all these situations allow for forgetting, losing, or being relieved of your valuables. Many people like to carry jewelry and other valuables in a small bag with them at all times till they reach the hotel, not giving it to a porter. This is a wise precaution.

Treat airline tickets as money, virtually cash. That's the way the airlines look at them. If your air tickets are lost or stolen, the airline will replace them, but you have to pay all over again—and you have to have cash or credit to pay for them. Moreover, if you were flying on a reduced-rate plan, such as an excursion rate, you will have to buy the balance of your travel at the full rate. What the airlines *will* do, if you report your loss promptly, is to put a stop to anyone's turning in your tickets for cash. Anyone who wants to can use them for travel, however—on the issuing airline or another—and even if they are unused you cannot get a refund for 90 days. The airlines have a computer to prevent passengers' booking space on more than one flight. I believe they could prevent someone's using stolen tickets if they wanted to. So far they will not do this.

At the hotel. When you register at a hotel, put *all* your valuables in a safe deposit box there. This is the most important rule in this entire list for the protection of your property. Most of your cash, most of your travelers' checks, your airline tickets, all valuable jewelry, any credit cards you don't need immediately, your passport or passports if you brought them, your check book, and anything else you do not need with you all the time should go in the safe deposit box at the hotel. There may be objections to this—wanting to have jewelry handy, disinclination to stop perhaps several times a day at the cashier's desk to have the box opened. The handier the jewelry is, the greater the risk you are taking. Calling frequently for your safe deposit box is the mark of the experienced traveler. Do not be deterred because some famous hotels had their deposit boxes burglarized. These cases are exceptions. And a hotel is not liable for valuables stolen from your room. Anyone who puts jewelry, money, or whatever in a suitcase and locks it thinking any safety is achieved thereby is very wrong, and he is even more mistaken if he thinks that there are few keys that will unlock that suitcase. And, of course, double lock your hotel door, or put the chain on, when you are inside, and do not open the door to someone who does not properly identify himself.

Going out. Carry a minimum of $50 (to appease a possible mugger). Carry some money elsewhere than in your wallet, in fact two other places. Cache some money in a relatively inaccessible place—a sock or stocking is good. If you are robbed you will then have something to fall back on. Keep a few dollars in a handy pocket as well, to pay for taxis, dispense tips, and make small purchases without reaching for your wallet or opening your handbag. If a woman is going out with her husband she should try to leave her purse behind (putting valuables in the hotel's safe, or course). She will feel less encumbered and there is no chance of a purse snatching—the most common kind of street robbery committed by young thieves.

A woman should keep a good grip on her handbag. She should put her arm through the strap and hold the purse against her body. The flap should open toward her side, not away from her. Obviously, carrying the purse by the strap alone is the least safe method. If she is diverted by something on the street or she is jostled, the first thing she should think of is the safety of her purse.

Here are some modern crooks' refinements on picking pockets and snatching purses:

Two crooks working together pull this trick—one gets in front of the victim, who is about to go through a turnstile or revolving door, then stops short. The victim, annoyed by being stopped, has his attention diverted. While he is waiting for the man in the front to find his change or decide to go through the door, the other crook crowds the victim from behind and lifts the wallet from pocket or purse and escapes. The first crook goes on through the turnstile or door and disappears. This is a trick used most often against women and is often not detected for several minutes.

Crooks sometimes cruise in a car, looking for someone to rob. The unhappy subject may be a person alone in a street or one of a small group. The car provides quick access for the thieves, and quick escape. They may stop the car and jump out, holding up the victim at gun or knife point, or snatch a purse. They then jump back in and make a quick getaway. A crook may also reach from a moving car (or in Europe a motor scooter) to snatch a purse. If this happens to you, let go of your purse *quickly*, to avoid physical injury.

As stated earlier, women sitting for a meal should put their purse between or in front of their feet, not beside their chair or on its back.

If you walk out of the hotel at night, go in a group (two couples are not a group), stay on streets that are well lighted and have plenty of people and get back to the hotel by 11 or 11:30 P.M. If you are in any doubt, take a cab, both ways, even for short distances.

Avoid getting in the midst of a suspicious group. If you approach a group of young men whose appearance you don't like, walk around all of them, not through them. Women and elderly people should not ride in an elevator with people they do not feel comfortable with. If they are on the ground floor, they should get out of the elevator and wait for another. It takes only a minute and is worth while.

Do not stop on a street where you feel unsafe. A common trick of thieves is to ask a pedestrian what time it is. This causes the victim to stop and also uncover his watch—so the thief determines whether it is worth stealing. If someone asks you the time, *keep walking*, and give the approximate time in a pleasant loud voice, without looking at your watch.

Do not stand near the edge of subway platforms. To do so is to run useless risks.

If you are held up. Realize that you are in a dangerous situation. Resistance is hazardous. Your personal safety, and that of the people with you, is more important than any money you can lose.

If you are armed with a gun, mace, or some other weapon, be sure it is legal. If you use it illegally, you can be in worse trouble. Also, realize that if you have a weapon, you are likely to want to use it. This can increase your danger, changing what might be simple robbery to something much more serious. I am convinced that most street crime is a form of economic activity intended to pay for dope. And users can be very bad characters. I think the best use of a weapon may often be to warn off potential attackers. If thieves surprise a victim and get close to him before he has a chance to draw his weapon, they are likely to turn his weapon against him.

It is wiser to open your wallet, without resistance, hold it so that the thief can see what money you have, and pass the money over to him. If he does not demand the wallet you have saved yourself a lot of future red tape—such as canceling credit cards.

What to do next. If you are the victim of a robbery, notify the police immediately. They will get you medical help if it is needed. If your hotel key is taken, notify security at the hotel.

Your next problem, particularly if you are away from home, is money. The credit card people say to notify them immediately if your cards are lost or stolen. Doing so will limit your liability to $50. If you have, in the hotel safe, a duplicate of the card that was stolen, it will give you the number of the card when you report the robbery. Do not use that duplicate card to get the money or credit you need—particularly replacement airline tickets and payment for your hotel—before "killing" the cards. Probably the thief will not use the credit cards immediately anyway. But to use the cards before killing the credit can make you liable if the cards are used for purchases.

If there was a check book or a blank check in the valuables taken from you, you may consider getting some cash before having the account closed—provided you still have a check. (This opportunity arises when your home bank, if large, has a branch in the foreign city you are visiting.) Here again, you run a risk, to be balanced against your need for survival.

In any case, act as fast as possible to get replacement for any stolen travelers' checks.

Inventory your loss in the robbery, promptly. Get a statement from the police that you reported the theft or robbery. This is important for income tax purposes. Also, have the locks on your house or apartment at home changed, if your keys were taken.

These tips about thieves come from experience, much of it gained first hand, which we wish we did not have.

(See "Home Security Checklist" in this chapter for tips about making your home secure when you leave it for a time.)

Time

Do you adjust your watch when you change time zones? Many people do. I don't if there is only an hour or two hours' difference. There are plenty of local clocks and watches on which to rely, and if I have to know local time it is easy to figure from home time on my own watch. Keeping my watch on home time immediately tells me what time it is at the office.

But if I am away from home three or more days, I always change my watch, even though the watch is not only a timepiece but also shows the calendar date and day of the week. Adjusting a calendar watch is somewhat complicated if you are going from east to west. When traveling from west to east, I just let it run down, allow the time to catch up, and then wind and set the watch.

Time Saver

If you and your spouse are traveling together, and there are two check-in lines at airport or hotel, split up. One stand in one line, the other person in the other line. The first one to reach the head of the line calls the other over.

Lest someone think this is immoral, look at it this way:

Suppose H gets to the head of the line first. The airline ticket or hotel room reservation for H and W would be processed together in any case. The person in line behind H is no worse off than he would have been if W had stood right beside H.

The situation would be different in a hotel line, at least, if two convention registrants who were not sharing the same room split and stood in separate lines. This could be unfair line-beating, because hotel reservations are processed separately.

Epilogue

At times in this book it may seem that I have made the job of meeting manager seem difficult. My warnings to the convention-goer to help him or her escape danger or unpleasantness in a large city may sound as if I thought people should stay home.

This is far from the case. The exchange of ideas, the debating of concepts, the spread of knowledge are essential for progress in business, education, and the professions—in fact, in all aspects of our culture. While other vehicles of information exist, none provides for interchange like the meeting. The man or woman who runs a good meeting makes possible that interchange. The job is challenging—to formulate general concepts, then particularize them into many detailed tasks, and finally to see that every task is exactly performed. The satisfaction of running a successful meeting is something only the meeting manager can fully appreciate, but the importance of what he does should be recognized by others.

The meeting-goer who conscientiously prepares for a conference and takes fullest advantage of what it offers is also an ingredient of a successful meeting. Without an audience there would be no one to hear, and the best prepared program would fall into a void.

If this book has helped the meeting manager plan and run a better conference, seminar, or convention, and the person attending a meeting get more from it and enjoy the break in the usual daily routine, the book will have been successful.

Yours for better meetings!

Index